Starting ... Business For Dummies, 3rd Edition

Cheat Sheet

United States Tax Deadlines

Note: Please check with your state government offices for due dates on sales taxes and license fees.

15th of every month: Prior month payroll tax deposit date (if you're on the monthly deposit system)

January 15: Estimated taxes due

January 31: Last day to distribute 1099s and W2s to people you paid during the prior year

January 31: Payroll reports for quarterly period ending 12/31 due

February 28: Last day to send the government copies of your 1099s and W2s

March 15: Calendar year corporation tax due

April 15: Deadline for Individual or Partnership Annual Tax return or deadline to file an extension

April 15: Estimated taxes due

April 30: Payroll reports for period ending 3/31 due

June 15: Estimated taxes due

July 31: Payroll reports for quarterly period ending 6/30 due

September 15: Estimated taxes due

October 31: Payroll reports for quarterly period ending 9/30 due

If the due date falls on a weekend or a federal holiday, the due date is the first business day after that date. See Chapter 15 for more information.

When Purchasing Merchandise to Sell

- Try to pay the lowest possible price for your item — buy at wholesale or less whenever possible.
- If you're the handy fix-it type, find items in need of minor repair and put them up for sale "like new."
- Search for unique items that may be common in your geographic area but hard to find in other places across the country.
- Attend estate sales — many a salable gem is hiding in someone's home.
- Visit closeout stores, liquidators, and auctions regularly.

When Taking Auction Photos

- Be sure that the item is clean, unwrinkled, and lint-free.
- Take the photo against a solid, undecorated background.
- Make sure the picture is in focus.
- Check that you have enough lighting to show the details of your item.
- Take second and third images to show specific details, such as a signature or a detail that better identifies your item.
- It's unnecessary to use an image that's more than 72 dpi for online purposes. Don't worry about megapixels.
- Try to keep the total size of *all* your pictures less than 50K for a smooth and swift download.

For Dummies: Bestselling Book Series for Beginners

Starting an eBay® Business For Dummies®, 3rd Edition

Cheat Sheet

eBay Time Chart

You need to know what time your auctions will close across the entire U.S. because you won't get top dollar for items that close while part of the country is asleep. Keep this page by your computer and refer to it every time you post an auction!

eBay	Pacific	Mountain	Central	Eastern
00:00	Midnight	1:00 a.m.	2:00 a.m.	3:00 a.m.
01:00	1:00 a.m.	2:00 a.m.	3:00 a.m.	4:00 a.m.
02:00	2:00 a.m.	3:00 a.m.	4:00 a.m.	5:00 a.m.
03:00	3:00 a.m.	4:00 a.m.	5:00 a.m.	6:00 a.m.
04:00	4:00 a.m.	5:00 a.m.	6:00 a.m.	7:00 a.m.
05:00	5:00 a.m.	6:00 a.m.	7:00 a.m.	8:00 a.m.
06:00	6:00 a.m.	7:00 a.m.	8:00 a.m.	9:00 a.m.
07:00	7:00 a.m.	8:00 a.m.	9:00 a.m.	10:00 a.m.
08:00	8:00 a.m.	9:00 a.m.	10:00 a.m.	11:00 a.m.
09:00	9:00 a.m.	10:00 a.m.	11:00 a.m.	Noon
10:00	10:00 a.m.	11:00 a.m.	Noon	1:00 p.m.
11:00	11:00 a.m.	Noon	1:00 p.m.	2:00 p.m.
12:00	Noon	1:00 p.m.	2:00 p.m.	3:00 p.m.
13:00	1:00 p.m.	2:00 p.m.	3:00 p.m.	4:00 p.m.
14:00	2:00 p.m.	3:00 p.m.	4:00 p.m.	5:00 p.m.
15:00	3:00 p.m.	4:00 p.m.	5:00 p.m.	6:00 p.m.
16:00	4:00 p.m.	5:00 p.m.	6:00 p.m.	7:00 p.m.
17:00	5:00 p.m.	6:00 p.m.	7:00 p.m.	8:00 p.m.
18:00	6:00 p.m.	7:00 p.m.	8:00 p.m.	9:00 p.m.
19:00	7:00 p.m.	8:00 p.m.	9:00 p.m.	10:00 p.m.
20:00	8:00 p.m.	9:00 p.m.	10:00 p.m.	11:00 p.m.
21:00	9:00 p.m.	10:00 p.m.	11:00 p.m.	Midnight
22:00	10:00 p.m.	10:00 p.m.	Midnight	1:00 a.m.
23:00	11:00 p.m.	Midnight	1:00 a.m.	2:00 a.m.

General Tips for Sellers

- Answer all e-mail questions from prospective bidders and buyers within twenty-four hours and check your e-mail hourly before the close of your auctions. (It can pay off in higher last-minute bidding.) Good customer service goes a long way in promoting and building your eBay business.

- When listing a new item, research it and be sure that you know its current value and the going price.

- Before listing, weigh your item and estimate the shipping cost. Be sure to list shipping (and handling) costs in your ad whether you use a flat rate or the shipping calculator for heavier packages.

- Always see how many other sellers are selling your item and try not to have your auction close within a few hours of another's.

- To encourage bidding, set the lowest possible starting bid for your item.

- Check the eBay guidelines to be sure that your item is permitted and that your listing doesn't violate any listing policies.

- Get to know the listing patterns of sellers who sell merchandise similar to yours, and try to close your auctions at different times or days.

For Dummies: Bestselling Book Series for Beginners

Starting an eBay® Business

FOR

DUMMIES®

Starting an eBay® Business

FOR

DUMMIES®

3RD EDITION

Marsha Collier

Wiley Publishing, Inc.

Starting an eBay® Business For Dummies® 3rd Edition
Published by
Wiley Publishing, Inc.
111 River Street
Hoboken, NJ 07030-5774

www.wiley.com

Copyright © 2007 by Wiley Publishing, Inc., Indianapolis, Indiana

Published by Wiley Publishing, Inc., Indianapolis, Indiana

Published simultaneously in Canada

For general information on our other products and services, please contact our Customer Care
Department within the U.S. at 800-762-2974, outside the U.S. at 317-572-3993, or fax 317-572-4002.

For technical support, please visit www.wiley.com/techsupport.

Wiley also publishes its books in a variety of electronic formats. Some content that appears in print may
not be available in electronic books.

Library of Congress Control Number: 2007933285

ISBN: 978-0-470-14924-9

Manufactured in the United States of America

10 9 8 7 6 5 4 3 2 1

WILEY

About the Author

Marsha Collier is one of the foremost eBay experts and educators in the world. With more than one million copies of her books in print, she is the top-selling eBay author. Her *eBay For Dummies* is the best-selling book for eBay beginners and her *eBay Business All-in-One Desk Reference For Dummies* is the best-selling title on operating an eBay business. In *Starting an eBay Business For Dummies,* Marsha combines her knowledge of business, marketing, and eBay savvy to help you make a smooth and quick transition from part-time seller to full-time moneymaker.

Marsha also shares her eBay business expertise through videos at Entrepreneur. com's "Entrepreneur's Coaches Corner." Her monthly column on Entrepreneur. com is also syndicated on many other major news sites. In addition, thousands of eBay fans also read her monthly newsletter, *Cool eBay Tools,* to keep up with the changes on the site.

Along with her writing, Marsha is also an experienced spokesperson. She was one of the original eBay University instructors as well as a regular presenter at eBay's annual convention, eBay Live. Marsha also hosted the highly acclaimed "Making Your Fortune Online," a PBS special on online business that premiered in 2005. Traveling across the country and recently in Singapore and Toronto, she continues to makes regular appearances on television, radio, and in print to discuss online commerce.

Marsha earned her eBay expertise as a longtime seller on the site. She began her eBay selling career in 1996 to earn extra money for her daughter's education. She grew her business to a full-time venture and was one of the first eBay PowerSellers. Nowadays you can find everything from autographed copies of her books to photo supplies, pet toys, and DVDs in her store, "Marsha Collier's Fabulous Finds," and on her Web site. More than anything, Marsha loves a great deal.

Marsha currently resides in Los Angeles, CA, and can be reached through her Web site, coolebaytools.com.

Dedication

This book is dedicated to the eBay entrepreneurs who have a zest for knowledge and the "stick-to-it-iveness" to follow through on their projects and stare success straight in the eye. It's dedicated also to those who are convinced that get-rich-quick schemes don't work and that, in the long run, hard work and loving what you do get the job done and lead to financial achievement and contentment.

Good luck in your endeavors. I know this book will help you get started.

Author's Acknowledgments

Updating a book like this is a challenge. Lots of people have helped, but the lion's share of assistance comes from the encouragement that I receive from the eBay community and those I've met when "doing it eBay."

Thank you to the eBay sellers referred to in this book for helping me show how eBay can reach out to the world: Jody Rogers and Asad Bangash (Beachcombers!), Robin Le Vine (Bubblefast), Dan Glasure (Dans Train Depot), Evan and Sandra Prytherch (EvanP), Stephen Kline (GalleryNow), Jonathan and Ellen White (Magic-By-Mail), Mary, Joanne, and Roz (MaryJoRoz_Aroma_Galaxy), Robert McMahan (McMahanPhoto), Jeff Stannard (Melrose_Stamp), and SallyJo Severance (SallyJo),

Then, of course, I thank the upper crust at Wiley. My publisher, Andy Cummings, and my acquisitions editor, Steven Hayes, have tried to reach "out-of-the-box" with some of my crazy ideas.

In this book, I had an amazing editor: Susan Pink. Susan was with me for the second edition and helped me upgrade this edition to make it even better. As always, thanks to Patti "Louise" Ruby, my technical editor and dear friend. This is the fifth book of mine that she's worked on as tech editor; I just can't think of a smarter person to go to for bouncing off ideas.

Publisher's Acknowledgments

We're proud of this book; please send us your comments through our online registration form located at www.dummies.com/register/.

Some of the people who helped bring this book to market include the following:

Acquisitions, Editorial, and Media Development

Project Editor: Susan Pink

Acquisitions Editor: Steve Hayes

Copy Editor: Susan Pink

Technical Editor: Patti Louise Ruby

Editorial Manager: Jodi Jensen

Media Development and Quality Assurance: Angela Denny, Kate Jenkins, Steven Kudirka, Kit Malone

Media Development Coordinator: Jenny Swisher

Media Project Supervisor: Laura Moss-Hollister

Editorial Assistant: Amanda Foxworth

Sr. Editorial Assistant: Cherie Case

Cartoons: Rich Tennant (www.the5thwave.com)

Composition Services

Project Coordinator: Heather Kolter

Layout and Graphics: Joyce Haughey, Stephanie D. Jumper, Laura Pence, Alicia B. South

Proofreaders: Aptara, John Greenough, Jessica Kramer

Indexer: Potomac Indexing

Anniversary Logo Design: Richard Pacifico

Special Help: Laura Bowman

Publishing and Editorial for Technology Dummies

Richard Swadley, Vice President and Executive Group Publisher

Andy Cummings, Vice President and Publisher

Mary Bednarek, Executive Acquisitions Director

Mary C. Corder, Editorial Director

Publishing for Consumer Dummies

Diane Graves Steele, Vice President and Publisher

Joyce Pepple, Acquisitions Director

Composition Services

Gerry Fahey, Vice President of Production Services

Debbie Stailey, Director of Composition Services

Contents at a Glance

Table of Contents

Introduction

You're here! You've made it! Welcome to the third edition of the best-selling book on eBay business: *Starting an eBay Business For Dummies.* This is the book you need to make that leap from casual seller (or buyer) to online mogul. You've probably been on eBay for a while and have seen that there really is a huge opportunity to make a part- or full-time living online. This book will serve as your manual to get organized and get your eBay business launched. Here you'll find information from how to handle your selling time more efficiently to stocking your store to the *real* way to set up your books and daily operations. I give you all the details about running a successful eBay business. I pass along not only my own experiences from eleven years of selling on eBay and thousands of interactions with eBay sellers, but also timesaving and moneysaving tips and lots of eBay secrets.

I've made a successful living while working out of my home for what seems like a lifetime (those corporate newspaper years fade further into the background as time passes), and I share my personal experiences to show that you, too, can run a successful home business. I started my own marketing and advertising business so that I could be at home and near my daughter. She's a big-time executive now (don't start counting the years — it's not polite), and I devote my time to selling on eBay (I'm a PowerSeller), running my Web site, and writing and teaching for eBay University. Through perseverance and dedication, my small homegrown business financed my home and my daughter's upbringing, private school, and college education. I know that the only limits to my eBay business are time. With the information in this book and some hard work, you too can expand to be an online success.

One thing that I can't guarantee is how much money you can earn. I've discovered — perhaps the hard way — that it takes a good deal of discipline to run a home business. Don't look for shortcuts — the time you spend and the amount of devotion you give your business will measure your success.

About This Book

Profits await! If you've read *eBay For Dummies,* you have the basics. You've probably picked up this book because you've heard stories about people making big money online, and you're interested in getting your piece of the pie.

Do you have a full-time job, but you'd like to sell on eBay part-time? eBay can easily supplement your income for the better things in life. Perhaps you're looking to make a career change, and jumping into an eBay business with both feet is just what you have in mind. If so, this is the book for you.

I've watched eBay change from a homey community of friendly collectors to a Wall Street giant with tens of thousands of categories of items and more than 222 million registered users worldwide. What are *you* waiting for? There's no time like the present to get started on your new career. Thousands of people around the world are setting up businesses online, and now is your time to take the leap of faith to begin a profitable enterprise. eBay gives you the tools, the customers, and the venue to market your wares. All you need is a bit of direction.

Starting an eBay Business For Dummies picks up where my *eBay For Dummies* leaves off. The tips I include here give you the opportunity to improve your eBay moneymaking ability, and can possibly turn an eBay novice into a professional running a booming eBay business. I also show the experienced user the prudent way to turn haphazard selling into an organized business. I've combined the fine points of eBay with real business and marketing tools to help you complete the journey from part-time seller to online entrepreneur.

In this book, you find the answers to some important questions as I take you through the following lessons:

- Reviewing what you know and introducing some of the finer points of eBay auctions
- Sprucing up your auctions to attract more bidders
- Dealing with customers and their needs
- Setting up your business in a professional manner
- Deciding how to handle inventory (and where to find it)
- Figuring out what you need to be in an eBay business . . . for *real*

What You're Not to Read

If you use this book the way you'd use a cookbook, jumping around from recipe to recipe (or chapter to chapter), you'll be able to find answers to particular questions. Or read the book from beginning to end if you'd like. Either way, be sure to keep the book handy to answer future questions as they come to you — there's a concise index.

Foolish Assumptions

Because you're reading this, I assume you're getting serious about selling on eBay and want to find out the fine points of just how to do that. Or perhaps you want to know how much is involved in an eBay business so that you can make the decision whether to give it a go.

If I have you figured out and you've decided that it's time to get serious, here are some other foolish assumptions I've made about you:

- ✔ You have a computer and an Internet connection.
- ✔ You've bought and sold on eBay and are familiar with how it works.
- ✔ You have an existing small business or you'd like to start one.
- ✔ You like the idea of not having to work set hours.
- ✔ You feel that working from home in jeans and a t-shirt is a great idea.

I must stop here and say that it would really help (especially if your total transactions on eBay are less than 100) if you read my beginning book, *eBay For Dummies,* 5th Edition. That book gives you all the basics you need to get started selling successfully.

If you can say yes to my foolish assumptions, you're off and running! Take a few moments to read the following section to get a feel for how I've put together this book.

How This Book Is Organized

This book has six parts. The parts stand on their own, which means that you can read Chapter 12 after reading Chapter 8 and maybe skip Chapter 13 altogether (but I know you won't because that's where I discuss the money!).

Part 1: Getting Serious about eBay

Reviewing what you know is always a great place to start. Considering the way eBay constantly changes, you'll probably find a little review worthwhile. So in Part I, I delve into the finer points of eBay. Perhaps you'll discover a thing or two you didn't know — or had forgotten.

Setting up your eBay store is important, and in this part I show you step by step the best way to do it — and give you tips to figure out when the timing is right for you to open your store.

Part II: Setting Up Shop

You need to decide what type of business you plan to run and what type of inventory you'll sell. Here's where I discuss how to find merchandise and the best way to sell it. I also give you the lowdown on eBay Motors, real estate, and some of the other unusual areas where you can sell.

You'll also find out how to research items — before you buy them to sell — so you'll know for how much (or whether) they'll sell on eBay.

I also discuss the importance of having your own Web site for online sales and how to set one up quickly and economically.

Part III: Business Is Business — Time to Get Serious

In Part III, I discuss exactly how to use available online and offline tools, implement auction management software, jazz up your auctions, and handle shipping efficiently and effectively. Because working with customers and collecting payments are important, too, you'll find that information here as well.

Most importantly, you also find out how to get free shipping material for your business delivered to your door, get your postal carrier to pick up your boxes at no charge, and insure your packages without standing in line at the post office.

Part IV: Your eBay Back Office

Setting up your business as a real business entity involves some nasty paperwork and red tape. I try to fill in the blanks in Part IV, as well as show you how to set up your bookkeeping. This is the place where you'll find a checklist of the items you'll need to run your online business.

You also need to know how to set up your home business space and how to store your stuff. I cover that here plus bunches more!

Part V: The Part of Tens

You can't write a *For Dummies* book without including the traditional Part of Tens. So in an untraditional manner, here are ten real-life stories of successful (and happy) people selling at eBay. You also find out about ten places to move your merchandise (if you want to sell elsewhere).

Part VI: Appendixes

I include a random collection of terms in Appendix A, the glossary. You're probably already familiar with many of these words, but others will be new to you. Refer to the glossary often as you peruse other parts of the book. There's also a short appendix on setting up a network at home.

Icons Used in This Book

All *For Dummies* books have cute little icons. I certainly wouldn't want to ruin your reading experience and leave them out. So, I selected a few and use them sparingly throughout the book. Be sure to take heed when you see them.

Here I share some of the interesting stories I've picked up from eBay sellers over the years. Because I believe that knowledge is enhanced through learning from the successes and mistakes of others, I include these little auction factoids so that you might gain some insight from them. After all, if someone else has learned from a unique trick, you can benefit by taking heed.

If there's something I need to interject — okay, something I'm jumping up and down to tell you but it won't fit directly into the text — I indicate it by placing this tip icon in front of the paragraph. You'll know the tip to follow will be right on target!

Do you really know people who tie string around their fingers to remember something? Me neither; but this icon gives me the opportunity to give you a brief reminder. Kinda like a sticky yellow Post-it note.

I like this picture of the bomb device that Wile E. Coyote slam-dunks in the cartoons In that vein, if you don't heed the warning indicated by the small petard, you may be "hoisted by your own petard," or made a victim of your own foolishness.

Where to Go from Here

Time to hunker down and delve into the book. If you have time, just turn the page and start from the beginning. If you're anxious and already have some questions you want answered, check out the handy index at the end of the book and research your query.

Take this information and study it. Being a success on eBay awaits you. I can't wait to hear your success stories if I meet you at eBay Live or at a book signing in your town.

My goal is to help you reach your goals. Feel free to visit my Web site and sign up for my free newsletter. That way you can stay up to date:

```
www.coolebaytools.com
```

Please e-mail me with any suggestions, additions, and comments. I want to hear from you and hope to update this book with your words of wisdom. (Humorous war stories are also gratefully accepted!). Please know that I read every e-mail I get, but I just can't answer every one. Know that your comments are truly appreciated and mean a lot to me.

Part I
Getting Serious about eBay

The 5th Wave   By Rich Tennant

"I don't understand why no one at eBay
is bidding on Junior's old baby clothes."

In this part . . .

When we've been doing something for a while (such as selling on eBay), often we forget some of the basics. eBay continually makes improvements, and some of its features are like hidden gems in a diamond mine. In this first part, I delve into the finer points of eBay with you. Perhaps you'll discover a thing or two you didn't know or had forgotten.

Chapter 1

Launching Your Business on eBay

In This Chapter

▶ Getting serious about your business

▶ Making decisions about what to sell

▶ Having what it takes to make a living online

▶ Running your business efficiently

So you've decided to step up to the plate and start that eBay business. You should first decide how much time you have to devote. I suggest that you don't quit your day job (yet). Instead, start expanding your sales in baby steps. You can sell part time and still be a business and have a nice chunk of extra income. A large portion of sellers, even eBay PowerSellers (those who gross more than $1000 a month in sales), work on eBay only part time.

eBay sellers come from all walks of life. A good number of stay-at-home moms are selling on eBay. And so many retirees are finding eBay a great place to supplement their income, that I wouldn't be surprised if the AARP creates a special eBay arm. If you're pulled out of your normal work routine and faced with a new lifestyle, you can easily make the transition to selling on eBay.

In this chapter, I talk about planning just how much time you'll be able to devote to your eBay business — and how to budget that time. I also talk about figuring out what to sell. Your eBay business won't grow overnight, but with dedication and persistence, you may just form your own online empire.

Getting Down to Bidness (er, Business)

Before launching any business, including an eBay business, you need to set your priorities. And to be successful at that business, you must apply some clear level of discipline.

I won't bore you with the now-legendary story of how Pierre Omidyar started eBay to help fulfill his girlfriend's Pez dispenser habit, blah, blah, blah. I *will* tell you that he started AuctionWeb.com (the original eBay Web site) with a laptop, a regular Internet service provider (ISP), and an old school desk. He and his buddy Jeff Skoll (a Stanford MBA) ran AuctionWeb twenty-four hours a day, seven days a week, all by themselves. When I began using the service, I had a lot of questions — and I always got prompt, friendly answers to my e-mails. When the site started attracting more traffic, Pierre's ISP began to complain about all the traffic and raised his monthly fees. To cover the higher costs, Pierre and Jeff began charging 25 cents to list an auction. Pierre was so busy running the site that the envelopes full of checks began to pile up — he didn't even have time to open the mail.

When Pierre incorporated eBay AuctionWeb in 1997 with his partner Jeff, they were each drawing a salary of $25,000. Their first office consisted of one room, and they had one part-time employee to handle the payments. They started small and grew. Now eBay is a respected, worldwide corporation, employing thousands of people and trading on the New York Stock Exchange.

Budgeting your time: eBay as a part-time moneymaker

A part-time eBay business can be very profitable. One thing that I stress in this book is that the more time and energy you spend on your eBay business, the more money you can make. That said, let's examine the lowest possible level of time that you should devote to your business.

Maybe you enjoy finding miscellaneous items to sell on eBay. You can find these items randomly in your day-to-day life. So let's suppose that you could spend at least a few hours (maybe two to three) a day on eBay. Now you must include the time it takes to write up your auctions. If you're selling only one type of item, allow about ten minutes to write your auction and photograph the item (or scan it) and upload it to eBay or a photo-hosting site.

How much time is required to perform these tasks varies from person to person and will improve according to your level of expertise. Regardless, every task in your eBay auction business takes time, and you must budget for that time. See the sidebar "Some handy eBay timesaving tips" for pointers.

You can take great photos and write brilliant descriptions, but cashmere sweaters won't sell for as much in the heat of summer as they do in winter. Doing your research can take up a good deal of time when you're selling a varied group of items. Only you can decide how much time you can afford to spend researching going rates for items on eBay.

Some handy eBay timesaving tips

Crunched for time? The following are some features you're sure to find handy:

- **HTML templates:** In Chapter 11, I give you some basic HTML templates for attractive auctions (and show you how to find more). These HTML templates cut your auction design time to a few minutes. Most experienced eBay sellers use preset templates to speed up the task of listing auctions, and this should be your goal.

- **The Turbo Lister program:** When you want to list a bunch of auctions at once, I recommend using the eBay Turbo Lister program. I estimate that Turbo Lister enables you to put together and upload ten auctions in just fifteen minutes. In Chapter 9, I run down the details on how to use this very cool tool.

- **The Selling Manager and Selling Manager Pro programs.** These eBay subscription programs can help you speed up the nuts and bolts of an ongoing eBay business when you're selling many items a week (more on the Selling Manager program in Chapter 9).

- **Relisting (or Sell Similar) feature:** When you sell the same item time after time, you can use Turbo Lister (it archives your listings so you can repeat them) or the handy eBay relisting or Sell Similar feature. When your auction ends on eBay, links pop up offering to relist your listing or to Sell Similar. If you want to run a different auction with a similar HTML format to the one that just ended, simply select the Sell Similar option and cut and paste the new title and description into the Sell Your Item page of your new listing. Use the Relist feature *only* when an item hasn't sold the first time, so it will qualify for a listing fee credit when it sells. Use Sell Similar to relist the same item after it fails to sell a second time.

- **Auction management software:** See the "Software you can use" section in this chapter, and also see Chapter 9, where I detail various programs to integrate into your eBay business.

You also have to consider how much time it takes to shop for your merchandise. You may have to travel to dealers, go to auctions, or spend time online discovering new ways to find your auction merchandise. Many sellers set aside a full day each week for this undertaking. Your merchandise is what makes you money, so don't skimp on the time you spend identifying products.

Here's a list of various activities that you must perform when doing business on eBay:

- Photograph the item.
- Upload the images to eBay Picture Services when you list or before listing to your ISP or third-party hosting service.
- Pack and weigh the item to determine the shipping cost.

✔ Choose an auction title with popular keywords.

✔ Write a concise and creative description.

✔ List the item for sale on eBay.

✔ Answer bidder questions.

✔ Send an end-of-listing e-mail (can be automated through PayPal).

✔ Carry out bookkeeping and banking.

✔ Address the label and affix postage.

✔ Ship the item safely and securely.

Time yourself to see how long it takes to accomplish each of these tasks. The time varies when you list multiple items, so think of the figures that you come up with as your *baseline,* a minimum amount of time that you must set aside. This information can help you decide how many hours per week or month you need to devote to running your part-time eBay business.

Jumping in with both feet: Making eBay a full-time job

As you can see in the list in the preceding section, the tasks required for your eBay business can be time consuming. But careful planning and scheduling can turn your business into an online empire.

The best way to go full time on eBay is to first run your business part time for a few months to iron out the wrinkles. After you become comfortable with eBay as a business (and decide that you enjoy selling and customer relations), you're ready to make the transition to full-time seller. The minimum gross monthly sales for a Bronze-level PowerSeller is $1000. If you plan your time efficiently, you can easily attain this goal. Head to Chapter 3 for more information on the PowerSeller program.

Running a full-time business on eBay is the perfect option for working parents who prefer staying at home with their children, retirees looking for a way to supplement their income, or those who'd just rather do something else than work for their boss. Read some real-life profiles of happy full-time sellers in Chapter 18.

See Figure 1-1 for an example of the eBay home page, the first stop for most visitors to eBay. Note how eBay makes an effort to reflect some sort of promotion to better market the items you put up for sale.

Figure 1-1:
The eBay
home page,
where it
all starts!

Deciding What to Sell

What should I sell? That is *the* million dollar question! In your quest for merchandise, you're bound to hear about soft goods and hard goods. *Soft,* or nondurable, goods are generally textile products, such as clothing, fabrics, and bedding. *Hard* goods are computer equipment, housewares, and anything else that's basically nondisposable.

Following are just a few points to consider when you're deciding what to sell:

- ✔ **Shipping costs:** Some differences exist between shipping hard and soft goods. Soft goods can fold up and be packed in standard box sizes, available from the USPS (U.S. Postal Service), or (better yet) in bubble or Tyvek envelopes for much lower shipping costs. Most hard goods come in their own boxes, which may or may not be individually shippable. You'll also need to use Styrofoam peanuts or bubble cushioning or double package the item in an oddly sized box. See Chapter 17 for the lowdown on shipping and packing.

- ✔ **Other shipping considerations:** Do you want to handle large boxes and deal with the hassles of shipping them?

- ✔ **Do you enjoy dealing with your products?** I would have been out of the eBay game years ago if I was forced to sell auto parts. Enjoying what you sell makes you an expert and a top-drawer seller.

> ✔ **Possible storage problems:** Do you have the room to store enough merchandise to keep you going? Soft goods can take up considerably less space than hard goods.

You don't always have to buy your items in bulk to make money on eBay. The first things you sell might be items you find in your garage or attic. To find out about some other fun ways to acquire goods to sell, check out the next section.

Turning your hobby into a business

C'mon, you have a hobby; everyone does! Did you collect stamps or coins as a kid? Play with Barbie dolls? Maybe your hobby is cars? Did you inherit a bunch of antiques? Been collecting Hummel figurines for a few years? eBay has a market for almost anything.

You can't possibly be an expert on everything. You need to keep up to date on the market for your items. Following more than four or five basic item groups may divert your attention from selling.

Selling within a particular category or two can be a good idea for repeat business. Should you decide to major in miscellany and sell anything and everything, you may not realize the highest possible prices for your items unless you thoroughly research them. This can be okay if you have a source that permits you to buy items at dirt-cheap prices.

Collectibles: Big business on eBay

Pierre Omidyar started eBay with the idea to trade collectible Pez dispensers. eBay now lists more than forty main categories of collectibles (see Figure 1-2), and those categories are divided into thousands of categories, subcategories, and sub-subcategories. Almost anything that you'd want to collect is here, from advertising memorabilia to Girl Scout pins to Zippo lighters!

If you have a collection of your own, eBay is a great way to find rare items. Because your collection is something dear to your heart and you've studied it on and off for years, you could probably call yourself an expert. Bingo — you're an expert at something! I recommend that you hone your skills to find things in your area of expertise at discount prices (you're liking this more and more, aren't you?) and then sell them on eBay for a profit. Start small and start with something you know.

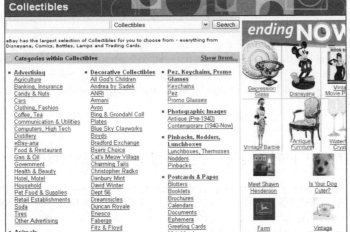

Figure 1-2:
The eBay
Collectibles
hub page
with links to
hundreds of
categories.

If there's one thing you know, it's fashion!

Are you one of those people who just knows how to put together a great
outfit? Do you find bargains at Goodwill but people think you've spent hundreds on your garb? Do you know where to get in-season closeouts before
anyone else does? Looks like you've found your market (see Figure 1-3).

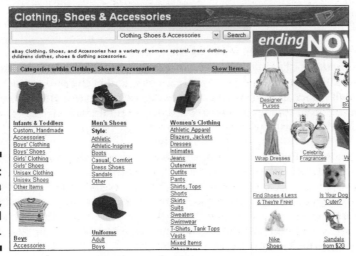

Figure 1-3:
eBay area
for clothing,
shoes, and
accessories.

Buy as many of those stylish designer wrap dresses (you-know-whose at you-know-where) as you can, and set them up on the mannequin you've bought to model your fashions for eBay photos. (For more on setting up fashion photos on eBay, check out Chapter 11.) Within a week, you just may be doubling your money — 'cause sweetie-darling, who knows fashion better than you?

If a ball, a wheel, or competition is involved — it's for you

I don't want to preach in generalities, but I think I'm pretty safe in saying that most guys like sports. Guys like to watch sports, play sports, and look good while they're doing it. I see that as opening up venues for a profitable empire on eBay. I don't want to leave out all the women who excel and participate in many sports. Women may have even more discriminating needs for their sporting endeavors! I know I do. My golf game stinks — but I do make a point to at least look good when I go out there, with respectable equipment and a fabulous outfit.

eBay has an amazing market going on right now for exercise equipment, and I don't even want to go into how much fishing equipment is selling on eBay. And the last time I looked, golf items totaled more than 111,000 listings! What a bonanza! New stuff, used stuff — it's all selling on eBay. It's enough to put your local pro shop out of business — or perhaps put *you* in business.

Including the whole family in the business

Sometimes just the idea of a part-time business can throw you into a tizzy. After all, don't you have enough to do? School, work, soccer, kids glued to the TV — you might sometimes feel as if you've no time for family time. However, the importance of family time is what brought me to eBay in the first place. I was working long hours in my own business, and at the end of the day, when my daughter Susan wanted to go shopping, perhaps for some Hello Kitty toy or a Barbie doll, I was just too tired. (Can you relate?)

I'd heard about AuctionWeb (eBay's original site name) from a friend and had bought some things online for my own collections. (Okay, you got me; I collected Star Trek stuff — call me geek with a capital *G*.) I'd also browsed around the site and found some popular toys selling for reasonable prices. So one evening I introduced Susan to AuctionWeb, and life has never been the same. We'd go to toy stores together right when they opened on Saturday morning, so we'd get first dibs on shipments of the hottest, newest toys. She'd go to the dolls and I'd go to the action figures. We'd buy several, go home, and post them for sale on eBay. We made money, yes, but the best part was our toy runs. They will always remain a special memory.

Susan has since graduated from college (she majored in business and marketing — must have been inspired by our eBay enterprise), but she still calls home when she finds a hot CD or closeouts of a top-selling item. We still purchase and list items together. The family that eBays together . . . always does.

My short trip down memory lane has a point: A family business can succeed and everyone can enjoy it. (Take a look at some of the family sellers I profile in Chapter 18.) I was in charge of the financing and the packing while Susan looked up ZIP codes on the Internet and put pins in a four-foot-by-five-foot map showing every city that we bought or sold from. She learned some excellent lessons in marketing, advertising, and geography, all in one swoop.

Toys, books, and music — oh MY!

Having children in your home brings you closer to the latest trends than you could ever imagine. I remember sitting at a Starbucks a couple of years ago watching some dads and their sons poring over notebooks full of Pokémon cards. (Actually, the kids were off playing somewhere and the dads were coveting the cards.)

And what about Star Wars? Star Trek? G.I. Joe? Can you say action figures? (If guys have them, they're not dolls — they're action figures.) If you have access to the latest and greatest toys, buy them up and sell them to those who can't find them in their neck of the woods.

If your home is like mine, books pile up by the tens! Old educational books that your children have outgrown (even college textbooks) can be turned into a profit. Remember that not every book is a classic that needs to be part of your library forever. Let another family get the pleasure of sharing children's tales!

If anything piles up faster than books, it's CDs, DVDs, and old VHS videos. Somehow the old lambada or macarena music doesn't hold the magic it once did. Or maybe, those Care Bears cartoons don't mesmerize the kids the way they used to. You can get rid of your own items and find plenty of stock at garage sales. Buy them cheap and make a couple of dollars.

Selling children's clothes

When I recently checked eBay for the number of listings of infant and toddler clothes up for sale, I found more than 198,000 — and the bidding was hot and heavy. For stay-at-home parents, selling infant and children's clothing is a super way to pick up extra income.

If you've had a baby, you know all too well that friends and relatives shower new moms with lots of cute outfits. If you're lucky, your baby gets to wear one or two of these (maybe only for a special picture) before outgrowing them. These adorable portrait outfits can earn you a profit on eBay. Many parents, with children a few steps behind yours, are looking for bargain clothing on eBay — a profitable hand-me-down community. As your children grow up (and out of their old clothes), earn some money while helping out another parent.

Bringing your existing business to eBay

Do you already have an existing business? eBay isn't only a marketplace where you're able to unload slow or out-of-season merchandise. You can also set up your store right on eBay (see Figure 1-4). An eBay store allows you to list a fixed-price item at a reduced fee and keep the item online until it's sold. When you run your regular auctions for special items, they will have a link to your store, thereby drawing in new shoppers to see your store merchandise.

Figure 1-4:
eBay Stores
central.

Here are a few ways you can expand your current business with eBay:

> ✔ **Open a second store on eBay:** How many people run stores that sell every item, every time? If you're a retailer, you've probably made a buying mistake or two. Many times the item that *isn't* selling in your store *is* selling like hotcakes in similar stores elsewhere in the country. eBay gives you the venue to sell those extra items to make room for more of what sells at your home base.

Perhaps you just need to raise some cash quickly. eBay has tens of thousands of categories in which you can liquidate regular stock or specialty items. For a caveat on what's verboten, check out Chapter 4.

✔ **Sell by mail order:** If you've been selling by mail order, what's been holding you back from selling on eBay? It costs you far less to list your item on eBay than to run an ad in any publication. Plus, on eBay, you get built-in buyers from every walk of life. If your item sells through the mail, it will sell through eBay.

✔ **Sell property:** Licensed real estate agents, take note. Plenty of land, homes, and condos are selling on eBay right now. List your properties online so that you can draw from a nationwide audience. When you offer listings on the Web, you're bound to get more action. Give it a whirl and read more about selling real estate on eBay in Chapter 2.

You won't find a cheaper landlord than eBay. Jump over to Chapter 5 if you really can't wait for more information about how to set up your eBay store.

Getting What It Takes to Sell

I've heard many sellers-to-be say they want to start a business on eBay so that they can relax. Since when is running any business a way to relax? Granted, you don't need a whole lot of money to get started on eBay and you won't have a boss breathing down your neck. But to run a successful eBay business, you need drive, determination, and your conscience to guide you, as well as a few solid tools, such as a computer and an Internet connection. In this section, I give you the lowdown on these things and more.

Computer hardware

First, you're gonna need a computer. In my basic assumptions about you (see the book's introduction), I figure that you have one and know how to use it. Your computer doesn't have to be the latest, fastest, and best available. It does help if your computer has a good deal of memory to process your Web browsing and image touchups. One of my eBay listing computers is an antique Pentium 3, an absolute turtle next to my new 4.3-GHz model. But combined with a high-speed Internet connection, my little machine enables me to run many eBay auctions easily.

Having a computer that will read all sorts of camera data cards is a timesaver. Instead of having to hardwire your camera and download images, you can just zip in the memory card and copy the pictures to your hard drive.

One thing to keep in mind is that hard drives are getting cheaper by the minute. The bigger your hard drive, the more space you'll have to store images for your auctions. (Individual pictures shouldn't take up much space because each should be 50K max.) Make sure that you set up a sensible filing system by using folders and subfolders.

Check out Chapter 11, where I talk more about the other stuff you might need, such as a scanner and a digital camera.

Connecting to the Internet

If you've been on eBay for any length of time, you know that your Internet connection turns into an appendage of your body. If your connection is down or you can't log on due to a power outage, you can't function and instead flounder around, babbling to yourself. I understand because I've been there. If you're selling in earnest, I recommend pulling the plug on your dial-up connection unless you have no choice.

Before investing in any broadband connection, visit `www.broadbandreports.com` (see Figure 1-5) and read the reviews of ISPs in your area. Users post their experiences with the many providers across the country, so you can get a good idea of what's in store in your neighborhood in the connection arena. The site also has more testing tools than you can imagine and will test the speed of your (or your friend's) Internet connection at no charge.

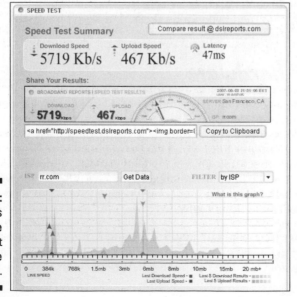

Figure 1-5: The results of the free speed test of my cable connection.

Dial-up connections

If you absolutely must use a dial-up connection, avail yourself of the many free trials that different Internet service providers (ISPs) offer to see which one gives your computer the fastest connection. After you find the fastest, be sure that it's reliable and has at least a 99 percent uptime rate.

Forty-four percent of the United States still logs on to the Internet with a dial-up connection, so what can be so wrong about a dial-up connection? This type of connection is painfully slow, and a listing with lots of images can take minutes to load. The average eBay users want to browse many listings and won't wait while your images load; they'll just go to the next listing.

To make the best use of your time when running your auctions and conducting research, you need to blast through the Internet. You need to answer e-mail, load images, and conduct your business without waiting around for snail's-pace connections. Although a modem is supposed to link up at 56K, FCC regulations state that it can't connect any faster than 53K. In practice, the highest connection I've ever experienced on a dial-up was 44K.

DSL

A confusing bunch of digital subscriber line (DSL) flavors (ADSL, IDSL, SDSL, and more) are available these days, ranging from reasonably priced to out of sight. DSL, when it works as advertised, is fast and reliable. A DSL line depends on the reliability of your telephone service: Crackling or unreliable phone lines can be a barrier to using DSL.

The main problem with a DSL connection is that your home or office needs to be no farther than 18,000 feet from your local telephone office. The service runs from $25 to $100 a month, and it might cost even more if you get DSL through a *booster* that boosts the signal to a location farther away than the minimum 18,000-foot border.

True DSL service can give you a connection as fast as 1.5MB per second download. (IDSL is only 144K.)

I had DSL for about a year and was initially blown away by the speed. Unfortunately, every time it rained (it does rain occasionally in Southern California), my service went out. I had to call time after time to get a service call. Sadly, this is a well-known drawback of DSL. Your local telephone company (telco in DSL-speak) owns your home or office phone lines. Because DSL goes over POTS (plain old telephone service), your DSL provider has to negotiate connection problems with the folks at your telephone company. As you might guess, one company often blames the other for your problems.

A friend of mine tried to get around this issue by getting DSL from the local phone company, which sounded great to me. It turned out to be not so great because it seems that the local phone companies tend to form companies to handle high-speed connections. So even though the two companies are technically the same, the two will still argue about who's responsible for your problems. Broadband with this much difficulty can be too much trouble.

Digital cable

Eureka, I think I've found the motherlode of connections: cable. If you can get digital cable television, you can probably get a blazingly fast cable Internet connection. Your cable company is probably replacing old cable lines with newfangled digital fiber-optic lines. These new lines can carry a crisp HD digital TV signal and an Internet connection as well. Fiber-optic lines have plenty of room to carry even more stuff (including telephone service), and I'm sure it won't be long before cable companies have some hot new services to sell us.

My digital cable Internet connection is generally fast and reliable. I can download 2 megabytes of data in only *eight seconds* (compared to almost seven minutes with a dial-up connection). So far, the service has been very reliable, and I've experienced little downtime. For around $40 a month, I consider my cable connection well worth the investment.

As far as the myth about more users on the line degrading the speed, a cable connection is more than capable of a 10 Mbps transfer. That's already about 10 times faster than DSL. It would take a whole lot of degrading to noticeably slow down your connection.

Choosing your eBay user ID

"What's in a name?" I believe that's how the old quote goes. On eBay, there's a whole lot in your name! When you choose your eBay user ID, it becomes your name — your identity — to all those who transact with you online. They don't know who you are; they know you only by the name they read in the seller's or bidder's spot.

Ever wonder why you don't see many banks named Joe and Fred's Savings and Loan? Even if Joe is the President and Fred is the Chairman of the Board, the casual attitude portrayed by their given names doesn't instill much confidence in the stability of the bank. Joe and Fred might be a better name for a plumbing supply company — or a great name for guys who sell plumbing tools on eBay! Joe and Fred strike me as the kind of friendly, trustworthy guys who might know something about plumbing.

The lowdown on user IDs

When choosing your user ID, keep the following points in mind:

✔ Your ID must contain at least two characters.

✔ It doesn't matter if you use uppercase; eBay displays your ID in all lowercase letters.

✔ You may use letters, numbers, and any symbol except @, ', <, >, and &.

✔ You can't use URLs as your user ID.

✔ You can't use the word *eBay* in your user ID; that privilege is reserved for eBay employees.

✔ Spaces aren't allowed; if you want to use two words, you can separate them by using the underscore key (press Shift and hyphen to type the underscore key). You may not use consecutive underscores.

✔ Do I have to tell you this? Don't use a name that's hateful or obscene; eBay (and the community) just won't permit it.

Does your retail business have a name? If you don't have your own business (yet), have you always known what you'd call it if you did? Your opportunity to set up your business can start with a good, solid, respectable-sounding business name. If you don't like respectable (it's too staid for you), go for trendy. Who knew what a Verizon was? Or a Cingular? Or a Bubblefast, which is one of my favorite eBay shipping suppliers.

Are you selling flamingo-themed items? How about pink_flamingos for your selling identity? Be creative; *you* know what best describes your product.

Stay away from negative-sounding names. If you really can't think up a good user ID, using your own name is fine.

You've no doubt seen a bunch of lousy user IDs out there. Here are a few examples of what not to use: ISellJunk, trashforsale, mystuffisgarbage.

eBay protects and does not reveal your e-mail address unless you're in a transaction with another member. If another user wants to contact you, he or she can do so by clicking the Contact Seller link on the item page. The e-mail will be sent to you through eBay's e-mail system.

If you decide to change your user ID, don't do it too often. Customers recognize you by name, and you may miss some repeat sales by changing it. Besides, eBay places a special icon next to your user ID to show others that you've changed it. This icon will stick with you for 30 days. Your feedback profile (permanent record) follows you to your new ID.

Finding your eBay feedback

The number that eBay lists next to your name is your feedback rating; see Figure 1-6 for my rating. Anyone on the Internet has only to click this number to know how you do business on eBay — and what other eBay users think of you. At the top of every user's feedback page is an excellent snapshot of all your eBay transactions for the past year, as well as detailed one- through five-star ratings. For the lowdown on feedback, go to Chapter 3.

Figure 1-6:
My eBay
feedback
rating.

If you're serious about this business thing and your feedback rating isn't as high as you'd like it to be, go online and buy some stuff. Even though eBay now distinguishes between buyer and seller feedback, the numbers will still grow. Feedback should always be posted for both buyers and sellers. Every positive feedback increases your rating by +1; a negative decreases it by –1. To get a high rating, you'd better be racking up those positives.

Making Your Auctions Run More Smoothly

In this section, I discuss a few more niceties that you'll need to round out your eBay home base. The following tools are important, but you must decide which ones you'll use. Some people prefer a totally automated office while others prefer to do things the old-fashioned way. One of my favorite eBay PowerSellers works with file folders, a hand-written ledger book, and hand-written labels. If it makes you happy, do it your way. I'm going to suggest a few options that will ease the pain of paperwork.

Software you can use

These days, software is available to accomplish just about anything. It would seem fitting that an all-encompassing software package exists that can help you with your auction, right? Well, maybe. It depends on how much you want your software to do and how much of your business you want to fully control. In this section, I describe some software examples that you might find useful.

Auction management

Auction management software can be a very good thing. It can automate tasks and make your record keeping easy. You can keep track of inventory, launch auctions, and print labels using one program. Unfortunately, most of these programs can be daunting when you first look at them (and even when you take a second look).

You have choices to make regarding the software: How much are you willing to spend for the software, and do you want to keep your inventory and information online? Maintaining your listing information online enables you to run your business from anywhere; you just log on and see your inventory. Online management software is tempting and professional, and may be worth your time and money.

A good many sellers prefer to keep their auction information on their own computers. This method is convenient and allows sellers to add a closer, more personal touch to their auctions and correspondence. Some folks say that keeping information local, on their own computer, is more suited to the small-time seller. I think it's a matter of preference.

In Chapter 9, I discuss the wide selection of management software available, including Marketworks, Channel Advisor, Auction Wizard 2000, and the eBay-owned Selling Manager.

HTML software

You may want to try some basic HTML software to practice your ad layouts. I tell you where to find some templates in Chapter 11, but you'll want to preview your auctions before you launch them. You might also enjoy my book *eBay Listings That Sell For Dummies* (co-authored with eBay tech maven Patti Louise Ruby). Half the book is on HTML and the other half helps you perfect your photography.

You can use a full-blown Web-page software package, such as FrontPage, to check out how your auction will look, or you may want to keep it simple. The simplest way is to use eBay's intuitive listing tool, which works in the same way as many word processing programs to format text. For more information, turn to Chapter 11.

Spreadsheets and bookkeeping

Many sellers keep their information in a simple spreadsheet program such as Excel. The program has all the functionality you need to handle inventory management and sales info.

For bookkeeping, I like QuickBooks, which is as complete as it gets. It's straightforward and professional, and it no longer requires that you have a basic knowledge of accounting. It also integrates with spreadsheets. In Chapter 16, I discuss QuickBooks in some detail.

Collecting the cash

Credit cards payments are the way to go for the bulk of your sales. Often, credit cards make the difference between a sale and no sale. People are getting savvy (and more comfortable) about using their credit cards online because they're becoming better informed about the security of online transactions and certain guarantees against fraud. So although you might truly love money orders, you need to take credit cards as well. In this section, I discuss another decision you need to make: Do you want your own private merchant account or would you rather run your credit card sales through an online payment service? For more about these options, read on.

Online payment services

Until you hit the big time, you should save yourself a bucket of trouble and go with the services of an online payment service such as the eBay-owned PayPal. PayPal offers excellent services, and their rates are on a sliding scale, according to your monthly dollar volume. Online payment services accept credit cards for you. They charge you a small fee and process the transaction with the credit card company. The auction payment is deposited in your designated bank account. Unless your sales go into tens of thousands of dollars a month, an online payment service is far more economical than having your own merchant account. For more about these services and accounts, see Chapter 13.

Your own merchant account

As you may or may not know (depending on the amount of spam in your e-mail), thousands of merchant credit card brokers guarantee that they can set you up so that you can take credit cards yourself. These people are merely middlemen. You have to pay for their services, either in an application fee or as part of a hefty percentage or by buying processing software. Some of these brokers are dependable businesses and others are nothing more than hustlers. If you have decent credit, you don't need these guys: Go straight to your bank!

Your bank knows your financial standing and creditworthiness better than anybody. It's the best place to start to get your own *merchant account,* an account in which your business accepts credit cards directly from your buyers. You pay a small percentage to the bank, but it's considerably less than what you pay to an online payment service. Some banks don't offer merchant accounts for Internet transactions because ultimately the bank is responsible for the merchandise related to the account if you fail to deliver the goods. Remember that your credit history and time with the bank play a part in whether or not you can get a merchant account.

The costs involved in opening a merchant account can vary, but you'll need between $300 and $2000 to get started. Here are some of the possible costs you may face:

- ✔ A monthly processing fee if you don't reach the monthly minimum set by your bank
- ✔ The discount rate (your bank's cut) of 15–45 cents per transaction
- ✔ About $700 for software that processes your transaction costs
- ✔ A monthly gateway fee of as much as $40 (an online connection to process charges)

This is quite an investment in time and effort. In Chapter 13, I get into the details of a merchant account and explain exactly where all these costs go.

Home base: Your Web site

eBay offers you a free page — the About Me page — that's the most important link to your business on eBay; see Chapter 3 for more information. The About Me page is part of your eBay store if you have one. You can insert a link on your About Me page that takes bidders to your listings. You can link also to your own Web site from the About Me page!

If you don't have your own Web site, I recommend that you get one, especially if you're serious about running an online business. Check out Chapter 8, where I provide some tips on finding a Web host and a simple way to put up your own Web site.

You can keep your complete inventory of items on your Web site and also list them in your eBay store as their selling season comes around. Remember that there's no listing or final value fee when you have repeat customers on your Web site.

Setting up your shop

Office and storage space are a must if you plan to get big. Many a business was started at the kitchen table (that's how Pierre started eBay), but to be serious with a business, you must draw definite lines between your home life and your online ventures. Concentrating when you have a lot of noise in the background is difficult, so when I say draw a line, I mean a physical line as well as an environmental one.

Your dedicated office

You must first separate the family from the hub of your business. Many eBay sellers use a spare bedroom. (I started my home business in a 10-by-12-foot room.) As time progresses and your business grows, you might have to move. I chose to sacrifice my detached two-car garage. I guess I could have made it into a one-car garage, but I decided to take over the whole thing instead.

Here's what I did: Zoning laws in Southern California require me to have a garage, so I put a false office wall in the back so that the garage door could open normally. I used that area for extra storage. My garage had been wired (for some guy who was going to use big-time power tools, I suppose) and had its own breaker box. I hired an electrician to come in and place outlets around my office and had a large window cut into the wall overlooking my backyard (to remove the claustrophobic feeling and for ventilation). I now had a window and electricity.

The phone man came by and brought a line into the garage; a friend installed double jacks all around to accommodate the two phone lines. I picked out some reasonably priced paneling and hired workmen to install it and to drop a paneled ceiling with florescent lights. Finally, I bought furniture from my local Goodwill store. Presto-chango — I had successfully transformed what was once a dark, musty garage into a bright, gleaming 18-by-20-foot *private* office. And here I successfully ran my advertising and marketing business for more than ten years.

You, too, have adjustments and decisions to make, just as I did, because you're going to need office space and storage space, too.

One PowerSeller that I know moved all the junk out of his basement and set up shop there. He now has three computers and employs his wife and a part-time *lister* (who puts his items up on eBay) to run the show. His basement office is networked and is as professional as any office.

Your eBay room

If you're able to set up an office similar to mine, your storage space should be covered for a while. For a real business, a closet just won't do, even though most sellers begin their eBay careers with an eBay closet. Seclude your stuff from your pets and family by moving it into another room. You'll also have to get shelving and more supplies to organize things. I talk more about this in Chapter 17.

Chapter 2

The Finer Points of eBay Selling

At first glance, eBay is this behemoth Web site with millions of listings that seems way too large for any novice to possibly master. On the surface, that's right. eBay is always growing and changing to meet the demands of its users. Under all the cosmetic changes, however, you always come back to the basics. eBay is still a traditional trading site: a community of buyers and sellers who follow rules and policies, making eBay a safe place to trade.

As anything expands, it must compartmentalize to be manageable. The folks at eBay have done this most handily. The original basic eight categories now number in the thousands. The category breakdown is far clearer and more concise than originally conceived. When a new trend begins, the eBay tech gurus evaluate the sales and, when necessary, add new categories.

All this growth has forced eBay to expand. Aside from the traditional eBay auctions, you'll now find multiple item (Dutch) auctions, private auctions, restricted auctions, and more. Whoa, that's confusing! In this chapter, I explain the eBay features by reviewing how you can transact your business. Armed with this knowledge, you can succeed with your listings — sooner than later.

Finding Where to Sell Your Stuff

The Internet is crowded with e-commerce sites selling everything possible. Many major portals also include auctions as part of their business. But the majority of buyers and sellers go to eBay. Why? Because eBay is the largest, attracting more buyers and sellers than any other site on the Web. More computers and electronics are sold on eBay than at Buy.com; more used cars are sold on eBay than in many states. Even name-brand manufacturers have opened outlets on eBay to sell directly to their customers.

Whether you're selling auto parts, toys, fine art, or land, eBay can work for you. But first, you have to find your niche. Sounds easy enough. After all, deciding where to put your stuff for sale is straightforward, right? Not necessarily. The task is complicated by the inclusion of thousands of categories on the eBay category overview page, shown in Figure 2-1.

Figure 2-1:
Just a portion of the vast eBay category overview page; numbers next to categories reflect the amount of active listings.

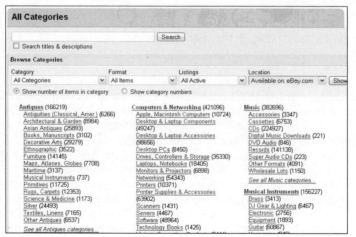

Consider the example of a Harry Potter toy. Harry Potter toys are hugely popular, with the continuing saga in both the books and the movies. (**Note:** You can replace Harry Potter with whatever the big pop-culture trend is when you read this book.) The easy choice is to list the item under *Toys & Hobbies: TV, Movie, Character Toys: Harry Potter*. But what about the category *Collectibles: Fantasy, Mythical & Magic: Harry Potter*? This is the point where you must decide whether you want to list in two categories and pay double (see the review of extra charges in Chapter 10) or count on the fact that your beautifully keyword-infested item title will drive prospective buyers who use the search engine directly to your item.

eBay supplies you with a great tool: *What are you selling?* is the first step in listing your item for sale. Type a few keywords that describe your item, and after you click the Sell button, the next page presents you with a list of categories where items similar to yours are listed, as shown in Figure 2-2. Each category in the results will indicate the percentage of matching items within the category.

Figure 2-2: eBay's Search for Categories feature.

Perhaps you aren't selling Harry Potter toys. Suppose you're selling a DVD of the movie *The Red Violin.* Would listing it in *DVD & Movies: DVD* be the right choice? Or would you reach an untapped audience of category browsers in the *Music: Musical Instruments: String: Violin?*

I once came across a lovely small book featuring the fashions of the 1960's fashion icon, Emilio Pucci. Do you think such a book should be listed in *Books: Non-Fiction?* I tried that category twice. Even with lowering my price, I couldn't sell the book. Then inspiration hit! I listed the book at my original starting price ($9.99) in the *Clothing, Shoes & Accessories > Vintage > Women's Clothing > 1965-76 (Mod, Hippie, Disco)* category. I had amazingly good luck going directly to the fans of 60's fashion. So much luck, in fact (the book sold for close to $40.00), that I found an inexpensive source for the book, bought a case, and listed them one at a time (so they would seem exclusive and I would continue to get the higher bids). During eighteen months, I bought and sold several dozen until I could no longer get a supply!

The popularity of categories varies from time to time. News stories, the time of year, hot trends, or whether Paris Hilton makes a comment about something can change a category's popularity in a nanosecond. How can you possibly know the best category for your item? Research your items regularly using my favorite tool: the awesome eBay search engine. (Visit Chapter 7 for more about using the search engine.) Searching for *completed listings,* I check items that have sold for the highest prices and see which category they were listed in. After you've found the right category for the item you're listing, give it a try. However, be sure to throw in a wildcard occasionally by trying alternatives.

After you've been selling a particular item for a while — and doing well with it — selling it in a different but related category can boost your sales. A little research now and then into where people are buying can go a long way to increasing your eBay sales.

Automotive? Go eBay Motors

Anything and everything automotive can go in the eBay Motors category (see Figure 2-3), and it will sell like giant tires at a monster truck rally. Following are just a few of the car-related items that fit in this category.

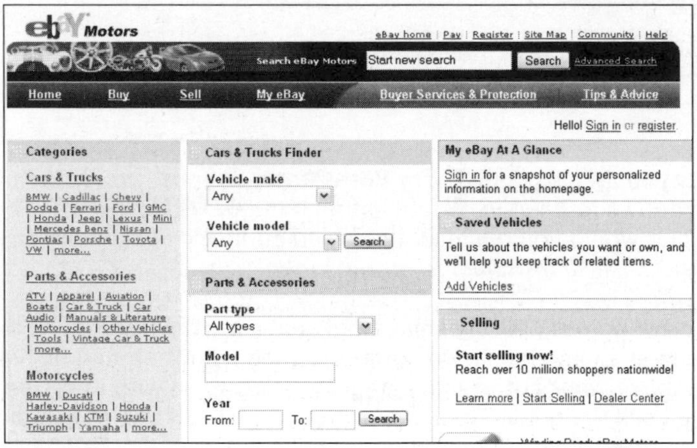

Figure 2-3: The eBay Motors home page.

Car parts

Have used car parts? eBay has an enormous market in used car parts. One seller I know goes to police impound sales and buys complete wrecks for close to nothing — just to save valuable parts that he can resell on eBay for big money. (Have you priced replacing your bumper lately? Yeow!)

New car parts are in demand, too. So if you catch a sale at your local auto parts store when it's blasting out door handles for a 1967 Corvette (a vehicle for which it's hard to find parts), it wouldn't hurt to pick up a few. Sooner or later, someone's bound to search eBay looking for them. If you're lucky enough to catch a trend, you'll make a healthy profit.

Cars

Yes, you can sell cars on eBay. In fact, car sales (used and new) have skyrocketed online thanks to the thousands of people who find eBay to be a trusted place to buy and sell used vehicles every day. Check out Figure 2-4 for an example of a used car auction. Selling vehicles on eBay is a natural business for you if you have access to good used cars, work as a mechanic, or have a contact at a dealership that lets you sell cars on eBay for a commission or on a consignment basis. (For the ins and outs of consignment selling, check out Chapter 6.)

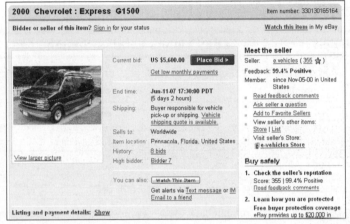

Figure 2-4: An eBay Motors auction for a previously owned van from seller e.vehicles.

eBay Motors and its partners offer useful tools to complete your sale. eBay Motors features a free passenger Vehicle Purchase Protection up to $20,000 (with a $100 buyer co-pay should you have a claim), one-click access to vehicle history reports, vehicle inspection and escrow services, and vehicle shipping quotes from Dependable Auto Shippers. Access eBay Motors and its services from the eBay home page or go directly to www.ebaymotors.com.

Here are just a few things to keep in mind if you plan to sell cars on eBay:

- ✔ Selling a car on eBay Motors is a bit different from selling on regular eBay, mainly in the fees area. Take a look at Table 2-1 for significant differences. In Chapter 10, I include a table of all basic eBay.com fees for listings, options, and final values.

- ✔ To sell a vehicle on eBay Motors, you must enter the Vehicle Identification Number (VIN) on the Create Your Listing page. This way, prospective buyers can access a vehicle history report.

✔ Although many people who have found the vehicle of their dreams on eBay are more than happy to take a one-way flight to the vehicle location and drive it home, shipping a vehicle is a reasonably priced alternative. You can make arrangements to ship a car quickly and simply. In Table 2-2, I list some sample costs for shipping cars around the country based on mileage.

✔ If your reserve isn't met in an eBay Motors auction, you may still offer the vehicle to the high bidder through the Second Chance option. More information on that later in this chapter. You may also reduce your reserve during the auction if you feel you've set your target price too high.

Table 2-1	eBay Motors Vehicle-Specific Fees	
Type of Vehicle	*Listing Fee*	*Transaction Fee**
Passenger vehicle	$40	$50
Motorcycles	$30	$40
Powersports	$30	$40
Powersports vehicles under 50cc	$3	$3
Other vehicles (trucks, trailers, planes, boats, etc.)	$40	$50
Reserve price in listing (refundable if the vehicle sells)	$5 to $10	Based on reserve price

* There is no final value fee for selling on eBay Motors. The transaction service fee is what you pay when your item gets a bid (or if you've used a reserve, when bidding meets your reserve price).

Table 2-2	Estimated Costs for Shipping a Car
Mileage	*Terminal-to-Terminal Cost*
Under 750	$350 to $650
751 to 1000	$450 to $750
1000 to 1500	$550 to $850
1501 to 2000	$650 to $950
2001 to 2500	$750 to $1100
2501 and over	$850 to $1150

REMEMBER

An item that you've listed on eBay Motors will appear in any search, whether potential buyers conduct a regular search on eBay.com or execute their search in eBay Motors.

Live auctions

eBay also holds live auctions, where you'll find rare and unusual items for sale. You can access the live auction area from a link on the home page or by going directly to www.ebayliveauctions.com.

To sell on eBay Live Auctions (shown in Figure 2-5), you must be a licensed auction houses or seller using a licensed auctioneer to control the bidding. eBay Live Auctions supplies buyers with exciting, nonstop, live auction action right on their desktop. Joining a live auction is a lot of fun. These auctions happen in real-time; you can see (and participate in) the bidding action on your screen as it's happening.

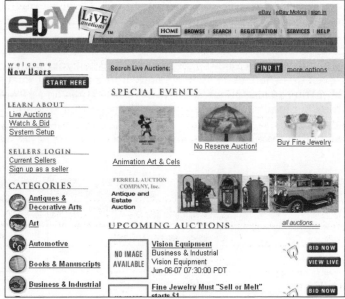

Figure 2-5: Nonstop bidding action on eBay Live Auctions!

Licensed auction houses run the live auctions from their locations, which are broadcast worldwide through eBay. You have to register individually for each auction in which you want to participate, and a buyer's premium is involved. More and more auctioneers are using this format to expand their customer bases.

As an eBay community member, you're able to bid on items featured in live auctions. As a matter of fact, I got waylaid for a few hours while writing this chapter, getting involved in bidding (and buying) in a coin auction! It's a good way to increase your own stock of merchandise to sell.

Real estate: Not quite an auction

eBay Real Estate isn't quite an auction. Because of the wide variety of laws governing the sale of real estate, eBay auctions of real property aren't legally binding offers to buy and sell. Putting your real estate up on eBay is an excellent way to advertise and attract potential buyers. When the auction ends, however, neither party is obligated (as they are in other eBay auctions) to complete the real estate transaction. The buyer and seller must get together to consummate the deal.

Nonetheless, eBay Real Estate sales are popular and the gross sales are growing by leaps and bounds. You don't have to be a professional real estate agent to use this category, although it may help when it comes to closing the deal. If you know land and your local real estate laws, eBay gives you the perfect venue to subdivide those 160 acres in Wyoming that Uncle Regis left you in his will.

For less than the cost of a newspaper ad, you can sell your home, condo, land, or even timeshare on eBay Real Estate in the auction format (see Figure 2-6). You can also choose to list your property in an ad format, accepting not bids but inquiries from prospective buyers from around the world. On the Create Your Listing form, shown in Figure 2-7, you must specify special information about your piece of real estate.

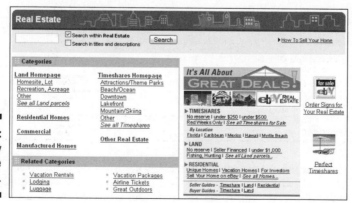

Figure 2-6:
eBay
Real Estate
home page.

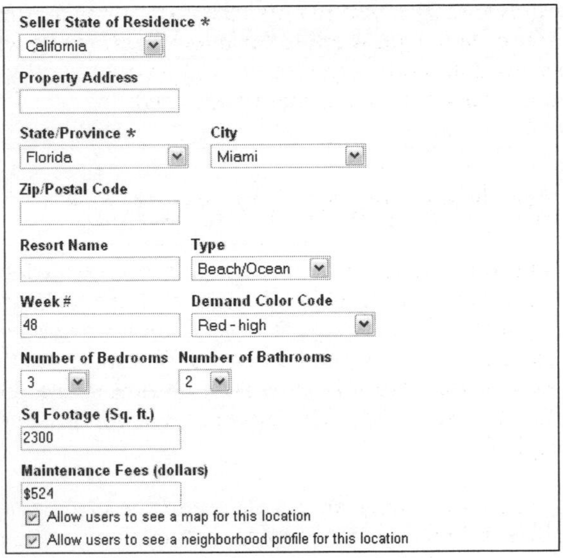

Figure 2-7:
Item
specifics for
selling a
timeshare.

In Tables 2-3 and 2-4, I provide a listing of fees that you can expect to encounter on eBay Real Estate.

Table 2-3	eBay Real Estate Timeshare, Land, and Manufactured Home Fees
Listing Type	*Fee Amount*
1-, 3-, 5-, 7-, or 10-day auction	$35
30-day auction	$50
30-day classified ad	$150
90-day classified ad	$300
Reserve less than $200 (refundable if reserve is met)	$2
Reserve $200 or more	1% (up to $50)
Final value fee	$35

Table 2-4 eBay Real Estate Residential, Commercial, and Other	
Listing Type	*Fee Amount*
1-, 3-, 5-, 7-, or 10-day auction	$100
30-day auction	$150
30-day classified ad	$150
90-day classified ad	$300
Reserve $200 or more (refundable if reserve is met)	1% (up to $50)
Final value fee	None

Fixed-Price Sales on eBay

To compete with other e-commerce sites, eBay now includes a *fixed-price sales* option. You put an item up for sale at a fixed price, and buyers pay the price that you're asking. Simple as that. Sellers are doing a great job at it, too.

You can also find fixed-price sales at eBay Stores and eBay Express (eBay's fixed-price, shopping cart venue at www.eBayExpress.com). Each eBay store is run by an eBay auction seller. eBay Stores has its own space on eBay — accessible in the following ways:

- Through the home page navigation bar by clicking eBay Express
- By clicking the eBay Stores link on the eBay home page
- By going straight to www.ebaystores.com from the Web

Potential buyers will be able to access your items from anywhere on the eBay site. The cost of an eBay store (see Table 2-5) compares favorably to any of the Web's megasite stores. There is no extra charge for your listings to appear in eBay Express.

Table 2-5 Basic eBay Stores Fees per 30 Days	
Type of Fee	*Fee Amount*
Monthly subscription fee	$15.95
Listing fee ($0.01 to $24.99 price)	$0.05
Listing fee ($25.00 and above price)	$0.10
Gallery picture	$0.01

Just as with auctions, fixed-price sales that are successful incur final value fees. eBay Express listings incur the same final value fees as auctions, but the final value fees for eBay Stores sales are higher. See Table 2-6.

For a complete overview on how to set up your own eBay store, check out Chapter 5.

Table 2-6	eBay Stores Final Value Fees
Closing Price	*Final Value Fee*
$0.01 to $25.00	**10%** of the selling price
$25.01 to $100.00	**10%** of the first $25.00 ($2.50) **plus 7%** of the remaining selling price
$100.01 to $1000.00	**10%** of the first $25.00 ($2.50) **plus 7%** of the next $25.01 to $100.00 ($5.25) **plus 5%** of the remaining selling price between $100.01 to $1000.00
$1000.01 and over	**10%** of the first $25.00 ($2.50) **plus 7%** of the next $25.01 to $100.00 ($5.25) **plus 5%** of the next $100.01 to $1000.00 ($45.00) **plus 3%** of the remaining selling price

Types of eBay Auctions

An auction is an auction is an auction, right? Naw. eBay has five types of auctions for your selling pleasure. Most of the time you'll run traditional auctions, but other auctions have their place, too. After you've been selling on eBay for a while, you may find that one of the other types of auctions also suits your needs. Keep in mind that eBay was founded on the regular auction format — the allure of "winning" is what brings users back to the site. In this section, I go over these auctions so that you fully understand what they are and when it's appropriate to use them.

Standard auctions

Auctions are the bread and butter of eBay. You can run a traditional auction for one, three, five, seven, or ten days, and when the auction closes, the highest bidder wins. I'm sure you've bid on several and I hope you've won a few. If you've tried selling, I suspect you've made some money running some of your own.

You begin the auction with an opening bid, and bidders bid up your opening price, competing with one another and building a healthy profit for you on your item.

If you'd like, you can set a *Buy It Now* option on your auction for an additional fee. By setting fixed selling prices at the get go, buyers have the option of buying your item outright. This is attractive for many users of the eBay system. The Buy It Now price you post should be the price at which you'd be happy to sell the item.

Even with a Buy It Now option, people can still bid on your item. After a bid is placed, the Buy It Now Option disappears and the item proceeds in a regular auction for the duration you indicated when you placed the listing.

Multiple Item (Dutch) auctions

When you've purchased an odd lot of five hundred kitchen knife sets or managed (legally, of course) to get your hands on a truckload of televisions that you want to sell as expeditiously as possible, you might want to use the Dutch (multiple item) auction. In the *Dutch auction* (see Figure 2-8 for an example), which can run for one, three, five, seven, or ten days, you list as many items as you'd like, and bidders can bid on as many items as they'd like. The final item price is set by the lowest successful bid at the time the auction closes.

Figure 2-8: A Dutch auction for coins in the Mexico, Coins category.

For example, suppose you want to sell five action figures on eBay in a Dutch auction. Your starting bid is $5 each. If five bidders each bid $5 for one figure, they each get a figure for $5. But if, say, two people bid $5, one person bids $7, and another bids $8, all five bidders win the action figure for the lowest final bid of $5.

In the following list, I highlight the details of the Dutch auction:

- The listing fee is based on your opening bid price (just like in a traditional auction), but it's multiplied by the number of items in your auction to a maximum listing fee of $4.80.

- The final auction value fees are on the same scale as in a standard auction, but they're based on the total dollar amount of all your completed sales in the listing.

- When bidders bid on your Dutch auction, they can bid on one or more items at one bid price. (The bid is multiplied by the number of items.)

- If the bidding gets hot and heavy, rebids must be in a higher total dollar amount than the total of that bidder's past bids.

- Bidders may reduce the quantity of the items for which they're bidding in your auction, but the dollar amount of the total bid price must be higher.

- All winning bidders pay the same price for their items, no matter how much they bid.

- The lowest successful bid when the auction closes is the price for which your items in that auction will be sold.

- If your item gets more bids than you have items, the lowest bidders are knocked out one by one, with the earliest bidders remaining on board the longest in the case of tie bids.

- When the auction closes, the earliest (by date and time) successful high bidders win their items.

- Higher bidders get the quantities they've asked for, and bidders can refuse partial quantities of the number of items in their bids.

For a large quantity of a special item, your Dutch auction may benefit from some of the eBay Featured auction options, which I detail in Chapter 10.

Reserve price auctions

In a *reserve price auction,* you're able to set an undisclosed minimum price for which your item will sell, thereby giving yourself a safety net. Figure 2-9 shows an auction in which the reserve has not yet been met. Using a reserve price auction protects the investment you have in an item. If, at the end of the auction, no bidder has met your undisclosed reserve price, you aren't obligated to sell the item, and the high bidder isn't required to purchase the item.

TEXAS RV LOT with LAKE ACCESS & Low Reserve!
Close to Lake Livingston-All Utilities Available!

Item number: 140123969351

You are signed in

Watch this item in My eBay

Current bid:	US $1,000.00 **Place Bid >**
	Reserve not met
End time:	**1 hour 25 mins** (Jun-06-07 16:55:23 PDT)
Shipping costs:	Not specified
Item location:	Texas, United States
History:	28 bids
High bidder:	Bidder 6

View larger picture

You can also: **Watch This Item**
Get alerts via Text message, IM or Cell phone
Email to a friend

Meet the seller
Seller: _____ (1194 ★)
Feedback: 99.8% Positive
Member: since Dec-27-00 in United States
• Read feedback comments
• Ask seller a question
• Add to Favorite Sellers
• View seller's other items

Buy safely
1. Check the seller's reputation
Score: 1194 | 99.8% Positive
Read feedback comments

Figure 2-9:
Note that a reserve has not been met for this auction.

For example, if you have a rare coin to auction, you can start the bidding at a low price to attract bidders to click your auction and read your infomercial-like description. If you start your bidding at too high a price, you might dissuade prospective bidders from even looking at your auction, and you won't tempt them to even bid. They may feel that the final selling price will be too high for their budgets.

Everyone on eBay is looking for a bargain or a truly rare item. If you can combine the mystical force of both of these needs in one auction, you have something special. The reserve price auction enables you to attempt — and perhaps achieve — this feat.

The fees for a reserve price auction are the same as those for a traditional auction with one exception. eBay charges between $1.00 and $50.00 for the privilege of running a reserve price auction. If the reserve price is $200.00 or more, the reserve price fee is 1 percent of the reserve price (with a maximum of $50.00). When your item sells, your reserve fee is refunded.

The reserve price auction is a safety net for the seller, but often an uncomfortable guessing game for the prospective bidder. To alleviate buyer anxiety, I recommend that you put reserve prices in the item's description. This allows bidders to decide whether the item will fit into their bidding budgets.

You can't use the reserve price option in a Dutch auction.

Restricted access auctions

eBay won't allow certain items to be sold in nonrestricted categories, so you must list them in the Mature Audiences category on eBay. eBay makes it easy for the user to find or avoid these types of auctions by making this area accessible only after the user enters a password and agrees to the terms and conditions of the area.

Items in the Mature Audiences area are not accessible through the regular eBay title search, nor are they listed in Newly Listed Items to those who haven't verified their identity.

Anyone who participates in Mature Audiences auctions on eBay, whether as a bidder or a seller, must have a credit card on file on eBay for verification (see Figure 2-10).

Terms of Use: Mature Audiences Category ("Terms of Use")

You must be a responsible adult over the age of 18 (or the age of consent in the jurisdiction from which this site is being accessed) to view the Adults-Only category pages. Materials available in this category include graphic visual depictions and descriptions of nudity and sexual activity. Federal, state or local laws may prohibit visiting this adult category if you are under 18 years of age. By entering your User ID and Password to access this site, to list an item, or to bid on an item in this category, you are making the following statements:

1. I am a member of the eBay community and I will follow the eBay User Agreement governing my use of the eBay web site.
2. I am willing to provide eBay with my valid credit card number and expiration date, which will be left on file with eBay in order to verify that I am at least 18 years of age.
3. I will not permit any person(s) under 18 years of age to have access to any of the materials contained within this site.
4. I am voluntarily choosing to access this category, because I want to view, read and/or hear the various materials that are available.
5. I understand and agree to abide by the standards and laws of the community in which I live or from which I am accessing this site.
6. By entering my User ID and Password and viewing any part of this adult category, I agree that I shall not hold eBay or its employees responsible for any materials located in the adult category, and I waive all claims against eBay relating to materials found at this site.
7. If I use these services in violation of these Terms and Use, I understand I may be in violation of local and/or federal laws and am solely responsible for my actions.
8. I am an adult, at least 18 years of age, and I have a legal right to possess adult material in my community.
9. I do not find pornographic images of nude adults, adults engaged in sexual acts or other sexual material to be offensive or objectionable.
10. I will exit from this site immediately if I am in any way offended by the sexual nature of any materials on this site.
11. By entering my User ID and Password at the bottom of these Terms of Use, and by listing, bidding an item, or entering the adult site, I agree to abide by these terms.

If you do not agree to these terms, click on the back button of your browser and exit this adult category page.

[Submit]

Figure 2-10: You must agree to the legalities to enter the Mature Audiences category.

Do not attempt to slip an adult-only auction into a nonrestricted category. eBay doesn't have a sense of humor when it comes to this violation of policy and may relocate or end your auction. eBay might even suspend you from its site.

Private auctions

Bidders' names are often kept private when dealing in the expensive fine art world. Likewise, to protect the innocent, eBay *private auctions* don't place bidders' names on the auction listing. No one needs to know just how much you choose to pay for something, especially if the item is rare and you really want it.

Not quite adult enough . . .

I was surprised to see a private auction listed on one of my favorite eBay seller's lists. She usually doesn't sell items like "Fringe Black BRA 36B SEXY SEXY SEXY," so I looked through this seller's past auctions. I saw that she didn't get any bids when she listed the bra in the restricted (Adult Only) area of eBay in the category Everything Else: Mature Audiences: Clothing, Accessory. When she put the bra up for private auction in the category Clothing & Accessories: Women's Clothing: Lingerie: Bras: General, she got five bidders and sold the item. I guess it wasn't sexy enough for the "adult" crowd!

As a seller, you have the option (at no extra charge) of listing your auction as a private auction. The option can be found in the How You're Selling portion of the Create Your Listing form. To find this option (should it be hidden), click Show/Hide Options in the top-right corner of the form, select Format, and then select Private Listing.

The eBay search page features an area where you can conduct a bidder search. You — and everyone else, including your family — can find the items you've bid on. One December, my daughter told me that she didn't want a particular item — something that I had just bid on — for Christmas. My creative daughter had been regularly perusing my bidding action on eBay to see what I was buying for the holidays! Buying from private auctions might have kept my Santa shopping secret.

The private auction is a useful tool for sellers who are selling bulk lots to other sellers. It maintains the privacy of the bidders, and customers can't do a bidder search to find out what sellers are paying for the loot they then plan to re-sell on eBay.

A great option for sales of items that are a bit racy or perhaps for purchases of items that may reveal something about the bidder, the private auction can save you the potential embarrassment associated with buying a girdle or buying the tie that flips over to reveal a racy half-nude female on the back.

Although the private auction is a useful tool, it may intimidate the novice user. On the other hand, if your customer base comes from experienced eBay users, and you're selling an item that may benefit by being auctioned in secret, you might want to try this option.

Running Your Auction

The basic plan for running an auction is the same for everyone, except for decisions regarding the timing of the auction and the starting price. If you speak to twenty different eBay sellers, you'll probably get twenty different answers about effective starting bids and when to end your auction. Until you develop your own philosophy, I'd like to give you some ideas to help you make a sound decision.

You can successfully promote your auctions online and offline, and can legally offer your item to the next highest bidder if the auction winner doesn't come through with payment. I discuss a few of these ideas in this section.

Starting the bidding

The most generally accepted theory about starting bids is that setting the bidding too high scares away new bids. Also, as in the case of the reserve price auction, if the bidding begins too high, novices might be afraid that the bidding will go too high and they'll never win the auction.

Some sellers begin the bidding at the price they paid for the item and an additional amount to cover fees, thereby protecting their investment. This is a good tactic, especially if you bought the item at a price far below the current going rate on eBay.

To determine the current going value for your item, I recommend using the Completed Listings search, which I explain in Chapter 7. If you know that the item is selling on eBay for a certain price and that there is a demand for it, starting the bidding at a reasonably low level can be a great way to increase bidding and attract prospective bidders to read your auction.

My years of advertising experience have taught me a lot of marketing lessons. If an item is in demand and people are actively buying, start the bidding low. Retail stores have done this for years with ads that feature prices starting at $9.99 or $14.98. Even television commercials advertising automobiles quote a low starting price. To get the car as shown in the ad, you may end up paying twice the quoted price.

When sellers know that they have an item that will sell, they begin their bidding as low as a dollar or even a penny. Because of the eBay *proxy bidding system* (which maintains your highest bid as secret, increasing it incrementally when you're bid against), it takes more bids (due to the smaller bidding increments) to bring the item up to the final selling price.

The downside is that new bidders who aren't familiar with the system may bid only the minimum required increment each time they bid. This can be frustrating, and they may quit bidding because it might take them several bids to top the current bid placed by someone who's familiar with the proxy bid system. Very few of us know the proxy increments by heart, so as a refresher, I give you the goods in Table 2-7.

Table 2-7	Proxy Bidding Increments
Current High Bid	*Bid Increment*
$0.01 to $0.99	$0.05
$1.00 to $4.99	$0.25
$5.00 to $24.99	$0.50
$25.00 to $99.99	$1.00
$100.00 to $249.99	$2.50
$250.00 to $499.99	$5.00
$500.00 to $999.99	$10.00
$1000.00 to $2499.99	$25.00
$2500.00 to $4999.99	$50.00
$5000.00 and up	$100.00

Auction timing

Another debatable philosophy is auction timing. People are always asking me how long to run auctions and what's the best day to end an auction. You have to evaluate your item and decide the best plan:

✔ **One-day auction:** This format can be very successful if you have an item that's the hot ticket for the moment on eBay. I used this format when I sold some *Friends* TV show memorabilia. The 24-hour auction opened midday before the final show and ended the next day — at a healthy profit!

One-day auctions also give you the benefit of pushing your auction to the top of the heap in the listings. Because eBay defaults to show the items ending first at the top of the page (just below Featured auctions), a one-day listing posts right up there!

Pirates of the Caribbean, er, Carribean?

Just before the *Pirates of the Caribbean* movie premiered, Disneyland gave out exclusive movie posters to their visitors. My daughter, savvy eBayer that she is, snagged several copies to sell on the site. She listed them (one at a time) when the movie opened and couldn't get more than the starting bid, $9.99, for each of them.

When we searched eBay for *pirates poster,* we found that the same posters with a misspelled title, Pirates of the Caribbean, were selling for as high as $30 each. We immediately changed her auctions to have the more popular (and misspelled) *Carribean* in the title and quickly saw those dollar signs! After selling out her initial stock, she found another seller who had ten for sale — in one auction — with the proper spelling in the title. She bought those as well (for $5 each) and sold them with misspelled titles on the site for between $15 and $27!

✔ **Three-day auction:** If the item's price will shoot up right after you post it, as in the heyday of Beanie Babies, a three-day auction works just fine. And it's great for those last-minute holiday shoppers looking for hard-to-find items.

With the Buy It Now feature, you can pretty much accomplish the same thing. When you list your item for sale, set a price at which you will sell the item; this is your target price. This price can be any amount, and if someone is willing to pay, it sells.

✔ **Five-day auction:** Five days will give you two days more than three and two days less than seven. That's about the size of it. If you just want an extended weekend auction, or if your item is a hot one, use it. Five-day auctions are useful during holiday rushes, when gift buying is the main reason for bidding.

✔ **Seven-day auction:** Tried-and-true advertising theory says that the longer you advertise your item, the more people will see it. On eBay, this means that you have more opportunity for people to bid on it. The seven-day auction is a staple for the bulk of eBay vendors. Seven days is long enough to cover weekend browsers and short enough to keep the auction interesting.

✔ **Ten-day auction:** Many veteran eBay sellers swear by the ten-day auction. Sure, eBay charges you an extra 40 cents for the privilege, but the extra three days of exposure (it can encompass two weekends) can easily net you more than 40 cents in profits.

If you're selling an esoteric collectible that doesn't appear on eBay often, run a ten-day auction to give it maximum exposure. Start it on a Friday, so it will cover the aforementioned two weekends worth of browsers. In my book, *eBay Timesaving Techniques For Dummies,* I examine in depth the opinions on how long to run an auction and what day or time to begin it.

Your auction closes exactly one, three, five, seven, or ten days — *to the minute* — after you start the auction. Be careful not to begin your auctions when you're up late at night and can't sleep: You don't want your auction to end at two in the morning when no one else is awake to bid on it. If you can't sleep, be productive and use Turbo Lister to prepare your listings ahead of time and upload them for future launching when the world is ready to shop.

The specific day you close your auction also is no longer as important as it was in the early days of eBay. Buyers browse the site seven days a week, 24 hours a day. The weekdays and the weekends are full of browsers, so it's hard to guesstimate when your perfect buyer will be browsing. Take a look at Figure 2-11, which is a screen shot outlining the days that all my items had hits during the past thirty days. This chart is part of a valuable tool called View Tracker, which is available from Sellathon.com. In Chapter 10, I show you how to combine your search engine research with this special kind of statistical counter to help you identify the best closing time for your items. (See Chapter 7 for the details about using the search engine as a valuable research tool.) The best person to figure out the closing information for your auctions is you. Use the tools, and over time you'll work out a pattern that works best.

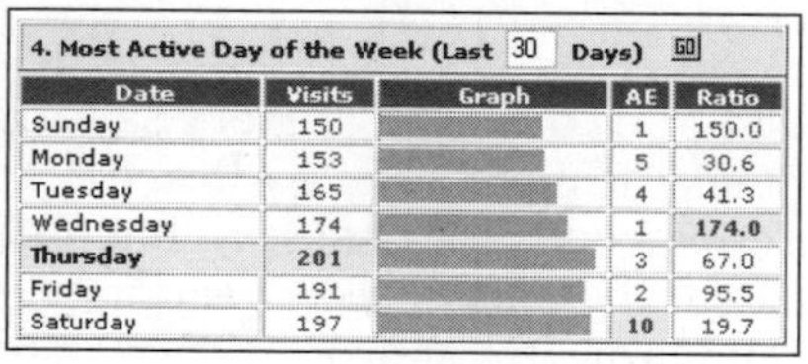

Figure 2-11:
Statistics
of hits on
my eBay
listings by
the day of
the week.

4. Most Active Day of the Week (Last 30 Days)				
Date	Visits	Graph	AE	Ratio
Sunday	150		1	150.0
Monday	153		5	30.6
Tuesday	165		4	41.3
Wednesday	174		1	174.0
Thursday	**201**		3	67.0
Friday	191		2	95.5
Saturday	197		10	19.7

A definite time *not* to close your auctions? Experience has taught many sellers never to close an auction on a national holiday. Memorial Day, the Fourth of July, and Veteran's Day may be bonanza sales days for retail shops, but eBay auction items closing on these days go at bargain prices. I guess everyone is out shopping at the brick-and-mortar stores.

Marketing your sales

How do you let people know about your listings? What do you do if all one hundred million users on eBay happen to not be on the site the week that your items are up for sale? You advertise.

Many mailing lists and newsgroups permit self-promotion. Find a group that features your type of items and post a bit of promotion. This works best if you have your own e-commerce Web site. Your site, which should be the hub for your sales, can give you an identity and level of professionalism that makes your business more official in the eyes of buyers. In Chapter 8, I detail the ins and outs of business sites on the Web.

When you have an eBay store, eBay allows you to send a number of e-mails to customers who request to be on your mailing list. Also, eBay will see to it that your store (and its listings) appears in searches on Google. Take a look at Figure 2-12, which shows my store in a Google search.

Figure 2-12: My eBay store listed on Google.

eBay to Go

A new feature on eBay allows you to transport your items to an outside site using JavaScript code. I've put one on my MySpace page (see Figure 2-13). To get code to insert in your listings, go to www.ebaytogo.com and make your own widget. Click the OK, Let's Go link, and on the next page, select which type of layout you'd like to use and follow the steps to select the items you want to promote. Just insert the code on any Web page on the Internet and visitors to that page will see your listings and be able to click to your items.

Figure 2-13:
eBay to
Go on
MySpace.

This widget is run by eBay's magic API (application program interface), which is far too technical for the likes of me — I'm an expert at buying and selling, not techie coding! Luckily, you don't need to be a techie to use this tool. It's automatically put on your site after you insert a bit of eBay-supplied HTML code into your Web page. The eBay API automatically updates your listings.

Voila! A virtual showroom.

Link buttons

eBay supplies some nice link buttons (see Figure 2-14) that you can use on your Web site. Visit the following address to add these links to your site's home page: `http://pages.ebay.com/services/buyandsell/link-buttons.html`.

I'm guessing that you already know all about your About Me page, a handy tool when it comes to marketing your auctions. In Chapter 3, I discuss the values of the About Me page. You should link to your Web site from your little home page on eBay.

Here's a great way to market future listings: When you're sending items after making a sale on eBay, include a list of items that you'll be selling soon (along with your thank-you note, of course) — especially ones that may appeal to that customer. If you schedule your auctions, you're given the auction number before the item is listed.

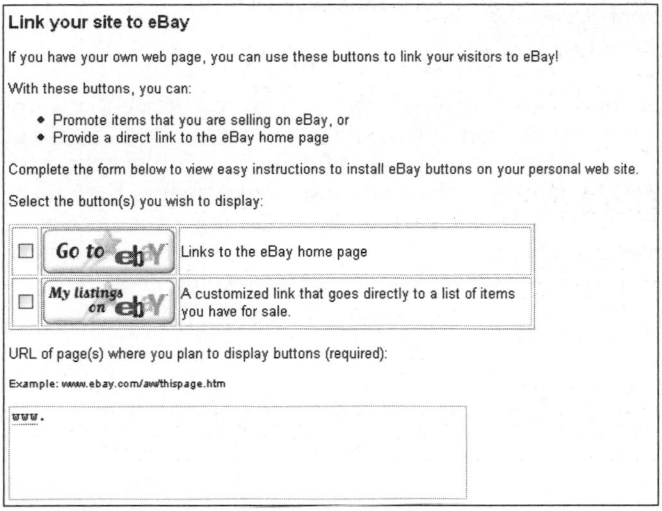

Link your site to eBay

If you have your own web page, you can use these buttons to link your visitors to eBay!

With these buttons, you can:

- Promote items that you are selling on eBay, or
- Provide a direct link to the eBay home page

Complete the form below to view easy instructions to install eBay buttons on your personal web site.

Select the button(s) you wish to display:

☐	Go to ebY	Links to the eBay home page
☐	My listings on ebY	A customized link that goes directly to a list of items you have for sale.

URL of page(s) where you plan to display buttons (required):

Example: www.ebay.com/aw/thispage.htm

uuu.

Figure 2-14:
The link
buttons.

Do not link your auction to your Web site. It's against eBay policy to possibly divert sales away from the auction site. *Do* link from your About Me page. See the "Linking from your auctions" section, later in this chapter, to find out just what you can and cannot link to and from.

A second chance

The Second Chance feature on eBay helps sellers legitimize something that previously went on behind closed doors and in violation of eBay policy. When a winner doesn't complete a sale, or you have multiple units of the same item, or the reserve price wasn't met but you are willing to accept the highest bid that didn't meet the reserve, the Second Chance feature allows sellers to offer the item to the next highest bidders.

You must still go through the proper channels and file your nonpaying bidder notice with eBay. After doing that, you can then send a Second Chance offer to any underbidder no more than sixty days after the end of the auction. Your final value fee is based on the price you receive when the offer is accepted.

In the Second Chance offer scenario, the seller can leave two feedbacks: one for the winner (nonpaying bidder) and one for the person who bought the item through the Second Chance offer transaction. The bidder to whom you proffer your Second Chance offer is covered by the eBay fraud protection program.

This feature does not apply to Dutch auctions.

Listing Violations

eBay does not sell merchandise. eBay is merely a venue that provides the location where others can put on a giant, e-commerce party (in other words, sell stuff). To provide a safe and profitable venue for its sellers, eBay must govern auctions that take place on its site. eBay makes the rules; you and I follow the rules. I like to think of eBay as the place that lets you hold your senior prom in its gym. When I was in school, my classmates and I had to follow the rules or see our prom cancelled. If we don't agree to follow eBay's rules, a safe and trusted eBay community can't exist.

Listing policies

eBay has some hard-and-fast rules about listing your items. You must list your item in the appropriate category (that only makes sense), and I highlight here a few other rules that you should keep in mind when listing. What I discuss in this section isn't a definitive list of eBay listing policies and rules. Take time to familiarize yourself with the User Agreement (which details all eBay policies and rules) at `pages.ebay.com/help/policies/uapp.html`. I recommend that you check the eBay User Agreement regularly for any policy changes.

Choice auctions

Your auction must be for one item only: the item that you specifically list in your auction. It's against the rules to give the bidder a choice of items, sizes, or colors. When you give your bidders a choice, it's an illegal sale on eBay and isn't covered under the PayPal Buyer Protection program. Anything that's negotiated outside the eBay system can lead to misrepresentation or fraud. You don't want to be caught up in that sort of grief and misery. If eBay catches you offering a choice, they will end the auction and credit the insertion fee to your account.

Duplicate auctions

Remember the old supply and demand theory from your economics class? When people list the same items repeatedly, they drive down the item's going price while ruining all the other sellers' opportunities to sell the item during that time frame.

eBay allows you fifteen identical listings at any time. If you're going to list an item that many times, be sure to list it in different categories. That's a rule, but it also makes sense. Nothing drives down the price of an item faster than closing identical auctions, one after another, in the same category. eBay also requires that you list your auction in a category that's relevant to your item.

Pre-selling: Not worth the hassle

A seller I once knew pre-sold Beanie Babies on eBay. She had a regular source that supplied her when the new toys came out, so she fell into a complacent attitude about listing pre-sales. Then her supplier didn't get the shipment. Motivated by the need to protect her feedback rating (and by the fear that she'd be accused of fraud), she ran all over town desperately trying to get the Beanies she needed to fill her orders. The Beanies were so rare that she ended up spending several hundred dollars more than what she had originally sold the toys for, just to keep her customers happy.

If you have multiple copies of something, a better solution is to run a Dutch auction for the total number of items you have for sale. Or perhaps run two Dutch auctions in different (but appropriate) categories.

If you're caught with more than fifteen identical auctions, eBay may end the additional auctions (any over fifteen).

Pre-sale listings

eBay doesn't like it when you try to sell something that's not in your hands (known as a *pre-sale listing*). Doing so is a dangerous game to play anyway. In many situations, being the first seller to put a very popular item up for sale can get you some pretty high bids. And if you can guarantee in your auction description that the item will be available to ship within thirty days of the purchase or the auction closing, you can run a pre-sale. However, I don't recommend even attempting a pre-sale listing if you're not completely sure that you'll have the item in time.

If you know that you'll have the item to ship — and it won't be lost on its way to you — you may list the item with the following requirement: You must state in your auction description that the item is a pre-sale and will be shipped thirty days from the end of the listing or purchase. You'll also have to use a little HTML here because the text must be coded with an HTML font no smaller than font size 3.

Before you set up such an auction, check out the Federal Trade Commission thirty-day rule covering these matters, which you can find at the following address: www.ftc.gov/bcp/conline/pubs/buspubs/mailorder.htm.

eBay Giving Works (charity) auctions

Tens of millions of dollars has been raised on eBay for charitable organizations (see the figure). If you represent a legitimate charity, you may run auctions on eBay to raise funds. Just follow these simple steps:

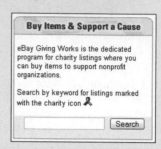

1. **Register your charity to be certified at MissionFish (`www.missionfish.org/register.jsp`).**

   Select the Register Your Nonprofit check box.

2. **Register on eBay and create a Seller account.**

3. **Go back to MissionFish and click the Register to Sell link.**

   Explain what your charity is, what it does, where the money goes, and so on. Set up the page to Show No Feedback and Show All Items. eBay will link this page to the Giving Works area.

4. **Create an eBay listing for your item.**

In the Pictures & Details section of the Sell form, click the Add link in the area titled Donate Percentage of Sale. Select your organization from the nonprofit directory and specify that 100% of the sale price will be donated to your organization.

Your listings will now get additional visibility through a specialized search reserved for eBay Giving Works and will have a ribbon icon in the title bars.

The eBay Giving Works page is accessible from a link on the home page or directly through `http://pages.ebay.com/giving works`.

Bonuses, giveaways, raffles, or prizes

Because eBay sells to every state in the United States, it must follow explicit laws governing giveaways and prizes. Each state has its own set of rules and regulations, so eBay doesn't allow individual sellers to come up with their own promotions. If your auction violates this rule, eBay might end it.

Keyword spamming

Keyword spamming is when you add words, usually brand names, to your auction description that don't describe what you're selling (for example, describing that little black dress as Givenchy-style when Givenchy has nothing to do with it). Sellers use keyword spamming to pull viewers to their auctions after viewers have searched for the brand name. To attract attention to their listings, some sellers use *not* or *like* along with the brand name, such as *like Givenchy.*

Keyword spamming actually causes your auction to fall under "potentially infringing" items for sale on eBay. Keyword spamming is a listing violation, and I mention it here because it affects all listings. The wording you choose when you run this kind of auction manipulates the eBay search engine and prospective bidders. For a complete discussion of keyword spamming, see Chapter 4.

Linking from your auctions

Few issues set sellers to arguing more than the rules on linking. In your auction item description, you *can* use the following links:

- ✔ One link to an additional page that gives further information about the item you're selling.
- ✔ A link that opens an e-mail window on the prospective buyer's browser so that the buyer can send you an e-mail.
- ✔ Links to more photo images of the item you're selling.
- ✔ Links to your other auctions on eBay and your eBay store listings.
- ✔ One link to your About Me page, in addition to the link next to your user ID that eBay provides.
- ✔ Links to vendors' sites that help you with your auctions. eBay considers listing services, software, and payment services to be third-party vendors. You can legally link to them as long as the HTML font is no larger than size 3; if you're using a logo, it must be no larger than 88 x 33 pixels. Most third-party vendors are well aware of these restrictions. They don't want their credits pulled from eBay, so the information they supply as a link generally falls within eBay's parameters.

In your auction description, you *cannot* link to the following:

- ✔ A page that offers to sell, trade, or purchase merchandise outside the eBay site.
- ✔ Any area on the Internet that offers merchandise considered illegal on eBay. See Chapter 4 for information on illegal items.
- ✔ Any site that encourages eBay bidders to place their bids outside eBay.
- ✔ Sites that solicit eBay user IDs and passwords.

Linking from your About Me page

eBay rules on your About Me page are pretty much the same as they are on the rest of the site. Because eBay gives you this page for self-promotion, *you* may link to your own business Web site from it (e-commerce or otherwise). Be sure not to link to other trading sites or to sites that offer the same merchandise for the same or a lower price. Read more about the About Me page do's and don'ts in Chapter 3.

Chapter 3

Cool eBay Tools

....

In This Chapter

▶ Making My eBay your home page

▶ Taking advantage of your About Me page

▶ Managing the business of your auction: eBay seller services

....

*e*Bay offers you an amazing variety of tools. But because the site is constantly changing, many users fail to notice when new tools appear on the
system. I must admit that I have fallen victim to the "Oh, I didn't know I could
do that" syndrome. When I poke around eBay and find a new cool tool or neat
shortcut, it's always an eye-opener!

eBay users frequently share with me some nugget of information that has
helped them along the way. And now I share these nuggets with you.

To stay on top of upcoming changes on eBay, you can subscribe to the
General Announcement e-mail. Unfortunately, eBay tends to fill these daily
missives with lots of promotional folderol, but a quick once-over will keep you
abreast of the many changes before they occur on the site. To sign up for this
e-mail, mouse over (hold your cursor still for a moment over) Community on
the navigation bar in the upper part of most eBay pages, and, from the drop-
down menu that appears, click Groups. On the Groups Center page, scroll
down to News & Events and click Announcements. On the resulting page, you
may join this group by clicking the eBay Announcements link.

Aside from the tools I tell you about in this chapter, the most important
shortcut I can give you is to remind you that when you sign in, but before you
start your business on eBay, select the Keep Me Signed In on This Computer
Unless I Sign Out check box. This permits you to close your window during
the day and reopen it later without having to sign in again.

If you have more than one user ID or share a computer with other people, be
sure to sign out when you're finished. The cookie system has been changed
on eBay. Now, as on other sites, your computer will maintain your sign-in
information for a twenty-four-hour period (or until you sign out).

In addition, eBay has developed some incredibly useful features, such as My eBay, which allows you to customize eBay for your home page. Another feature, the About Me page, lets you tell the story of your business to the world as well as find out (with a click of the mouse) about the people you plan on buying from. To get the lowdown on my favorite cool eBay tools, read on.

My eBay

The first tool eBay gives you is your My eBay page. Every time you sign on to the site, this page will pop up on your screen with a cheery, "My eBay — Hello, marsha_c (substitute your user ID for mine)," followed by your current feedback rating. The My eBay page is the perfect tool for running a small eBay business. It's no longer a step-by-step list of what you're bidding on and selling; it's an out-and-out Swiss Army knife of eBay tools.

Access the My eBay page by clicking the My eBay button in the eBay navigation bar, which appears at the top of every eBay page. You'll see that if you mouse over one of the five selections, a drop-down menu appears. You can go directly to the main pages by clicking the navigation bar. But if you know that you want to go to one of the specialized areas, you can mouse over and click the individual links. A sample is shown in Figure 3-1.

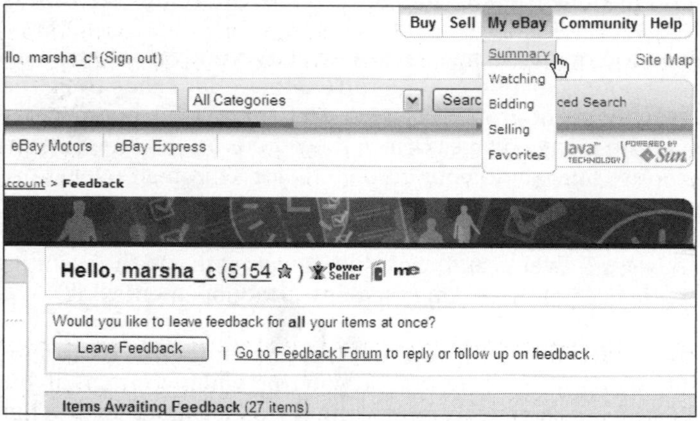

Figure 3-1: The eBay navigation bar appears at the top of every eBay page; each link has a drop-down menu.

When you arrive at your My eBay page, you see a summary of the business that you have in progress on the site (see Figure 3-2). Each comment has a link, so you can investigate the progress of the transactions.

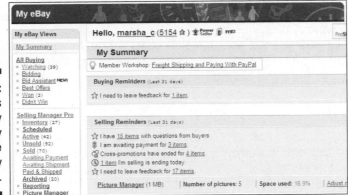

Figure 3-2: This is the My Summary entrance page for my business.

Most My eBay areas are divided into several areas (My Summary, All Buying, All Selling, Want It Now, My Messages, All Favorites, My Account, My Reviews and Guides, and the Dispute Console), which you can visit by clicking links in the My eBay Views area on the left side of the page. The top link of each My eBay area presents you with a summary of the activity in that area. The links below the top link take you to specific data, without having to scroll through a long page.

At the bottom of My eBay Views is another area with Related Links to services and to answers you may need while doing business at eBay. The task-specific pages of My eBay may show a <u>More</u> link in this additional links box. Click the More link and you're presented with a page of links related to the page you're on.

The links in the Related Links box are different depending on the page, with buying-related links on the All Buying page, selling-related links on the All Selling page, account-related links on the My Account page, and so forth. When you have a question regarding some eBay procedure, you'll find these links handy.

Setting a desktop shortcut to your My eBay page

People often tell me that they'd like a direct link from their computer desktop to their My eBay page. If you use Internet Explorer as your browser, just follow these steps:

1. **Sign in and go to your My eBay page.**

2. **In your browser's toolbar, choose File⇨ Send⇨Shortcut to Desktop.**

That's it. A clickable shortcut to your My eBay area is placed on your computer's desktop.

At the bottom of each of the Views is a mini tote board, giving you a snapshot of your financial business dealings. In the Buying area, it displays the number of items you're bidding on and the dollar amount of all your winning bids. In the Selling area, you see the number of items and the dollar amounts bid (see Figure 3-3).

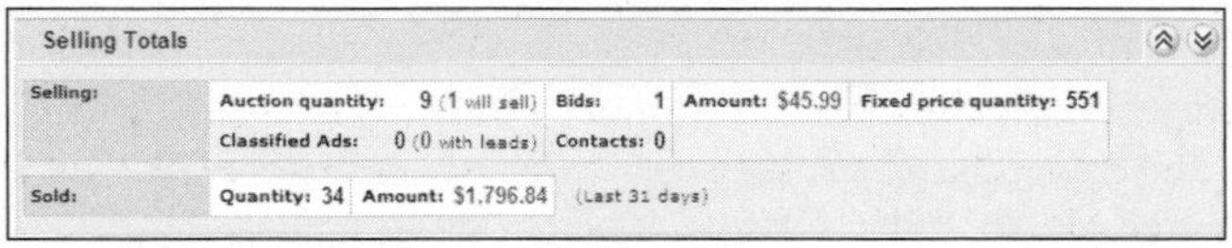

Figure 3-3:
My Selling
Totals tote
board.

Selling Totals					⊗ ⊗
Selling:	Auction quantity:	9 (1 will sell)	Bids:	1	Amount: $45.99	Fixed price quantity: 551
	Classified Ads:	0 (0 with leads)	Contacts: 0		
Sold:	Quantity: 34	Amount: $1,796.84	(Last 31 days)		

All Buying

Here it is: All Buying is the hub for keeping track of your bids, your wins, items you're watching, and any items you didn't win. Although you plan to sell more than you buy at eBay, I'm sure you'll occasionally find something to buy if only to turn around and resell it. I've found many a bargain item at eBay that I've re-sold immediately at a profit. Plus, I purchase most of my shipping supplies on eBay. (In Chapter 17, I reference a few eBay sources with great prices and fast shipping.)

Items I'm Bidding On

When you place a bid, eBay automatically registers it in the Items I'm Bidding On area, such as the one shown in Figure 3-4.

Figure 3-4:
Keeping
track of your
bidding on
My eBay.

If you're shopping on eBay, make the bidding page a daily stop so you can see the status of your bids:

✔ Bid amounts in green indicate that you're the high bidder in the auction.

✔ Bid amounts in red indicate that your bid is losing. If you decide to increase your bid, simply click the auction title to go to the auction.

✔ Dutch auctions appear in black. To determine whether you retain high bidder status in a Dutch auction, you have to go to the actual auction.

✔ The My Max Bid column reminds you of the amount of your highest bid; if you see a bid that surpasses your own, you'll know it's time to throw in another bid (or throw in the towel).

✔ The Bidding Totals box, at the top of the Bidding page, lists the current dollar amount you're spending and the number of items you're currently winning in pending auctions. You'll see the total amount you've bid and a separate total representing auctions you're winning.

✔ As auctions on which you've bid end, they automatically transfer to the Won and Didn't Win pages, based on your success or failure in the bidding process.

You can make notations on your bidding or item watching, for example, to help you organize your gift giving. (See the note I added in Figure 3-5.) Click to place a check mark next to the item you want to annotate, click the Add Note button, and then add the information.

Figure 3-5: My Father's Day notation on my bid.

Items I've Won

Clicking the Won link in the bidding area displays all the items you've won as far back as the last sixty days. The default is thirty-one days, which should suffice for most transactions. The Items I've Won page is a great place to keep track of items that you're waiting to receive from the seller. It's also a convenient way to keep track of your expenditures, should you be buying for resale. Helpful features on this page include the following:

- ✔ **Check box:** Click the box to add a check mark, and you can indicate that you'd like to add a note to your record or remove it from the list.

- ✔ **Seller's user ID:** It always helps to remember the seller's name, and this link sends you to the seller's Member Profile (feedback page) where you can send an e-mail to the seller.

- ✔ **Listing title:** A link to the auction. I always use this when an item arrives so that I can be sure that the item I received is exactly as advertised.

- ✔ **Item number:** The auction number for your records.

- ✔ **Auction sale date:** A convenient way to see whether your item is slow in shipping. After a week, it doesn't hurt to drop the seller an e-mail to check on the shipping status.

- ✔ **Sale price** and **quantity:** Helps you keep track of the money you've spent. Works with the totals in the tote board.

- ✔ **Action:** The drop-down menu displays different commands based on the status of your transaction. You can click a link to pay for the item through PayPal, view the payment status on paid items, mark the item paid if you paid through other payment methods, or leave feedback once you've received the item and are satisfied that it's what you ordered.

- ✔ **Icons:** At the end of each item's listing are three icons that appear dimmed until the selected action is taken. A dollar sign indicates whether you've paid for the item, a star indicates that you've left feedback, and a quote bubble indicates whether feedback has been left for you.

When you receive an item and leave feedback, select the check box next to the item and then click the Remove button to remove the completed transaction from view.

Items I'm Watching

Have you ever seen an auction that made you think, "I don't want to bid on this just now, but I'd like to buy it if it's a bargain"? Clicking the Watching link from the My eBay All Buying box will bring you to the Items I'm Watching page (see Figure 3-6), one of the most powerful features of the My eBay area. This page lists each auction with a countdown (time left) timer, so you know exactly when the auction will close. When an auction on your watch list gets close to ending, you can swoop down and make the kill — if the price is right.

Also a handy marketing tool, the Watching page allows you to store auctions from competitive sellers. That way, you can monitor the status of items similar to ones you plan to sell later and see whether the items are selling high or low, helping you to decide whether it's a good time to sell.

Figure 3-6:
Sit back and
observe at
My eBay.

You've probably seen the Watch This Item link at the top of each auction page. If you're watching items (eBay allows you to monitor one hundred auctions at a time), you'll see a notation on the page, indicating how many auctions you're currently watching.

My number-one reason for using the watch list function is that it allows me to keep my bargain hunting quiet. Everybody — including the competition — knows when you're bidding on an item; nobody knows when you're watching the deals like a hawk. When you're looking for bargains to buy and resell, you may not want to tip off the competition by letting them know you're bidding.

Selling

eBay provides some smooth management tools on your Selling page. You can track items you currently have up for auction and items you've sold. It's a quick way to get a snapshot of the dollar value of your auctions as they proceed. Although this page isn't as good for marketing information (detailed counters are best — see Chapter 9), it's a pretty good way to tell at a glance how your items are faring.

Items I'm Selling

With the Items I'm Selling page, shown in Figure 3-7, you can keep an eye on your store items, your fixed-price sales, and the progress of your auctions. You can see how many bids your auctions have, whether your reserves have been met, and how long before the auction will close. By clicking an item title, you can visit the listing to make sure your pictures are appearing or to check your counter.

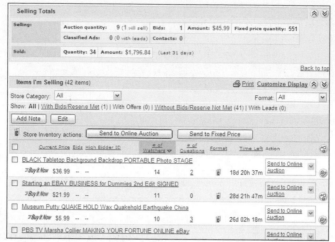

Figure 3-7:
The Items
I'm Selling
at My eBay.

Many people watch auctions and don't bid until the last minute, so you may not see a lot of bidding activity on your page. The # of Watchers feature can give you important information on the progress of your auctions.

The auctions that appear in green have received one or more bids (and met any reserves you've set). Auctions in red haven't received any bids or the set reserve price hasn't been met. Dutch auctions aren't color-coded and appear in black.

At the top of the Items I'm Selling area, eBay lists the current price of all items, including items that have been bid on but that haven't met your reserve. The total dollar amount of the items that will sell when the auction is over appears below these totals. On the right side of your listings, eBay has a column for icons.

The tech crew is always adding more features to these pages. Occasionally, go to the top right of these pages and click the Customize Display link. Here, you see a chart of additional options that you may display on the page. They will vary depending on the page.

Items I've Sold

Click the Sold link in the All Selling Views area and you'll come to the Items I've Sold area. The Items I've Sold area keeps your sales in a concise place, as shown in Figure 3-8. You can use it in lieu of fancy auction management software until you're selling lots of items. If you're selling hundreds of items, your list will probably be too long to monitor individual auctions, but you can view the total current price of the items that will sell.

Figure 3-8:
The Items
I've Sold
page in
My eBay.

If you're selling more than twenty items a week, consider using eBay's Selling Manager to give you a more complete auction management solution. See Chapter 9 for the lowdown on how to make this tool work for you.

The Items I've Sold page has the following features, which I'm sure you'll find helpful in completing your transactions:

- **Check box:** Click here to add a personal note to your record or to remove an item from your list.

- **Buyer's user ID** and **feedback rating:** The eBay ID of the winner of the sale. Click it to go to the user's Member Profile, where you can use eBay's e-mail sever to contact the buyer.

- **Quantity:** If the sale was for multiple items, the number of items is displayed here.

- **Item title:** A direct link to the auction. You can click this link to check on your auction and see the other bidders, should you want to make a Second Chance offer.

- **Item number:** The auction number for your records.

- **Sale price:** The final selling price for your item.

- **Total price:** The final selling price plus the shipping amount.

- **Sale date:** Keep an eye on the end date so that you can be sure you get your payment as agreed.

- **Action:** Here's where you find a hidden, drop-down menu that works with the icons to the right and offers links to various actions that you can take. Some of the more popular options are

- **Mark paid:** If the customer hasn't paid using PayPal, indicate their method of payment (after you receive it).

- **View payment status:** See a copy of the payment receipt if the buyer paid using PayPal, or see a notation you inserted regarding other payment methods.

- **Print shipping label:** You can print a shipping label from here. See Chapter 14 for more professional options.

- **Leave feedback:** Leave feedback with a single click once you've heard that the item arrived safely and your customer is happy. For more information on leaving feedback, check out the section "Feedback: Your permanent record," later in this chapter.

- **Mark shipped:** After you've shipped the item, click here to indicate that it's on the way.

- **Second Chance offer:** Make a Second Chance offer to one of your underbidders if you have multiple items for sale.

- **Relist:** Here you can relist your item on the site.

✔ **Icons:** My eBay has several icons that appear dimmed until you perform an action with the Action command. You may also click the icons at the top of the list to sort your listings by actions completed, although most sellers prefer to keep the listings in the default chronological order:

- **Shopping cart:** The buyer has completed checkout (supplying a shipping address and planned payment method).

- **Dollar sign:** The buyer has paid using PayPal, or you've used the drop-down menu to indicate that the buyer has paid with a different form of payment (such as a money order or a personal check).

- **Shipping box:** The item has shipped.

- **Star:** You've left feedback.

- **Comment bubble:** The buyer has left feedback. A plus sign (+) indicates a positive comment, and a minus sign (–) indicates a negative comment.

All Favorites

If you sell and have an interest in a few categories, look no further than the My eBay All Favorites pages, which give you some links for checking out what's hot and what's not. The All Favorites pages help you track trends and find some bargains to resell at eBay.

Favorite Categories

eBay allows you to store hot links for four categories. These links give you the chance to quickly check out the competition.

Before you list some of a popular item, estimate the date and hour that other auctions selling that item will close. Then go into the category and check to be sure that your auction won't be closing during a flood of auctions for the same item. Nothing kills profits more than closing an auction in the middle of a series of auctions selling the same thing. You can watch the final values drop one at a time.

Favorite Searches

Another tool that comes in handy for sellers as well as buyers is Searches (see Figure 3-9). You can list as many as one hundred favorite searches; when you want to check one out, simply click the Search Now link next to the item.

My Favorite Searches (34 searches)			Add new Search
Show: All | Searches (6) | Want It Now Searches (0)			
Delete			
☐ Name of Search ▲	Search Criteria	Email Settings	Action
☐ "camp ocala"	"camp ocala" Sort: Ending First	Not receiving emails	Sign up for Emails
☐ "case of"	"case of"	Not receiving emails	Sign up for Emails
☐ (Sekkisei,kose)	(Sekkisei,kose) Category: Health & Beauty	Not receiving emails	Sign up for Emails
☐ Abramovitz oil	Abramovitz oil	Not receiving emails	Sign up for Emails
☐ altair 880*	altair 880*	Not receiving emails	Sign up for Emails

Figure 3-9: Some of my favorite searches (this month).

You can view, change, and delete saved searches, or indicate that you'd like to receive e-mail notification when a new item is listed. To add an item to the list, run a search from any search bar on any eBay page and click the Save This Search link that appears at the top of the search results page. The next time you reload your My eBay All Favorites page, your new favorite will be listed.

Keeping track of favorite searches is a valuable tool when you're looking for particular items to resell and want to find them at bargain-basement prices. Be sure to take advantage of asterisks (wildcard characters) and alternate spellings so you can catch items with misspellings in the title. These are your best bets for low prices. (See Chapter 7 for the lowdown on the search engine and how it can help your sales.)

If you choose to receive e-mail when your search locates a new listing, you can request that you receive notification from seven days to a year. You're allowed to receive new listing e-mails on any or all of your hundred searches. Just click the drop-down menu and click the Sign Up For Emails link (refer to Figure 3-9). eBay sends its robot to check listings each night, so you'll get notification of a new listing the next morning.

Favorite Sellers

Favorite Sellers is where I keep a list of people who sell items similar to what I sell. I can check up on them and see what they're selling, when they're selling it, and for how much. It's a helpful tool that has prevented me from listing an item at the same time as one of their auctions.

Favorite Sellers is also handy when your competition is selling an item that you plan to sell, but at a deeply discounted price. When that happens, don't offer yours until they sell out of the item, at which time the price will most likely go back up — supply and demand, remember? I have a few quality wholesalers and liquidators under my favorite sellers, too, and search for lots that I can resell at a profit.

To add a seller to your Favorite Sellers list, click the Add New Seller or Store link in the upper-left corner of the page. On the page that appears, type the seller's user ID.

My Account

Your eBay account summary page (see mine in Figure 3-10) lets you know how much you owe eBay and how much they will charge your credit card that month. This is a quick way to check your last invoice, payments and credits, and your account; all the links are located in one area.

You can also access your PayPal account to see, for example, when deposits were credited to your checking account. (For a complete picture of how to sign up and use PayPal, visit Chapter 13.)

Personal Information

The Personal Information page holds all the links to your personal information at eBay. This is where you can change your e-mail address, user ID, password, and credit card information, and edit or create your About Me page. You can also change or access any registration or credit card information that you have on file at eBay.

My Seller Account Summary	☆ ☰
Account Activity	
Previous invoice amount (05/31/07): (View invoices)	US $178.37
Payments and credits since last invoice:	-US $0.60
Fees since last invoice: (View account status)	US $48.91
Current balance:	**US $226.68**

My PayPal Account Information 🖉	☆ ☰

View and update your PayPal account information and profile summary. Clicking the links below will take you to PayPal's secure website.

- Go to My Account Overview
- View Account History
- Update Profile Summary (account information, financial information, and selling preferences)

To view and update your PayPal user preferences on eBay: click here.

Recent Feedback (View all feedback)			☆ ☰
Comment	From	Date/Time	Item #
⊕ As described..fast ship...works great! Thanks!	Buyer: ▬▬▬ (737 ☆)	Jun-05-07 17:55	120061200825
⊕ Smooth transaction. Fast shipping. Great experience! A+++	Buyer: ▬▬ (169 ☆)	Jun-05-07 06:30	120061200825
⊕ Super Fast shipping.Thanx again	Buyer: ▬▬ (433 ☆)	Jun-01-07 16:41	120061200825

Figure 3-10: The My Account summary page.

The Personal Information page has a link for adding a wireless e-mail address for your cell phone or handheld device. What a great idea: eBay can send End of Auction notices right to your WAP-enabled cell phone. The trouble is, sometimes these messages can get lost in cellular space. So don't count on always getting immediate updates.

Addresses

On the Addresses page, you can see the address you used to register on eBay and edit (when necessary) your payment address and primary shipping address.

Preferences

A nifty feature of the eBay Preferences page is the opportunity to customize how you run your eBay business. There are sections on your buying, selling, communication, and general preferences. This is an important area for you to check out because setting some of these tools can make your selling career on eBay go far more smoothly. You can change the following:

- **Notification Preferences:** Tell eBay whether (and how) you'd like to be notified every time a function occurs in your eBay account. You can customize buying, selling, and other transaction details, notifications, and legal notices issued by eBay.

- **Selling Preferences:** In this area, you take control of how eBay helps you run your business. Here you can customize your checkout procedures, offer shipping discounts, and more. Most importantly, this is the place where you can decide to block certain buyers before they bid or buy from you. Figure 3-11 shows my eBay buyer requirements. By clicking the Edit link, you can block the following:

- **Buyers in countries to which I don't ship:** Every eBay seller (until they find out about this option) has had an item won from someone in a country to which they choose not to ship. You may choose not to ship for any number of reasons. Maybe you don't want to ship internationally and accept foreign payments (along with the extra fees from PayPal), or you don't want to risk your packages getting lost in a foreign postal system. When you get a sale like this, you are basically forced to go through with the sale — or risk negative feedback. By indicating that you do not want to accept business from buyers in particular countries, you avoid this problem.

- **Buyers with a negative feedback score:** If you don't want to accept customers who have been rapidly building negative feedback, you can remove them from your business here. You have a choice of barring people with a –1, –2, or –3 total feedback score (indicating these people have more negatives than positives).

- **Buyers with unpaid item strikes:** You may prevent those who have had two unpaid item strikes within the last thirty days. This is a good idea. If they haven't paid for two items in the last thirty days, they're likely not to go through with your transaction, thereby costing you time and money.

- **Buyers who may bid on several of my items and not pay for them:** This title is a bit misleading. As often happens in any commerce, some people think shopping is a game. Many hyper-caffeinated (to be kind) eBay joy riders will ferret out a particular seller and buy every item they have for sale, with absolutely no intention of paying. They seem to think this is fun.

  I know several major sellers who went to bed with several hundred items up for sale — only to wake up to find everything sold. After the initial blush of victory, they realized that everything was bought by the same buyer — often someone with a new account or a low feedback rating. If that's not bad enough, they check their feedback and find that the buyer left negative feedback for every item they bought. eBay is cooperative in helping to clean up this mess, but all items need to be relisted, and the entire repair process is hugely time consuming. Save yourself some grief and limit your buyers here.

- **Buyers without a PayPal account:** You may choose to bar buyers who don't have a PayPal account, but why? New buyers are the core of eBay, and signing up for a PayPal account is a simple task for those who want to pay you with a credit card.

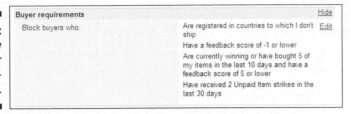

Figure 3-11:
My eBay
Buyer
require-
ments.

- ✔ **Member to Member Communication:** Once you've set up an account with Skype, you can insert your Skype ID here and indicate that prospective buyers may contact you through Skype. They then can contact you through chat or Skype voice.

- ✔ **General Preferences:** Here's where you can set up all the other fun stuff that has to do with your eBay business. Check it out. It changes as eBay adds option, so it's worth visiting on a regular basis.

If all the information on the My eBay pages seems daunting (indeed it is), you can adjust how your My eBay pages are displayed. In the General Preferences area, open the My eBay link by clicking the Show link in that area. (Take a look at Figure 3-12 to see what happens when you click the Show link.) You can then set your My eBay pages to Display Help Content in My eBay. That way, you'll have help links at the bottom of the pages should you get lost or merely confused.

Figure 3-12:
Changing
your prefer-
ences to
display help.

Feedback

Feedback is a crucial area. Clicking here shows you feedback you need to leave and your last few feedback comments. This information is easier accessed elsewhere.

PayPal

Links in the PayPal area allow you to view and update your PayPal account information and profile summary. Clicking the links will take you directly to the PayPal Web site.

Half.com Account

Old-time eBay sellers have been threatened over and over with the possible demise of Half.com (eBay's fixed-price media marketplace), and yet it still hangs on. If you sell or buy on Half.com, you can access your information and transactions from the Half.com Account area.

Seller Account

If you want to check to see how much you owe eBay for your listing and sale, or want to make a payment, the Seller Account area is the place to go.

Subscriptions

When you subscribe to any of the eBay services, such as Selling Manager Pro or Sales Reports Plus, the Subscriptions area is where you can cancel, upgrade, or edit your level of subscriptions.

The About Me Page

If you're on eBay, you *need* an About Me page. I hate to harp, but eBay is a community and all eBay members are members of that community. Checking out the About Me page of people you conduct business with gives you an opportunity to get to know them. Because eBay is a cyberspace market, you have no other way to let prospective bidders know that you're a real person. Don't you shop at some stores because you like the owners or people who work there? The About Me page is your first step toward establishing a professional and trusted identity at eBay.

The About Me page enables you to personalize your business to prospective bidders. (See Figure 3-13 for an example.) Your About Me page also becomes your About the Seller page if you have an eBay store.

An About Me page benefits you also when you buy. Sellers usually like to know about their bidders to build confidence in their trading partners. If you've put up an About Me page, you're halfway there.

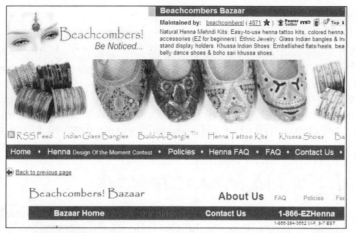

Figure 3-13:
An excellent
example of
an About
Me page
from Beach-
combers!

If you don't have an About Me page, put this book down and set one up immediately. It doesn't have to be a work of art; just get something up there to tell the rest of the community who you are. You can always go back later and add to or redesign it.

When you plan your About Me page, consider adding the following:

✔ Who you are and where you live.

✔ Your hobbies. If you collect things, here's where to let the world know.

✔ Whether you run your eBay business full time or part time and whether you have another career. This is more integral information about you; let the world know.

✔ The type of merchandise that your business revolves around. Promote it here; tell the reader why your merchandise and service are the best!

✔ Your most recent feedback and a list of your current auctions.

To create your page, click the Me icon next to any user's name, scroll to the bottom of the About Me page that appears, find the line that reads "To create your own About Me page, click here," and click. You can also click the About Me page link in the Personal Information of My Account area. Or go to `http://members.ebay.com/aw-cgi/eBayISAPI.dll?AboutMeLogin`. Then follow the simple preformatted template for your first page and work from there.

eBay Seller Services

Most eBay users don't know the extent of eBay's seller-specific services. And sometimes sellers are so involved with their auctions that they don't take the time to find out about new helper tools. So I've gone deep into the eBay pond to locate a few excellent tools to help you with your online business. Even if you've used some of these before, it might be time to revisit them because eBay has implemented quite a few changes during the past year.

Bidder management tools

Did you know that you don't have to accept bids from just anyone? Although many people include notices in their auction descriptions attempting to qualify bidders ahead of time, this doesn't always prevent them from bidding on your auction. Alas, part of the business is watching your bidders. With bidder management tools, you can save yourself a good deal of grief.

Canceling bids

You could have any number of reasons for wanting to cancel someone's bid. Perhaps an international bidder has bid on an auction in which you clearly state you don't ship overseas. Here are a few more legitimate reasons for canceling a bid:

- The bidder contacts you to back out of the bid; choosing to be a nice guy, you let him or her out of the deal.

- Your bidder has several negative feedbacks and hasn't gone through with other transactions that he or she has won.

- You're unable to verify the bidder's identity through e-mail or the phone.

- You need to cancel the auction (see following tip).

I don't recommend canceling an auction unless you absolutely have to because it's just bad business. People rely on your auctions being up for the stated amount of time. They may be planning to bid at the last minute, or they may just want to watch the action for a while. You may lose potential buyers by ending your listing early.

For whatever reason you're canceling someone's bid, you should first e-mail that person and clearly explain why you're doing so. Your bid cancellation appears in the auction's bidding history and becomes part of the auction's official record. For that reason, I recommend that you leave a concise, unemotional, one-line explanation on the cancellation form as to why you've cancelled the bid.

To get to the bid cancellation form, go to the Related Links box on the My eBay page and click the word *more,* which appears at the bottom. On the resulting page, you will find a Cancel Bids link. You can also get to the cancellation form directly by typing the following in your browser: `offer.ebay.com/ws/eBayISAPI.dll?CancelBidShow`.

End your listing early

You may decide to end a listing early for any number of reasons. If any bids are on your auction before you end it, you'd be duty-bound to sell to the highest bidder. So before ending an auction early, it's polite to e-mail everyone in your bidder list, explaining why you're canceling bids and closing the auction. If an egregious error in the item's description is forcing you to take this action, let your bidders know whether you're planning to relist the item with the correct information.

Only after canceling all bids should you go ahead and close your auction. To end your listing, use the drop-down menu next to the item in your Items I'm Selling area. Click the End Item link. You can also go directly to `http://cgi3.ebay.com/aw-cgi/eBayISAPI.dll?EndingMyAuction`.

Following are some legitimate reasons for closing your auction:

- **You no longer want to sell the item:** Your account may be subject to a "Non-Selling Seller" warning unless you have a really good reason. (See Chapter 4 for more details.)

- **An error occurred in the minimum bid or reserve amount:** Perhaps your wife said that she really loves that lamp and you'd better get some good money for it, but you started the auction at $1.00 with no reserve.

- **The listing has a major error in it:** Maybe you misspelled a critical keyword in the title.

- **The item was somehow lost or broken:** Your dog ate it?

Blocking buyers

If you don't want certain buyers bidding on your auctions, you can remove their capability to do so. Setting up a list of bidders that you don't want to do business with is legal on eBay. If someone whom you've blocked tries to bid on your auction, the bid won't go through. A message will be displayed notifying the person that he or she is not able to bid on the listing and to contact the seller for more information.

You can block as many as one thousand users from bidding on your auctions. However, I recommend that you use this option only when absolutely necessary. Situations — and people — change, and it's best to try to clear up problems with particular bidders.

You can reinstate a bidder at any time by going to the Buyer Blocked Bidder/Buyer list at `http://pages.ebay.com/services/buyandsell/bidder management.html`. Click the Add an eBay User to My Blocked Bidder/Buyer List link. The resulting page will allow you to delete the bidder's user ID from the Blocked list.

ID Verify

ID Verify establishes that you are who you say you are. It also enables you to perform specialized eBay functions if you choose not to supply eBay with a credit card when you register. ID Verify has a one-time charge of $5, and Equifax (one of the nation's largest credit security companies) conducts the verification. It is not a credit check. Your personal information is checked alongside consumer and business databases for consistency so that Equifax can verify that you are who you say you are.

If you aren't quite ready to get the SquareTrade seal (see Chapter 4) for your auctions or you find the monthly fees involved in the seal currently prohibitive, ID Verify is the next best thing. Following are the extra functions you can perform without supplying your credit card:

- Buy an item for more than $15,000 through the eBay Buy It Now feature
- List and offer the Buy It Now or Best Offer options
- Place a bid above $15,000
- Bid on eBay Live Auctions
- Open an eBay store
- Sell and access items in the eBay Mature Audiences category

Feedback: Your permanent record

Just like your high school permanent record, your eBay feedback follows you forever at eBay. If you change your user ID, it's there. If you change your e-mail address, it's there. When you click the feedback number next to a user's ID, the user's eBay ID card (see Figure 3-14) is displayed. The information shown will tell you a lot about your bidder.

The most obvious tip-off to someone's feedback is the star you see next to the user ID. Different colored stars are awarded as folks reach milestones in their feedback ratings. To decipher the star colors and see what they mean, click the help link, and type the words *star rating*.

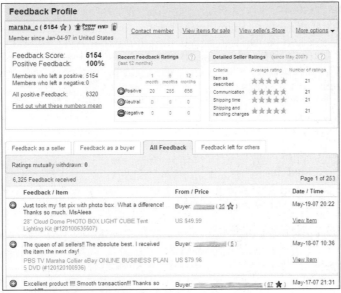

Figure 3-14:
The eBay
Feedback
page with
an overall
profile and
an ID card,
summarizin
g recent
comments
and your
detailed
Star ratings.

Your feedback means a great deal to people who visit your auctions. By glancing at your feedback page, they can see

- Whether you're an experienced eBay user
- Your eBay history
- When you started at eBay
- How many bid retractions you've had in the past six months

This is valuable information for both the buyer and the seller because it helps to evaluate whether you're the type of person who would make a responsible trading partner.

Worried about negative feedback? There are two possible ways to get negative feedback points removed from your record. One, you can file for mediation with SquareTrade (see Chapter 4 on how to do this). Two, if you and the person who posted the feedback are both in agreement, you can file for Mutual Feedback Withdrawal by going to http://feedback.ebay.com/ws1/eBayISAPI.dll?MFWrequest. Enter the item number and continue filing the form. If the person who posted the feedback agrees to remove the negative feedback, eBay will oblige.

Leaving feedback

Everyone in the eBay community is honor-bound to leave feedback. Sometimes when you've had a truly dreadful experience, you hate to leave negative or neutral feedback, but if you don't, you're not helping anyone. The point of feedback is not to show what a great person you are but to show future sellers or bidders where the rotten apples lie. So, when leaving feedback, be truthful and unemotional and state just the facts.

Feedback is important, so you should be sure to leave some for every transaction you take part in. If a week has passed since you've shipped an item, and you haven't heard from the bidder or seen any feedback, drop that bidder an e-mail. Write "Thanks for your purchase. Are you happy with the item?" Also emphasize that you'll be glad to leave positive feedback after you've heard a reply, and ask for the same in return.

Never leave feedback on a sale until you're absolutely, positively sure that the buyer has received the product and is happy with the deal. Many inexperienced sellers leave feedback the minute they get their money, but experience can teach them that it ain't over till it's over. A package can get lost or damaged, or the bidder may be unhappy for some reason. A buyer may also want to return an item for no good reason, turning a seemingly smooth transaction into a nightmare. You get only one feedback per transaction, so use it wisely. You can't go back and say that the buyer damaged the product and then tried to return it.

eBay provides so many different links to leave feedback that I could probably write an entire chapter on it. But I don't want you to fall asleep while reading, so I go through only the most convenient methods:

- ✔ Go to your auction page and click the Leave Feedback link, which appears on the left.

- ✔ Click the number (in parentheses) next to the other user's name. When you're on that user's feedback page, click the Leave Feedback link.

- ✔ Click the Leave Feedback link in the drop-down menu next to the completed sale on the Items I've Sold page in your My eBay page.

- ✔ Visit the feedback forum (this link shows up on the bottom of every page) and click the link that shows all pending feedback for the past ninety days. When you've fallen behind in leaving feedback, this is a super-fast way to catch up.

Reply to feedback received

You may occasionally get feedback that you feel compelled to respond to. Did you know that you could? If the feedback is neutral or negative, I recommend that you cover yourself by explaining the situation for future bidders to see.

If you receive a negative feedback rating, a well-meaning admission of guilt would work. You could say something like, "Unfortunately, shipping was delayed and I regret the situation." Prospective bidders will see that you've addressed the problem instead of just letting it go.

To respond to feedback, follow these steps:

1. **In the My eBay Views area on your My eBay page, click the Feedback link under My Account.**

2. **On the feedback page, click the Go to Feedback Forum link at the top of the page.**

3. **On the resulting page, click the Reply to Feedback Received link.**

   The Reply to Feedback Received page appears, as shown in Figure 3-15.

Figure 3-15: Review and respond to your feedbacks.

4. **Scroll to find the feedback comment that you want to respond to and click the Reply link.**

5. **Type your response, and then click the Leave Response button.**

The eBay PowerSeller program

I'm sure you've seen that PowerSeller logo on auctions. eBay PowerSellers represent the largest gross sales users on eBay. The requirements for becoming a PowerSeller follow:

✔ You must have a gross monthly dollar volume of $1000 (Bronze level); $3000 (Silver level); $10,000 (Gold level); $25,000 (Platinum level); or $150,000 (Titanium level). To remain a PowerSeller, you must maintain your level's minimum gross sales for the past three months and keep current with all the other requirements. To advance up the PowerSeller chain, you must reach and maintain the next level of gross sales for an average of three months.

If you miss your minimum gross sales for three months, eBay gives you a grace period. After that time, if you don't meet the minimum gross figures for your level, you may be moved down to the prior level or be removed from the PowerSeller program.

✔ You must have at least one hundred feedback comments, with 98 percent positive. To calculate your feedback percentage, divide your number of positive feedbacks by your number of total feedbacks (negatives plus positives).

✔ You must average a minimum monthly total of four listings in the past three months.

PowerSellers enjoy many benefits:

Level	Priority eSupport	Toll-free phone #	Account Manager
Bronze	Yes	No	No
Silver	Yes	Yes	No
Gold	Yes	Yes	Yes
Platinum	Yes	Yes	Yes
Titanium	Yes	Yes	Yes

The best thing about being a PowerSeller is the awesome level of customer service you receive, called Priority eSupport. When a PowerSeller dashes off an e-mail to a special customer service department, a reply comes back at the speed of light.

eBay doesn't require you to show the PowerSeller logo in your descriptions when you attain that level. Some PowerSellers don't include the logo in their auctions because they'd rather be perceived as regular folks on eBay.

eBay auction software

eBay has developed a fantastic software program called Turbo Lister, which is free and downloadable from the site. They also have an online Selling Manager to manage your auctions. For a breakdown of these software products and others to ease the seller's burden, skip to Chapter 9.

PayPal Buyer Protection

When a buyer pays with PayPal, he or she is covered with its fraud protection program. Tangible items sold on eBay that can be shipped (and are paid through PayPal) are covered to $200. (Intangibles, such as services, licenses, and other access to digital content aren't covered.) PayPal covers some items sold by the most reputable sellers up to $2000 of the final selling price. The amount at which your sales are covered is indicated at the bottom of the Meet the Seller area on each listing page.

The plan covers only fraud, not damaged packages. The United States Postal Service offers insurance as an option, so I guess this means if your package arrives damaged and isn't insured, the buyer is out of luck and you're going to get some bad feedback unless you make things right. The protection program covers eBay buyers only when they're defrauded, the item is never shipped, or the item is significantly different from the auction description. When you ship an item through the USPS, PayPal will accept a delivery confirmation number that has been scanned at arrival as proof of delivery. If the item you send is valued over $250, PayPal requires that you get a signature delivery confirmation to protect the seller. The policy does *not* cover sellers for anything — so don't ship that item until you're darn sure the check has cleared!

Once a buyer files a successful claim against you, the money they paid you is whisked out of your PayPal account immediately.

Note that there is also a PayPal Seller Protection program; see Chapter 13 for details on how to stay protected.

eBay education

eBay offers many forms of training and education. No matter how advanced you are, it's fun to go to eBay University and take a refresher course on the basics. You can also find some cool online interactive tutorials as you make your way through eBay. When you can, take a moment and watch them — you might just see one or two new features that you didn't know about. More information about eBay education is available at www.eBay.com/education.

eBay University

The eBay traveling tent show goes across the country, hosting thousands of eBay members, spreading the eBay word to the masses. You get a chance to meet some wonderful people who work for eBay and enjoy answering questions. eBay University follows two tracks:

 ✔ **Basic Selling:** A beginning class for new sellers that lays out the basics so they can progress from there.

 ✔ **Beyond the Basics:** A tutorial on eBay tools for advanced sellers.

Find out where classes are being held by going to www.eBay.com/university.

Online workshops

eBay has ongoing online workshops that allow you to participate through a chat screen. eBay members and staff give the one-hour workshops. eBay records and archives many interesting classes in the eBay education area, so you can see the classes after they premiere as well. Remember to take the opinions passed on in these workshops as just that, opinions. Weigh the ideas and balance them against what you've learned and what you know rather than accept them as gospel.

Chapter 4

Safe Selling Equals Profitable Sales

*T*here are a lot of *shoulds* in this world. You *should* do this and you *should* do that. I don't know who's in charge of the *shoulds,* but certain things just make life work better. You may or may not take any of the advice on these pages, but they'll make your eBay business thrive with a minimum of anguish. If you've ever had an auction pulled by eBay, you know what anguish truly feels like.

In the real world, we have to take responsibility for our own actions. If we buy a fifty-two-inch plasma television for $250 from some guy selling them out of the back of a truck, who do we have to blame when we take it home and it doesn't work? You get what you pay for, and you have no consumer protection from the seller of the possibly "hot" TVs. Responsible consumerism is every buyer's job. Lawsuits get filed — and some are won — when someone feels they've been ripped off, but my best advice is that if you stay clean in your online business, you'll keep clean.

eBay is a community, and the community was founded on the following five basic values:

- ✔ We believe people are basically good.

- ✔ We believe everyone has something to contribute.

- ✔ We believe that an honest, open environment can bring out the best in people.

- ✔ We recognize and respect everyone as a unique individual.

- ✔ We encourage you to treat others the way that you want to be treated.

eBay is committed to these values, and it says so right on its Web site. eBay believes that community members should "honor these values — whether buying, selling, or chatting." So *should* we all.

Is What You Want to Sell Legal?

Although eBay is based in California and therefore must abide by California law, sellers do business all over the United States. Therefore, items sold on eBay must be governed by the laws of every other state as well. As a seller, you're ultimately responsible for the legality of the items you sell and the way that you transact business on eBay. Yes, you're able to sell thousands of different items on eBay. But do you know what you aren't allowed to sell on eBay?

The eBay User Agreement outlines all eBay rules and regulations regarding what you can and can't sell as well as all aspects of doing business at eBay. If you've never ever read the User Agreement, you really should — at least once. You can find it at the following address:

```
http://pages.ebay.com/help/policies/user-agreement.html
```

These policies can change from time to time. As an active seller, you should make sure that you're notified of any changes. To request that you be notified when eBay makes changes to the User Agreement or Privacy Policy, as well as to control any correspondence you receive from eBay, follow these steps:

1. **Sign in with your user ID and password.**

   You have to sign in with your password before the Legal and Policy Notification Preferences page appears.

2. **Go to your My eBay page. In the My eBay Views section on the left side of the page, click the Preferences link under My Account.**

3. **On the resulting Preferences page, click the Show link, next to Legal and Policy Notifications.**

4. **Click Edit.**

5. **Click to put check marks in the check boxes below the Email column (see Figure 4-1).**

   This enables you to receive important information that may affect how you run your business.

6. **Click Save to save your changes.**

Figure 4-1: Change notifications here.

My eBay > My Account > Preferences > **Notification Preferences**

Legal and Policy Notification Preferences   Help

Choose which notifications you'd like to receive, then click the **Save** button below.

Legal and Policy Notifications	Email
User Agreement changes Notify me if the current User Agreement changes.	☑
Privacy Policy changes Notify me if the current Privacy Policy changes.	☑

[Save]   Cancel | View change history

Note: It may take up to 10 days to process changes to these preferences.

The preceding procedure for changing notifications will work on any of the options on this page. Take a moment and go through each of your options to be sure everything is set up the way you like it.

By now, you should have a firm grasp of the rules and regulations for listing auctions (if not, check out Chapter 2). But in addition to knowing the rules for listing items, you must consider the items themselves. In this section, I detail the three categories of items to be wary of: prohibited, restricted, and infringing. Some are banned, period. Others fall in a gray area. You're responsible for what you sell, so you'd better know what's legal and what's not.

You may think it's okay to give away a regulated or banned item as a bonus item with your auction. Think again. Even giving away such items for free doesn't save you from potential legal responsibility.

Prohibited items

A *prohibited item* is banned from sale on eBay. You can't sell a prohibited item under any circumstance. Take a look at the following list. A little common sense tells you there's good reason for not selling these items, including liability issues for the seller (what if you sold alcohol to a minor? — that's against the law).

The following is a list of items prohibited as of this writing, so don't try to sell 'em at eBay:

    Academic software

    Alcohol*

    Animals and wildlife products

    Beta software

Bonuses, prizes, giveaway, and raffles

Bootleg recordings

Catalogs (current issues) and Web sales

Catalytic converters and test pipes

Counterfeit currency or stamps

Counterfeit items

Credit cards

Describing drugs and drug-like substances

Drugs and drug paraphernalia

Embargoed goods

Enabling duplication of copy-protected material

Encouraging illegal activity or infringement

Faces, names, and signatures

Fireworks

Government and Transit documents and uniforms

Government IDs and licenses

Human parts and remains**

Listing no item for sale

Lockpicking devices

Lottery tickets

Mailing lists and personal information

Mod chips, game enhancers, and boot discs

Movie prints (35mm and 70mm)

Multilevel marketing, pyramid, and matrix programs

Postage meters

Prescription drugs

Promotional copies of media

Recalled items

Reproduction political memorabilia

Satellite and cable TV descramblers

Stocks and other securities***

Stolen property

Surveillance equipment

Tobacco

Travel****

USDA-prohibited plants and seeds

Used cosmetics

*Alcohol may be allowed if the value of the item lies in the collectible container (bottle) exceeding the alcohol's retail price. The item should not be currently available at a retail outlet. The auction should state that the container has not been opened, and the seller should be sure that the buyer is over twenty-one. eBay does allow licensed and vetted sellers of wine to sell on the site. For more information visit `http://pages.ebay.com/help/policies/alcohol.html`.

**Skulls, skeletons, and items that may contain human hair are permissible as long as they're used for educational purposes.

***Old or collectible stock certificates may be sold provided that they're cancelled or are from a company that no longer exists.

****All sellers listing airline tickets, cruises, vacation packages, or lodging must be verified by SquareTrade.

Check the following address for updates:

`http://pages.ebay.com/help/policies/items-ov.html`

Restricted items

A *restricted item* is iffy — determining whether or not you can sell it is tricky. Under certain circumstances, you may be able to list the item for sale. To fully understand if and when you can list a restricted item, visit the links that I highlight in Table 4-1.

When alcohol becomes collectible

Many people collect rare and antique bottles of liquor or wine. I even sold a bottle of Korbel champagne designed by Frank Sinatra on eBay in 1998. Korbel bottles have featured artwork by designer Nicole Miller and comedienne Whoopi Goldberg as well as designs by Tony Bennett and Jane Seymour.

People also collect Jim Beam bottles, Dug's decanters, and miniatures that are even more valuable when they're full. You *can* sell these on eBay as long as you fulfill the following requirements:

✔ The value of the item is in the collectible container, not its contents.

✔ The auction description should state that the container has not been opened, but any incidental contents are not intended for consumption.

✔ The item must not be available at any retail outlet, and the container must have a value that substantially exceeds the current retail price of the alcohol in the container.

✔ Sellers should take steps to ensure that the buyer of these collectibles is of lawful age in the buyer's and seller's jurisdictions (generally 21 years old).

Table 4-1	Restricted Items and Where to Find the Rules Regulating Them
Can I Sell This?	*Go Here to Find Out**
Alcohol	`/alcohol.html`
Artifacts	`/artifacts.html`
Autographed items	`/autographs.html`
Celebrity material	`/celebrity-material.html`
Cell phone (wireless) service contracts	`/cellphone-services.html`
Charity or fundraising	`/fundraising.html`
Compilation and informational material	`/compilation.html`

Can I Sell This?	*Go Here to Find Out**
Contracts and tickets	`/contracts.html`
Downloadable media	`/downloadable.html`
Electronics equipment	`/electronics.html`
Event tickets	`/event-tickets.html`
Firearms, weapons, and knives	`/firearms-weapons-knives.html`
Gift cards	`/gift.html`
Food	`/food.html`
Hazardous, restricted, and perishable items	`/hazardous-materials.html`
Imported goods	`/importation.html`
International trading — buyers	`/international-trading.html`
Manufacturers' coupons	`/manufacturers-coupons.html`
Mature audiences	`/mature audiences.html`
Medical devices	`/medical-devices.html`
OEM software	`/oem.html`
Offensive material	`/offensive.html`
Pesticides	`/pesticides.html`
Plants and seeds	`/plantsandseeds.html`
Police-related items	`/police.html`
Pre-sale listings	`/pre-sale.html`
Prohibited services *(wink, wink)*	`/prohibited-services.html`
Real estate	`/real-estate.html`
Slot machines	`/slot-machines.html`
Stock certificates	`/stocks.html`
Transit and shipping-related items	`/transit-shipping.html`
Used clothing	`/used-clothing.html`
United States embargoed goods from prohibited countries	`/embargo.html`
Weapons and knives	`/weapons.html`

* *All URLs begin with* `http://pages.ebay.com/help/policies`

The Chanel-style purse

I once listed a quilted leather women's purse that had a gold chain strap, which I described as a Chanel-style purse. Within two hours, I received an Informational alert from the eBay listing police. I described the item to the best of my ability, but found that it became a potentially infringing item. My use of the brand name *Chanel* caused my auction to come under the violation of keyword spamming (more on that in the section "Potentially infringing items").

In its informational alert, eBay described my violation:

> "Keyword spamming is the practice of adding words, including brand names, which do not directly describe the item you are selling. The addition of these words may not have been intentional, but including them in this manner diverts members to your listing inappropriately."

Ooops! You can see how my ingenuous listing was actually a violation of policy. Think twice before you add brand names to your auction description. Thankfully, the eBay police judge each violation on a case-by-case basis. Because my record is clear, I merely got a reprimand. Had my violation been more deliberate, I might have been suspended.

Note: In addition, in your title, you may not use a brand name along with the words *not* or *like*. As in Chanel-*like* purse or *not* Chanel. This is also considered a violation of the keyword spamming policy.

To see the Chanel USA statement on violations, visit its About Me page. The violations apply to many items that may be listed at eBay: `http://members.ebay.com/aboutme/chanelusa/`.

Potentially infringing items

Potentially infringing items follow a slippery slope. If you list a potentially infringing item, you may infringe on existing copyrights, trademarks, registrations, or the like. Get the idea? These items are prohibited for your own protection.

Items falling under the potentially infringing category are generally copyrighted or trademarked items, such as software, promotional items, and games. Even using a brand name in your auction as part of a description (known as *keyword spamming*) may get you into trouble.

Keyword spamming manipulates the eBay search engine by including an unrelated item in the listing for a copyrighted or trademarked item, and then diverting bidders to an auction of other merchandise. This is frustrating to the person trying to use the search engine to find a particular item and unfair to members who have properly listed their items.

Keyword spamming can take many forms. Some merely mislead the prospective bidder while others are legal infringements. A few of the most common are

- Superfluous brand names in the title or item description
- Using something like "not brand X" in the title or item description
- Improper trademark usage
- Lists of keywords
- Hidden text — white text on a white background or hidden text in HTML code. The white text shows up in the search but is not visible to the naked eye. Sneaky, eh?
- Drop-down boxes

To get the latest on eBay's keyword spamming policy, go to

```
http://pages.ebay.com/help/policies/keyword-spam.html
```

Repeating various nontrademarked keywords can get you in trouble as well. eBay permits the use of as many as five synonyms when listing an item for sale. A permissible example of this might be: purse, handbag, pocketbook, satchel, and bag. Adding many nontrademarked keywords would cause the auction to come up in more searches.

The eBay Verified Rights Owners program

eBay can't possibly check every auction for authenticity. But to help protect trademarked items, it formed the Verified Rights Owners (VeRO) program. Trademark and copyright owners expend large amounts of energy to develop and maintain control over the quality of their products. If you buy a "designer" purse from a guy on the street for $20, it's probably counterfeit, so don't go selling it on eBay. eBay works with VeRO program members to educate the community about such items. They work also with verified owners of trademarks and copyrights to remove auctions that infringe on their products. If eBay doesn't close a suspicious or blatantly infringing auction, both you and eBay are liable for the violation.

To become a member of the VeRO program, the owners of copyrights and trademarks must supply eBay with proof of ownership. If you are a legitimate owner and someone on the site has violated your rights, download the Notice of Infringement form at

```
http://pages.ebay.com/help/community/notice-infringe2.pdf
```

Note: eBay cooperates with law enforcement. Should you be a violator, they may give your name and street address to a VeRO program member.

To view a list of other VeRO members' About Me pages, go to

```
http://pages.ebay.com/help/community/vero-aboutme.html
```

Trading Violations

Both buyers and sellers can commit trading violations by attempting to manipulate the outcome of an auction or a sale. Many of the violations aren't necessarily buyer or seller exclusive, but apply to both. Regardless of the nature of a violation, such bad behavior harms everyone who's part of the eBay community.

As a valued member of the community, it's partially your responsibility to look out for such violations — so that eBay continues to be a safe venue in which to do business. Should you see a violation, report it immediately to the eBay Security Center (see "eBay's Security Center," later in this chapter). In this section, I detail many common violations so that you can be on the outlook for them — and I'll just assume that you won't be committing any yourself.

We need to be watchdogs because we need to protect the other users in our community. Don't feel like a squealer if you make a report. Remember that it takes just one rotten apple to spoil the basket, so if you see a violation, do your duty and report it.

When the competition doesn't play fair

Unfortunately, you may sometimes encounter non-community-minded sellers who interfere with your auctions or sales. This interference can take on several forms, such as sellers who illegally drive up bids or "steal" bidders.

Again, should you fall victim to bad deeds, be sure to report the bad-deed-doer's actions immediately. (Check out "Taking Action: What to Do When Someone Breaks the Rules," later in this chapter.) eBay will take some sort of disciplinary action. Penalties range from formal warnings and temporary suspension to indefinite suspension. eBay reviews each incident on a case-by-case basis before passing judgment.

Shill bidding

Shill bidding is the practice of placing a bid on an auction to artificially inflate the final value. It's the bane of every eBay user (whether buyer or seller) and undermines community trust. Shill bidding is a violation of the Federal wire-fraud statute, which encompasses the practice of entering into interstate commerce to defraud — it's a felony and not something to toy with!

The practice of shill bidding has been a part of auctions from their beginnings. To prevent the suspicion of shill bidding, people in the same family, those who share the same computer, and folks who work or live together should not bid on each other's items.

Should you ever even dream of participating in any sort of auction manipulation, I urge you to think twice. You might think you're smart by using another e-mail address and username, but that doesn't work. Every time you log on to your ISP, your connection carries an IP address. So no matter what name or computer you use, your connection will identify you. eBay can use this number to track you through its site.

Shill bidders are fairly easy to recognize, even for the eBay user who isn't privy to things such as IP addresses. By checking a bidder's auction history, you can easily determine a user's bidding pattern. A bidder who constantly bids up items and never wins is suspicious.

Spurious sellers often employ shill bidding to increase the number of bids on an item to more quickly make it a hot item. This doesn't mean that all hot auctions are products of shill bidding; it means that hot auctions are desirable and pull in lots of extra bids (due to the herd mentality). Rogues would like all their auctions to be hot and may take any road to ensure that they are.

Transaction interference

Have you ever received an e-mail from an eBay seller offering you an item that you're currently bidding on for a lower price? This is called *transaction interference,* and it can prevent sellers from gaining the highest bid possible.

Transaction interference occurs also when a troublemaker who has it "in" for a particular seller e-mails bidders participating in the seller's current auctions to warn them away from completing the auction. Tales of woe and much bitterness usually accompany such e-mails. If a bidder has a problem with a seller, that bidder can — and should — file a report with eBay and leave negative feedback for that seller. This sort of e-mail barrage can potentially fall under the category of libel and isn't a safe thing to practice. If you receive an e-mail like this, ignore its message but report it to eBay.

Transaction interception

They say the criminal mind is complex; when it comes to transaction interception, it certainly is! *Transaction interception* occurs when an eBay scalawag keeps track of closing auctions and then, when the auction is finished, e-mails the winner as if the scalawag were the seller. The e-mail often looks official and is congratulatory, politely asking for payment. Interceptors usually use a post office box for such mischief. This behavior goes beyond being a trading violation — it's stealing.

The best way to protect yourself from such miscreants is to accept payments through a payment service, such as PayPal, by using a Pay Now link. For more about setting up a payment service account, see Chapter 13.

Fee avoidance

Basically, *fee avoidance* is the practice of evading paying eBay fees by going around the eBay system. You can commit fee avoidance in many ways — sometimes without even realizing it. Read this section carefully so that you don't fall into this violation by mistake.

You're guilty of fee avoidance if you

✔ Use an eBay member's contact information in an attempt to sell, off the eBay site, a listed item

✔ Use an eBay member's contact information to sell, off the eBay site, an item from a closed auction in which the reserve wasn't met

✔ Close your auction early so you can sell the item to someone who has e-mailed you with an offer to buy the item

✔ Cancel bids to end your auction before it legally closes so you can sell the item to someone who has e-mailed you with an offer of a higher price

✔ Offer duplicates of your item to the unsuccessful bidders in your auction, unless you use the Second Chance option

Take a look at the discussion on listing policies in Chapter 2 for listing violations that also might fall into this category.

Excessive shipping charges

Although the excessive shipping charges violation falls somewhat in the Fee Avoidance category, it has a rule all to itself. You, as a seller, are required to charge reasonable shipping and handling fees. You may not charge a shipping fee that's disproportionate to the item you are selling. Charging $15 to ship a cell phone accessory is a good example of unwarranted charges. A cell phone accessory can most likely be shipped First Class — or at the very most at the one-pound rate.

I know; you're saying that you see lots of sellers violating this rule, but this is a firm policy. Should you want to report another seller's shameless shipping charges, just click the Report This Item link at the bottom of every listing page. If sellers are flagrant about breaking this rule and enough complaints are in their record, they can be suspended from eBay.

Nonselling seller

Refusing to accept payment from the winning bidder and refusing to complete the transaction is simply wrong. Very, very bad form! You are legally and morally bound to complete any transaction in which you enter.

Baaad bidders

Nothing can ruin a seller's day like a difficult bidder, such as someone who asks questions that are clearly answered already in your auction description or someone who asks you to close the auction so that he or she can buy the item offline. Sheesh — you'd think no one read the rules. From the nonpaying bidder to the unwelcome and shady, you might encounter the buyers I describe here.

Bid shielding

When two or more eBay members work together to defraud you out of real auction profits, they're guilty of *bid shielding*. One member, lets call him Joe, places an early bid on your item, with a *proxy bid*. (An automatic bid that increases your bid to outbid any competition, up to the highest amount you specify.) Immediately, the accomplice (we'll call her Ann) places a very high proxy bid to drive it to the max or beyond. If legitimate bidders bid, they only ratchet up the second bidder's bid — they don't outbid the high bidder's proxy. When the auction is coming to it's twelve-hour bid freeze, the high bidder (Ann) retracts her bid, thereby granting the winning bid to her buddy (Joe), the original low bidder. The ultimate point of bid shielding is that it increases the bid to such a high level that normal bidding by authentic bidders is discouraged and they stop watching the listing.

This illegal bidding process is used not only to get bargain-priced merchandise but also to drive bidders away from competitors' auctions by artificially inflating the high bid level.

Unwelcome bidder

In this business, you might think that you couldn't possibly regard anyone as an *unwelcome bidder,* but you just might. Remember how you painstakingly explain your terms in your auction description? That's lost on people who don't take the time to read those descriptions or choose to ignore them. Consider the following points:

- ✔ You state in your description that you ship only within the United States, but you see a bidder with an e-mail address that ends in .jp (Japan), .au (Australia), .uk (United Kingdom), or whatever.

- ✔ A prospective buyer has three Unpaid Item strikes on his or her account in the past thirty days and decides to bid or buy your item. You probably won't get paid, but you still have the hassle of cleaning up and trying to get fee refunds.

- ✔ You don't want bidders who have a negative feedback, but someone fitting that description bids on your auction.

 ✔ You decide to cancel a bid for one of the previous two reasons, but the bidder continues to bid on your auction.

 ✔ You've blocked a particular bidder who's now using a secondary account to bid on your auctions.

To solve these issues before they occur, you can set your Selling Preferences to prevent bad bidding from ruining your sales. Visit Chapter 3 for instructions on how to block people who could ruin your sales.

Nonpaying buyers

If there's one thing that just ain't tolerated at eBay, it's *unpaid items.* eBay reminds all potential buyers, before they place a bid, that "If you are the winning buyer, you will enter into a legally binding contract to purchase the item from the seller." You'd think that was clear enough, but sadly, many people out there think bidding and buying on eBay is a game. If you see a high bidder on your auction who has very low or negative feedback, dropping a line reiterating eBay policy never hurts.

How you, as a seller, communicate with the high bidder is also important. Many times a well-written, congenial, businesslike e-mail can cajole the basically good person into sending payment. To see some samples that get the job done, drop by Chapter 12.

I've been selling and buying on eBay for more than eleven years. During that time, I've had to file only twenty nonpaying buyer alerts (see the steps a bit later in this section). I think that nonpaying buyers tend to bid on certain types of items. After you've seen some unpaid items, you'll get an idea of which items to stay away from. My items? A gas-powered scooter, a video game, and some Beanie Babies. Serious collector or business items have never been an issue.

To reduce the number of nonpaying buyers, eBay has established that all eBay users are indefinitely suspended if they have three nonpaying buyer alerts filed against them. An *indefinite suspension* is a suspension of members' privileges to use the eBay site for more than sixty days, with no definite reinstatement date. If users attempt to re-register at eBay and use the system under new IDs, they risk being referred to the United States Attorney General's Office for the Northern District of California for criminal prosecution.

Before filing an unpaid item dispute, give the winner a second chance to send payment. If you still don't receive payment, follow these steps to recoup your final value fees and be eligible for the nonpaying buyer relist credit:

1. **As soon as you have a winner, contact him or her.**

2. **If you don't hear from the winner within three days of the auction's end time, send a payment reminder:**

   a. **Go to the My eBay Views area on the My eBay page. Under Selling, click the Sold link.**

   b. **Click the View Payment Status link next to the pertinent auction.**

   c. **Click the Send a Payment Reminder link.**

   You may send a reminder between three and thirty days after the auction closes.

If you still don't hear from or receive money from your high bidder, it's time to swing into action by filing an alert.

You must file the alert no earlier than seven days and no later than forty-five days after the auction has ended.

Follow these steps to file an unpaid item dispute:

1. **In the My eBay Views area of the My eBay page, click the Dispute Console link.**

   Alternately, go to the following address:

   ```
   http://rebulk.ebay.com/ws/eBayISAPI.dll?CreateDispute
   ```

2. **Check the Dispute Console to select the transaction that is eligible for filing.**

   eBay sends the buyer an e-mail, and the buyer has the right to respond in the dispute management process.

Eight days after filing an unpaid item dispute, you may close the dispute and apply for a final value fee credit in the Dispute Console. At this point, eBay offers several options. To close the dispute, you must select one of the following:

- ✔ **We've completed the transaction and we're both satisfied.** You received your payment and you're ready to ship! The buyer will not receive an undeserved Unpaid Item strike.

- ✔ **We've agreed not to complete the transaction.** If you feel sorry for the buyer or believe their tale of woe as to how they cannot possibly buy your item, you can select this option. The buyer won't get a strike on his or her permanent record, and you will receive a final value fee credit. (The item is eligible for the standard relist credit.)

✔ **I no longer wish to communicate with or wait for the buyer.** You've had it — either no response or no payment. The buyer receives their well-deserved Unpaid Item strike and you get your final value fee credit. (This item is eligible for a relist credit.)

You must file for your final value fee credit within sixty days of the transaction's close.

Don't forget! When you file for your final value fee credit, you also have the option of blocking that buyer from participating in your sales.

If you work things out with the winner, you may remove the unpaid item strike within ninety days of the close of the listing. eBay sends an e-mail to notify the winner that the strike has been removed at your request. You'll find the link to remove the warning at your Dispute Console:

1. **Go to the My eBay page. Scroll down the My eBay Views to the Dispute Console link and click it.**

2. **On the Dispute Console page, next to the dispute in question, select Cancel the Unpaid Item Strike for This Dispute from the drop down menu.**

3. **Click Confirm to remove the Unpaid Item strike.**

   An e-mail is sent to the buyer letting the buyer know that the strike has been removed and his or her reputation is clear.

In the case of Multiple Item listings or eBay store items, you may file an unpaid item strike only *once* per listing. You may file against as many buyers as necessary in that one alert, but you can't go back and file more strikes later. You may remove an unpaid item strike at any time.

Not knowing who's who

eBay members have user IDs rather than expose their e-mail addresses for all to see. However, you must supply eBay with your contact information. When you register with eBay, its software immediately checks your primary phone number area code against your ZIP code to verify that the two numbers are from the same city. If you've supplied incompatible codes, the eBay servers will recognize that and ask you to reinput the correct codes.

An eBay member who's involved in a transaction with you can get your phone number by clicking Advanced Search next to the eBay search box and then clicking the Find Contact Information link under the Members area on the left side of the page.

Don't be lured by phishing

Fraudulent e-mail has become a common occurrence. Without warning, a request for confirmation of your personal details arrives allegedly from your bank, Internet ISP, credit card company, PayPal, or even eBay. These e-mails are *phishing* for your personal information and passwords to defraud you of your money or your identity.

These e-mails look just like a legitimate e-mail from the company that holds your data. If you follow the links in the e-mail to "update" your information, you'll be brought to a Web page that duplicates a legitimate Web page. How can you protect yourself from these scammers?

✔ **Never go to the Web site in question from the link in the e-mail.** Open up a new browser and type the URL that you normally use to enter the site. After you log in, you'll know whether there's a problem with any of your information.

✔ **Always look for secure Web site information.** If you're logged onto a secure Web site, the URL will begin with `https://` rather than the standard `http://`. You'll also see a lock symbol in the status bar at the bottom of your browser window.

✔ **Regularly log onto your Internet accounts.** By keeping in regular contact with your providers, you'll know about issues with your accounts before they have a chance to cause a problem.

✔ **Report the e-mail.** If you receive an e-mail supposedly from PayPal, forward the e-mail to `spoof@paypal.com`. Forward an e-mail purportedly from eBay to `spoof@ebay.com`.

I take things into my own hands by checking the suspicious e-mail's underlying code. You can do this if you use Internet Explorer and Outlook, by opening the e-mail, right-clicking it, and choosing View Source. When you view the HTML code, you'll be able to see the actual URL of the site that would get your response if you click the link, as shown in the figure.

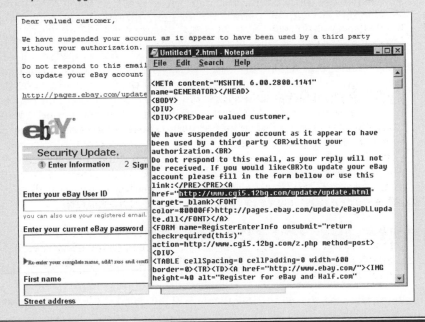

When you arrive at the page, you can then request contact information, as shown in Figure 4-2.

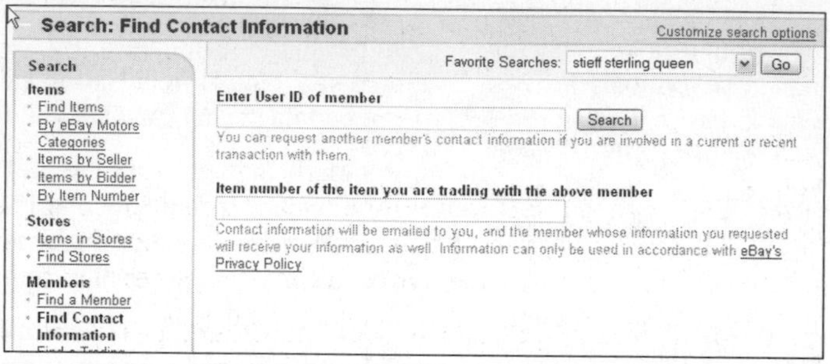

Figure 4-2: eBay's Member contact information form.

To be on the up-and-up at eBay (and to keep others honest, too), make sure that you

- ✔ **Have your current phone number on file at eBay:** If a buyer can't reach you, you're in violation and you *can* be disciplined.

- ✔ **Have your current e-mail address on file:** If your buyer continually gets e-mail bounced back from your e-mail address, you could get in big trouble.

- ✔ **Report all underage buyers:** If you suspect that a buyer in one of your transactions is underage (eBay requires that all users be over 18), eBay may close the account. Underage buyers may be using their parent's credit card without permission, or perhaps even a stolen card, for registration.

- ✔ **Verify e-mail purportedly coming from an eBay employee:** If someone e-mails you claiming to work for eBay, be sure to check it out before replying. When eBay employees conduct personal business on the site, company policy requires that they use a personal noncompany e-mail address for their user registration. If you suspect someone is impersonating an eBay employee for harmful purposes, contact the eBay Security Center.

Taking Action: What to Do When Someone Breaks the Rules

You need to take a business-like approach to problems at eBay, whatever those problems may be. In previous sections of this chapter, I outline eBay's many rules, as well as the bad deeds and bad seeds you're likely to encounter while doing business on eBay.

As a member of the eBay community, you have the responsibility of knowing and abiding by eBay's rules and regulations. This responsibility includes notifying eBay when someone tries to sell an illegal item (see "Is What You Want to Sell Legal?" earlier in this chapter), an integral part of keeping eBay a safe and lucrative place to do business. In this section, I discuss who to call when someone breaks the rules and what to do when a third party is necessary.

Here are the basic steps you can follow:

- ✔ **Contact the buyer:** If you're involved in a transaction, get the buyer's contact information by using the instructions outlined above. Then call the buyer to see whether you can diplomatically resolve the situation.

- ✔ **Seek out eBay security:** Use the Security Center to report any shady actions, policy violations, or possible fraud, such as a community member impersonating an employee or a suspicious auction. Likened to the front desk at your local police station, eBay's Security Center report form gets results. On an item's page, scroll to the bottom and click the Report this item link. On most other eBay pages, click the Security Center link, which usually appears at the bottom. Then select the issue you want to report and select the Report a Problem check box. Alternatively, you can go directly to

  ```
  http://contact.ebay.com/ws/eBayISAPI.dll?ShowCUPortal
  ```

  You'll find an all-purpose security form on this page to help you in your eBay transactions. These forms will be routed to the right department for action.

- ✔ **Apply for online resolution:** SquareTrade (`www.squaretrade.com`) offers online dispute resolution services and mediation for eBay members. See the following section on how to involve SquareTrade.

- ✔ **Contact the National Fraud Information Center (NFIC):** If you feel you've become a victim of fraud, be sure to file a report through eBay channels. To really bring down wrath on your nemesis, report them to the NFIC by calling 1-800-876-7060.

- ✔ **Contact local law enforcement:** If you become the target of a check-bouncer, contact the local law enforcement in your bidder's hometown. eBay will supply any information necessary to help law enforcement clear the world of fraud. Provide eBay with the name of the local law enforcement officer, agency, telephone number, and case number or police report number. Also include the offending user's ID and the auction item's number. For a state-by-state list of the possible criminal penalties, visit

  ```
  www.ckfraud.org/penalties.html#criminal
  ```

SquareTrade to the rescue

Threats of suing each other, filing fraud charges, and screaming back and forth don't really accomplish anything when you're in the middle of a dispute at eBay. Back in the olden days of eBay, when you weren't able to respond to feedback, users threw negative feedback back and forth willy-nilly, which resulted in some vile flame wars.

You can handle this in eBay's Dispute Console, or you can take it off eBay and go to SquareTrade. When you're selling regularly at eBay, you will undoubtedly run into a disgruntled buyer or two. SquareTrade, a Web-based dispute resolution company, waits in the wings to pull you out of the most difficult situations. SquareTrade pioneered large-scale online dispute resolution and has handled more than two million disputes across 120 countries in five languages, helping consumers and merchants mediate resolutions to e-commerce disputes.

Should you find yourself in an inexorably difficult situation with one of your buyers, and you'd like to take the situation up a notch, go to the following page, shown in Figure 4-3:

```
http://www.squaretrade.com/cnt/jsp/odr/overview_odr.jsp?
            marketplace_name=ebay
```

After you click the File a Case link on this page and answer a few questions regarding the situation, SquareTrade generates and sends an e-mail to the other party, giving instructions on how to respond. From this point, the case information and all related responses appear on a private, password-protected page on the SquareTrade site.

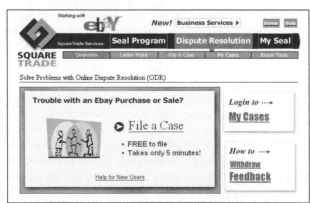

Figure 4-3:
SquareTrade
Dispute
Resolution
start page.

SquareTrade offers three main services to eBay members, which I discuss in this section:

- ✔ Online dispute resolution through direct negotiation
- ✔ Professional mediation
- ✔ SquareTrade Seal

Online dispute resolution

Online dispute resolution is a fast, private, and convenient way to resolve your auction disputes — and it's *free*. Both you and the buyer work together through the SquareTrade Web-based system. Online dispute resolution (ODR) works whether your transaction is in the United States or in another country.

The SquareTrade Web-based negotiation tool is automated, and you and the other party get to communicate on neutral ground. When (and if) the buyer responds, the two of you can work out the situation online and without human interaction. If you're unable to reach a solution, you need to move on to professional mediation (see the following section).

SquareTrade states that problems are usually solved in ten to fourteen days and 85 percent of all cases are resolved without going to mediation. The process will run a quicker course if both people in the transaction are at their computers and answer e-mail during the day.

Participation in ODR is voluntary. If a buyer is set on defrauding you, he or she probably isn't going to engage in a resolution process. If you get no response to your ODR, report your situation to the Security Center.

Professional mediation

If push comes to shove, and in auction disputes it certainly may, you might have to resort to professional mediation. A *mediator,* who is neither a lawyer nor a judge, but an impartial professional, works with both parties to bring the situation to a convivial conclusion. This service is available for a reasonable fee of $29.95 per issue.

If both parties participating in dispute resolution agree to mediation, each party communicates with only the assigned mediator, who communicates with both parties through the same case page. Your case page shows only your communications with the mediator. The mediator reviews both sides of the story to find a mutually acceptable solution to the problem. He or she tries to understand the interests, perspectives, and preferred solutions of both parties, and tries to help both parties understand the other's position.

The mediator is there to disperse highly charged emotions commonly associated with disputes and recommends a resolution only if both parties agree to have the mediator do so. By using the mediation service, you do not lose your right to go to court if things aren't worked out.

SquareTrade seal

A SquareTrade seal lets prospective bidders know that you deal with customers promptly and honestly. Should you choose to get a SquareTrade seal, SquareTrade inserts it into your auctions automatically. (Each seal icon contains a digital watermark with an encrypted expiration date.) You can use the seal in your auctions only if SquareTrade approves you.

Your SquareTrade seal approval is based on several points:

- **Identity verification:** SquareTrade verifies your identity using the information you provide through a third party.

- **Superior selling record:** SquareTrade runs your eBay feedback history through five individual checks. It has an advanced system based on its extensive experience of dispute resolution that allows it to evaluate the quality and quantity of eBay feedback.

- **Dispute resolution:** They check whether you have a history of resolving disputes.

- **Commitment to standards:** You pledge to meet the SquareTrade standards regarding selling and to respond to disputes within two business days.

After you have a seal, you must continue to uphold SquareTrade standards and maintain an acceptable feedback rating. The nifty little personalized seal icon will appear on each of your auctions. Users can click the icon to access your own Seal Display page on the SquareTrade site.

The SquareTrade seal is a fee program — an affordable and good idea if you're in this business for the long run. The seal tells prospective buyers that you care about good customer service and don't tolerate fraudulent activity. It also says that you abide by the SquareTrade selling and customer service standards, which dictate that you will

- Disclose contact information and credentials

- Provide clear and accurate descriptions of goods and services in your auctions

- Clearly disclose pricing, including all applicable fees

- List clear policies on after-sales services, such as refunds and warranties

✔ Maintain privacy policies

✔ Conduct transactions only on secure sites

✔ Respond to any disputes filed against you within two business days

To provide a much higher level of security for your buyers, you can bond your auctions using BuySAFE. Your listings will display the BuySAFE seal, which backs them with a bond up to $25,000. Doing so increases buyer confidence and also protects you. See Chapter 10 for more information.

eBay's Security Center

The Security Center is the eBay version of the FBI. By rooting out evildoers, it serves and protects — and puts up with an immense amount of e-mail from users.

If you see an item on eBay that isn't allowed (see "Is What You Want to Sell Legal?"), be sure to make eBay aware of the auction. The Community Watch team will then take over and investigate the item and, when necessary, end the auction and warn the seller.

When you click the Security Center link, which is at the bottom of most eBay pages, you see the page shown in Figure 4-4. Click the Report Problem button to get action. You then fill out a step-by-step customer service report. Alternatively, you can get to the Security Center customer service reporting form at `http://contact.ebay.com/ws/eBayISAPI.dll?ShowCUPortal`.

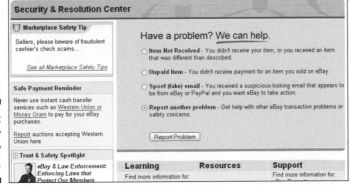

Figure 4-4: The eBay Security Center.

Chapter 5

Expanding Sales with an eBay Store

*I*f you're doing well selling your items on eBay auctions, why open a store? Have you used the eBay Buy It Now feature in one of your listings? Did It work? In an eBay store, all items are set at a fixed price and are online until cancelled (or listed at least thirty days), so it's kind of like a giant collection of Buy It Now featured items. Get the idea?

When you open a store, you have just three main rules to remember and apply: location, location, location. If you were going to open a brick-and-mortar store, you could open it in the corner strip mall, a shopping center, or even somewhere downtown. You'd have to decide in what location your store would do best; that goes for an online store as well. You'll find tons of locations to open an online store, including online malls (when you can find them) and sites such as Amazon.com, Yahoo!, and, of course, eBay.

You have to pay rent for your online store, but opening and running an online store isn't nearly as expensive as a store in the real world (where you also have to pay electrical bills, maintenance bills, and more). Plus, the ratio of rent to sales makes an online store a much easier financial decision, and your exposure can be huge.

In this chapter, I show you, step by step, how to hang out your virtual shingle and get business booming by opening your own eBay store.

Online Stores Galore

Amazon.com, Yahoo!, and eBay make up the big three of the online stores. They are the top locations and get the most visitors. These sites garnered an astounding number of *unique* visitors (that counts *all* of one person's visits to the sites just *once* a month) within any given day.

No doubt feeling competition from Yahoo! and Amazon.com, eBay decided to open its doors (in July 2001) to sellers who wanted to open their own stores. Fixed-price stores were a normal progression for eBay in its quest to continue as the world's marketplace. And eBay Stores make sense: It benefits all current eBay sellers and opens doors to new shoppers who don't want to deal with auctions.

eBay is an online marketplace that specializes in giving you a place to sell *your* stuff, not *theirs*. It doesn't stock a stick of merchandise, and it isn't in competition with you. In addition to its staggering number of visitors, eBay offers you the most reasonable store rent. You may be able to get an introductory rate for the first few months on any of these services, but the ongoing rates are static. To see what I mean, check out the costs in Tables 5-1 and 5-2.

Table 5-1	Online Starter Store Monthly Costs		
	eBay	*Yahoo! Shopping*	*Amazon Pro Merchant*
Basic rent	$15.95	$39.95	$39.99
Setup fee	0	$50.00	0
Listing fee	$0.05 to $0.10	0	0
Final value (transaction) fee	See Table 5-2	1.5%	5% to 15%

Table 5-2	eBay Stores Final Transaction Fees
Selling Price	*Final Value Fees*
$0.01 to $25.00	10%
$25.01 to $100.00	10% of the first $25.00 (**$2.50**) plus 7% of the remaining value to $100
$100.01 to $1000.00	10% of the first $25.00 (**$2.50**) plus 7% of the amount between $25.01 to $100.00 (**$5.25**) plus 5% of the remaining value to $1000
$1000.01 and over	10% of the first $25.00 (**$2.50**) plus 7% of the amount between $25.01 to $100.00 (**$5.25**) plus 5% of the amount between $100.01 to $1000.00 (**$45.00**) plus 3% of the remaining value

Even the basic ($15.95) eBay store gives you so many extras:

- **Selling Manager:** This is the super eBay software that replaces your All Selling page in My eBay. I use it and love it. The $4.99 a month fee is waived with your basic store.

- **Five custom pages:** You can use custom pages to customize the look of your store, make different landing pages, list store policies, and make the store your own. (I use only a few custom pages and it suits me fine!)

- **Web address:** Your store has its very own Internet address (URL). This way you can drive buyers directly to your store. Mine is `www.stores.ebay.com/Marsha-Colliers-Fabulous-Finds`.

- **Promotion boxes:** By using the promotion boxes, you can highlight featured merchandise on the top of your store pages.

- **Three hundred store categories:** You sell sporting goods in one category, women's fashion in another, fine art in one more. . . . You have up to three hundred custom categories for your varied merchandise.

- **Custom store header:** Get your own brand by designing a graphic store header.

- **Markdown Manager:** Hold a sale in your store! Select items to discount for a period of time and offer discounted pricing! You can run sales on up to 250 two hundred fifty listings a day.

- **Vacation hold:** Ever wish you could make your listings temporarily unavailable, or let your customers know you'll be out of town? This great feature allows you to do just that.

- **Picture Manager:** Host pictures on eBay's servers for no extra charge. Basic store owners get 1 MB free.

- **E-mail marketing:** Basic store owners can send up to five thousand e-mail newsletters a month to those who have selected you as a favorite seller. You can find customized e-newsletters and promotional e-mail layouts in your store's marketing area.

- **Listing feeds:** eBay automatically distributes your listings to buyers, search engines, and comparison shopping sites via online feeds.

- **Downloadable business card and stationery templates:** If you've ever wanted collateral to go with your eBay store and have wondered about the legalities of using the eBay logo, you're not alone. eBay offers pre-designed (perfectly legal to use) downloadable templates for store owners to use. Just print them on your color printer and you're set!

- **Search engine keyword management:** You may customize search engine keywords in Manage My Store to improve your store's page rankings in the search engines to which eBay feeds.

- **Traffic reports:** Use the eBay store traffic report to improve your merchandising and listing strategies.

✔ **Store referral credit:** If you refer new customers to your store from flyers, e-mails, and other Web sites, you can get a 75 percent rebate on Final Value Fees. Visit `pages.ebay.com/storefronts/referral-credit-faq.html` for full details.

I don't think it's going to take a rocket scientist to convince you that having a space in eBay Stores (see Figure 5-1) is better than setting up shop anywhere else. No one I know of gives you more features and improves your chances to grow a business. I know that stores aren't based on auctions, but fixed-price store listings are as easy to handle as auctions.

Figure 5-1: eBay Stores opening page.

To review current prices and rules before opening your store, go to `pages.ebay.com/storefronts/subscriptions.html`.

Your eBay Store Name

You've decided to take the plunge and open an eBay store. Do you have an eBay user ID? Have you thought of a good name for your store? Your store name doesn't have to match your eBay user ID, but they're more recognizable if they relate to each other. You can use your company name, your business name, or a name that describes your business. I recommend that you use the same name for your eBay store that you plan to use in all your online businesses. By doing so, you'll begin to create an identity (or as the pros call it, a *brand*) that customers will come to recognize and trust.

Mind your underscores and hyphens

If you want to use your eBay user ID for your store name, you can — unless it contains a hyphen (-) or an underscore (_). Remember how eBay recommends that you break up words in your user ID with a dash or an underscore? Uh oh, that's no good for an eBay store name. I'm in that situation. My user ID is marsha_c; without the underscore, it translates into a user ID that someone else has already taken! Even though it hasn't been used since 1999, someone else has it, which means I can't use it. (marsha_c is probably a crummy name for a store anyway!)

A favorite seller of mine — mrswarren — realized that mrswarren isn't a good name for a store either. So she named her store Pretty Girlie Things, which suits her merchandise to a T.

Your online eBay store should not replace your e-commerce-enabled Web site (see Chapter 8); it should be an extension of it. When people shop at your eBay store, you must take the opportunity to make them customers of your Web site through your store's About the Seller page (which is also your About Me page on eBay). Good deal!

Setting up Shop

It's time to get down to business. Go to the eBay Stores hub from the link on eBay's home page and click the Why Open an eBay Store link in the upper-right corner of the screen (refer to Figure 5-1). This takes you to the seller's hub of eBay Stores, as shown in Figure 5-2. If you click all the links you see here, you get the company line about how good an eBay store can be for your business. You already know how good an eBay store can be for your business, so skip the propaganda and get right down to business (but don't forget to check for any policy changes that may affect your store's operations).

Before you click that link to open your store, ask yourself two questions:

✔ **Can I make a serious commitment to my eBay store?** A store is a commitment. It won't work for you unless you work for it. You have to have the merchandise to fill it and the discipline to continue listing store and auction items. Your store is a daily, monthly, and yearly obligation. You can close your store temporarily, but eBay will reserve your store name for only thirty days. After that, you have to come up with a new name (and your competition may have taken over your famous store name).

Figure 5-2:
The seller's
welcome
page to
eBay
Stores.

✔ **Will I work for my eBay store even when I don't feel like it?** You have to be prepared for the times when you're sick or just don't feel like shipping, but orders are waiting to go out. You have to do the work anyway; it's all part of the commitment.

eBay gives you the venue, but it's in your own hands to make your mercantile efforts a success. If you can handle these two responsibilities, read on!

If you're serious and ready to move on, click the Open a Store link in the upper-right corner of the page (refer to Figure 5-2). You're escorted to a page reminding you that eBay stores fall under the same User Agreement that you agreed to when you began selling on eBay. Click the Continue button to access the Build Your Store pages similar to the image in Figure 5-3. Because I have an eBay store, eBay allows me to make changes and redesign my store at any time.

You need to make a few decisions to create a good store. So before building your store, read the following sections.

Depending on the whims and changes on eBay, the order in which you have to make these decisions may change, but these are choices that you must make:

1. **Choose a color theme.**

    eBay provides some elegant color and graphics themes (see Figure 5-3). You can change the color scheme or layout later, so until you have time to go hog-wild and design a custom masterpiece, choose one of the fourteen clearly organized layouts, either predesigned or with easily customizable themes. Don't select something overly bright and vibrant; you want something that's easy on the eyes, which is more conducive to a comfortable selling environment.

You have the option of selecting a store theme that doesn't require you to insert a custom logo or banner. I highly recommend against it. You need to establish a unifying brand for your online business.

2. **Click Continue.**

3. **Type your new store's name.**

   You've decided on a store name, right? Your eBay store name can't exceed thirty-five characters. Before you type it, double-check that you aren't infringing on anyone's copyrights or trademarks. You also can't use any permutation of eBay trademarks in your store's name.

4. **Type a short description of your store.**

   When I say short, I mean *short*. The paragraph you're reading is 249 characters, and you have only *300* characters to give a whiz-bang, electric description of your store and merchandise. You can't use HTML coding to doll up the description, and you can't use links. Just the facts please, and a little bit of dazzle.

   The importance of this description is huge. When people search eBay stores and descriptions, the keyword information you put here is referenced. Also, if the store header contains your description (as in the Classic style themes), search engines such as Google and Yahoo! will look in this description for the keywords to classify and list your store.

   Write your copy ahead of time in Word. Then, still in Word, highlight the text and choose Tools⇨Word Count. Word gives you the word count of the highlighted text. Check the character count with spaces, to be sure your text fits.

5. **Select a graphic to jazz up the look of your store.**

   You can use one of eBay's clip-art style banners or create a custom 310-x-90-pixel one. If you use one of eBay's graphics, you must promise (hand over heart) that you won't keep it there for long. (See the text after this set of steps for info on designing your own graphics — or hiring someone to do it.)

6. **Click Continue.**

   Now you should have an idea of what your store will look like. You are about to open an eBay storefront (drumroll, please).

7. **Sign up for the basic store ($15.95 a month), and click the Start My Subscription Now button.**

Your store is now live on the Internet with nothing up for sale — yet.

8. **Click the supplied link to get in the trenches and customize your store further.**

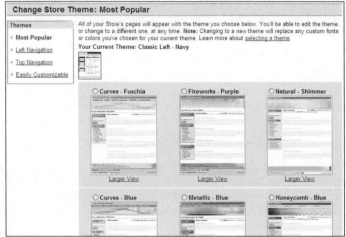

Figure 5-3:
Select the store theme.

If you're wondering in which category your store will be listed on the eBay Stores home page, it's all up to you. eBay checks the items as you list them in the standard eBay category format. For example, if you have six books listed in the Books: Fiction and Nonfiction category and five items in the Cameras & Photo category, you'll be in the listings for both of those categories. Your custom store categories (read on) will be used to classify items only in your store.

If you use one of eBay's prefab graphics, people shopping your eBay store will know that you aren't serious enough about your business to design a simple and basic logo. I've had many years of experience in advertising and marketing, and I must tell you that a custom look will beat out clip art any day. Your store is special — put forth the effort to make it shine.

If you have a graphics program, design a graphic with your store's name. Start with something simple; you can always change it later when you have more time. Save the image as a GIF or a JPG, and upload it to the site where you host your images (your own Web site, your ISP, or a hosting service).

A bunch of talented graphic artists make their living selling custom Web graphics on eBay. If you aren't comfortable designing, search eBay for *web banner* or *banner design*. Graphic banners on eBay sell for about $10 to $20 — certainly worth the price in the time you'll save.

Running Your Store

As part of your store subscription, your My eBay selling area is replaced with eBay's Selling Manager. Selling Manager gives you easy access to customize your store at any time by going to the Manage My Store box, on the lower right of your Selling Manager summary page, shown in Figure 5-4.

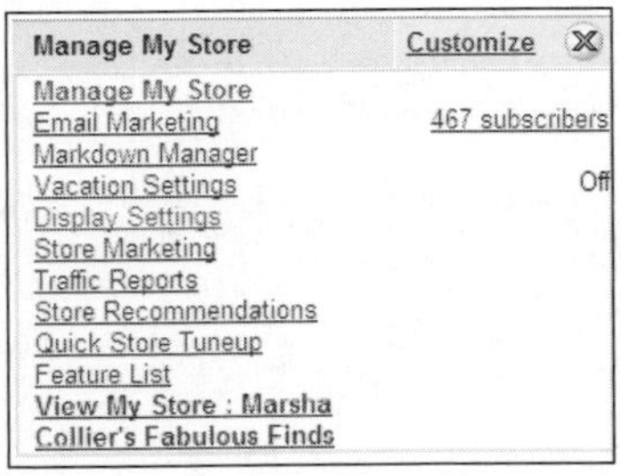

Figure 5-4:
Here's where you can perform all the necessary tasks for running your store.

Manage My Store   Customize ☒

Manage My Store
Email Marketing   467 subscribers
Markdown Manager
Vacation Settings   Off
Display Settings
Store Marketing
Traffic Reports
Store Recommendations
Quick Store Tuneup
Feature List
View My Store : Marsha
Collier's Fabulous Finds

Store design

In the Store Design area (see the screen shot of mine in Figure 5-5), you can perform major tasks required for your store.

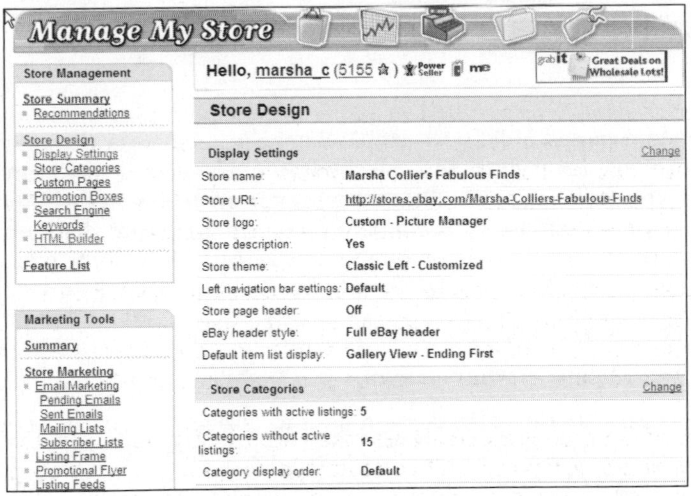

Figure 5-5:
My eBay Store Design area, where I can easily change the look and feel of my store.

Manage My Store

Hello, **marsha_c** (5155 ☆) **Power Seller** **me**   grab**it** Great Deals on Wholesale Lots!

Store Management

Store Summary
• Recommendations

Store Design
• Display Settings
• Store Categories
• Custom Pages
• Promotion Boxes
• Search Engine Keywords
• HTML Builder

Feature List

Marketing Tools

Summary

Store Marketing
• Email Marketing
   Pending Emails
   Sent Emails
   Mailing Lists
   Subscriber Lists
• Listing Frame
• Promotional Flyer
• Listing Feeds

Store Design

Display Settings   Change

Store name: Marsha Collier's Fabulous Finds
Store URL: http://stores.ebay.com/Marsha-Colliers-Fabulous-Finds
Store logo: Custom - Picture Manager
Store description: Yes
Store theme: Classic Left - Customized
Left navigation bar settings: Default
Store page header: Off
eBay header style: Full eBay header
Default item list display: Gallery View - Ending First

Store Categories   Change

Categories with active listings: 5
Categories without active listings: 15
Category display order: Default

Here are a just few of the tasks you should consider revisiting:

✔ **Store design:** You can always go back here to change the name of your store or the theme of your pages. You can also change the way your items are displayed: gallery view (as shown in Figure 5-6) or list view. Neither view is inherently better, but I like the gallery view because it shows the thumbnail gallery pictures of my items.

You should also select the order in which your items will sort. Highest Priced First, Lowest Priced First, Items Ending First, or Newly Listed First. I like Items Ending First as my sort, so that buyers can get the chance to swoop in on items closing soon.

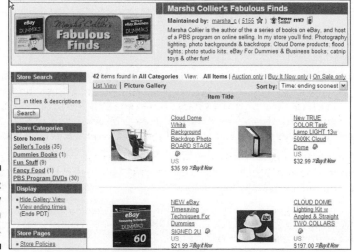

Figure 5-6: My eBay store in gallery view.

✔ **Custom pages:** Most successful eBay sellers have (at the very least) a store policies page. Figure 5-7 shows you the one for my store. When you set up a policies page, eBay supplies you with a choice of layouts. Just click the Create New Page link to select the template that you want to use. Don't freak out if you don't know HTML, eBay helps you out with an easy-to-use HTML generator, as in the Sell Your Item form.

Following are some important policies to include:

• **Indicate to what locations you'll ship.**

• **Specify the sales tax you plan to collect.** If your state doesn't require you to collect sales tax, leave the area blank. If it does, select your state and indicate the proper sales tax. Most states won't require you to collect sales tax unless the sale is shipped to your home state. Check the links in Chapter 15 to verify your state's sales tax regulations.

Terms and Conditions Payment and shipment terms may vary on individual items.	Payment methods	Pay Pal [VISA] [cards] [CHECK] Money Order/Cashiers Check All credit Card payments are graciously accepted through PayPal only.
	Store ship-to locations	Depending on the item, I will gladly ship Internationally. Because of DVD regions and electrical differences, some of my items may not be appropriate in some countries. United States shipments are sent via Priority Mail unless requested ahead of time. THANK YOU!
	Shipping & Handling	Buyer Pays Shipping and handling.
	Sales tax	8.25% if shipped to CA Resale numbers accepted please email after auction.
	Customer service & return policy	All items are guaranteed to be exactly as stated in the auction description. Any defective merchandise will be cheerfully replaced.
Additional Store Information		I research and personally test out many items to find the most useful and economical items to help eBay sellers. The items that make the grade are the ones I sell in my store!

Figure 5-7: My eBay store policies page.

- **State your customer service and return policy.** Fill in the information regarding how you handle refunds, exchanges, and so on. If you're a member of SquareTrade (see Chapter 4) or BuySAFE, mention here that you subscribe to its policies. Be sure to include whatever additional store information you think is pertinent.

You can also set up a custom home page for your store, but it's not a popular option. Most sellers feel It's best to let your visitors go right to the listings of what you're selling.

✔ **Custom categories:** Here's where you really make your store your own. You may name up to three hundred custom categories that relate to the varied items you sell in your store.

✔ **Promotion boxes:** Set up some promotion boxes and change them every month or so to keep your store's look fresh. Select items for promotion that work well with the particular selling season.

✔ **Search engine keywords:** Check out this area to see the keywords that eBay forwards to the major Web shopping and search feeds. If you think there are better keywords, be sure to add them.

Marketing tools

Under the Marketing tools heading, you can perform many tasks that help bring customers to your store. You have the option of clicking a Summary page, which gives you a quick look at how your store's marketing features are currently set. You have a lot of options in this area. Here are a few of the many offered:

✔ **Email marketing:** When you want to design an e-mail campaign to your buyers, you have all the tools here. Create an e-mail newsletter, create one for sending later, manage your subscriber lists — all from one convenient area.

✔ **Listing frame:** Select this option once you get an eBay store. Don't ask questions, just do it. The custom listing header display is one of the best tools you can use to bring people into your store (see how effective it is in my listing in Figure 5-8). Click the link and select the option to Show Your Custom Listing Header on all your eBay auctions and fixed-price sales. This will encourage shoppers to visit your eBay store when they browse your eBay listings. When customizing, be sure to include your store logo as well as a store search box.

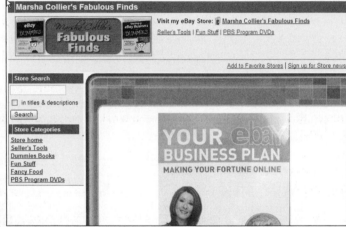

Figure 5-8:
A store listing frame surrounding one of my auctions.

Item promotions

eBay has added some excellent ways to promote your store. As an eBay store owner, you have access to promotional tools that other sellers can't use. One of the most valuable of these is cross-promotions — there's no charge to use it either!

✔ **Cross-promotions:** The cross-promotion box appears after a buyer places a bid on or purchases an item from an eBay seller. The beauty of having a store is that the cross-promotion box appears *twice:* once with your regular listings and again with a different assortment of items (if you want), after someone buys an item. Best of all? You get to select which categories' items are selected from to display with your individual auctions. Figure 5-9 shows a cross-promotion box that appears when someone views one of my auctions.

Figure 5-9:
A cross-promotion in one of my eBay auctions.

You can set up the promotions so that they default to show other items from related store categories. Again, every listing has two sets of options: one for when a user views your listings and the other for when someone bids or wins your item.

✔ **Markdown Manager:** So you say you have to raise some cash to buy new merchandise? Why not run a sale? By clicking here you can select items to put on sale. After they've been marked down, they will appear branded as "On Sale."

Logos and branding

As a store owner, you can customize just about everything that you do on eBay. In Logos and Branding, you can add a store banner and a personalized message (if you'd like) on your end-of-auction e-mails and on your eBay checkout invoices. Figure 5-10 shows an invoice customized with my logo and message.

Create an About the Seller page

If you haven't already created an eBay About Me page, do it now! The About Me page becomes the About the Seller page in your store. This page is a primary tool for promoting sales. (See Chapter 3 regarding About Me pages.) You can put this page together in about ten minutes — max — with eBay's handy and easy-to-use templates!

Figure 5-10: Super promotion for your business: Your eBay store logo can appear on your eBay invoices as well as your e-mails.

Manage your items

We've all listed items on eBay, so I don't plan on boring you with a tutorial on how to list your items here (although I give you some listing and photo image tips in Chapter 11). Following are the main differences between listing an item in your store and listing an auction on eBay:

- ✔ You have to assign your item to one of the prescribed store categories that you designated while setting up your store. If your new item falls into a category that you haven't defined, you can always go back to your store and add a category (as many as three hundred) or put the item in the eBay-generated Other Items category.

- ✔ You don't place a minimum bid or a reserve price on your store items because everything you list in your eBay store is a Buy It Now (fixed-price) item.

- ✔ Listings in an eBay store can be put up for sale for thirty days or on a GTC (good till cancelled) basis.

The items you list in your eBay store *will not* appear in the regular eBay site title search unless less than twenty of that item are listed on eBay. Then your items will be listed below the regular search results as items found in eBay stores. Your items *will* be seen if one of your buyers does a Seller or Stores search from the eBay Search page. That's why you pay only 5 or 10 cents per listing for thirty days. You *must* put a link in your auctions to your eBay store — and tell the auction browsers that you have more stuff for them that they "can't find in a regular eBay search."

Dressing Up Your Listings

eBay has more tempting options that you can use to spruce up your store items. These options work exactly like the ones eBay offers for your auctions (see Chapter 10). When choosing whether to use these options, remember that your eBay store items appear only when someone searches in eBay stores. eBay store items don't appear in a regular eBay search, so the Gallery option may be the most beneficial option at this time. Check out Table 5-3 for a rundown of the optional feature and their associated fees.

Table 5-3	eBay Optional Store Features
Feature	*Every 30 Days*
Featured Plus!	$19.95
Item subtitle	$0.02
Gallery	$0.01
Listing Designer	$0.10
Highlight	$5.00
Border	$3.00
Boldface title	$1.00

Making a Sale

From the buyer's point of view, shopping at an eBay store is much different than winning an auction. eBay stores feature fixed-price sales; the buyer will get the merchandise as soon as you can ship it (instead of waiting for the auction to run its course). Even though your auctions show up on your store's home page, all regular listings in your eBay store are Buy It Now items.

When a buyer makes a purchase from an eBay store, here's what happens:

1. The buyer clicks the Buy It Now button on the listing page. The Review Payments page appears, where the buyer can review the purchase. This page contains the shipping amount you specified when you listed the item.

2. The buyer provides shipping information (required). When eBay notifies you that a sale has been made, you have all the information you need. You don't have to scurry around looking for the return address on the envelope when the payment arrives.

3. The buyer reviews the transaction and then clicks the confirm button. The information about the sale is e-mailed to you, and the buyer receives confirmation of the sale.

Your eBay store will be an essential backup to your auctions. It's a great place to put out-of-season items, accessories for the items you sell actively, and even consignment items between relisting. Considering the price of an eBay store, you have to make only a few sales per month to pay for it — and when your sales start to build, your efforts will be greatly rewarded!

Part II
Setting Up Shop

The 5th Wave   By Rich Tennant

In this part . . .

Your hobby is what you love, and I'm betting you have a houseful of duplicate items — the perfect stuff to start to sell on eBay! Or why not buy from other collectors locally and become a specialist on eBay? Or perhaps you'd like to sell inventory from an existing business or for others on consignment. Or maybe you want to start buying wholesale merchandise like the big boys.

As you can see, the options are countless. In this part, I talk about how to find merchandise to sell, the best way to sell it, and your ever-important Web site.

Chapter 6

Finding Merchandise to Up Your Profits

· ·

· ·

*Y*ou're probably wondering just how you can possibly get enough merchandise to list as many as twenty (maybe fifty?) items a day. You're thinking that there aren't possibly enough sources out there to fulfill that kind of volume. Success on eBay isn't easy. Despite the e-mail claims of the huge money that can be made on eBay, it's like everything else. No one has a magic formula. (The only people who really make money from those e-mails are the ones who send them to hopeful new sellers.) Many hours and a good deal of perspiration — along with loads of inspiration — are necessary to make a good living selling online. You *can* do it — if you apply the same amount of effort in acquiring merchandise.

One of my favorite mottoes is "Buy off-season, sell on-season." You can get great bargains on winter merchandise in the heat of summer. January's a great time to stock up on Christmas decorations, and the value of those trendy vintage aluminum trees doubles in November and December. Cashmere sweaters, too! In the winter, you can get great deals on closeout summer sports merchandise. It's all in the timing.

How are you going to acquire the products you need? I've spent hours, days, weeks, okay, even months trying to work out the best ways to stock an eBay business. Ultimately this depends on you, your personality, and the type of merchandise you plan to sell. I've tried many of the tactics that I discuss in this chapter, as have some eBay sellers that I know, and I pass on the secrets and caveats that each of us discovered along the way.

Dollar Stores

Dollar stores come in all shapes and sizes. They can be filled with junk or treasure, and it takes a practiced eye to separate the wheat from the chaff. Many an item can be found here that makes for great practice for beginning sellers — and often goes for ten times what they paid. Try going in with a teenager, and see whether he or she reacts to any of the items for sale. Sometimes only one in five visits works out, but you'll know when you see the item — and at these prices you can afford to go deep! Stock at these stores doesn't stay on the shelf for too long; if you pass on an item, it may not be there when you return for it the next day. Maybe another savvy eBay seller picked up the values.

99¢ Only stores

The crème de la crème of the dollar-type stores on the West Coast are the 99¢ Only stores. (Okay, $.99 isn't $1.00, but I still think it qualifies as a dollar store!) You can find these stores in California, Nevada, Arizona, and Texas. The highest price in the store is 99¢, and some items can be bought for as little as 29¢.

The bulk of the items sold at 99¢ Only stores are closeouts or special opportunity buys. When a company changes its labels, for example, it might sell all remaining stock with the old labels to 99¢ Only. I've found some profitable books, Olympics memorabilia, and pop culture items at this store. You can go a long way here by being nice. Befriend the store manager, who might alert you when merchandise that matches your specialty comes in. The chain is expanding rapidly, so visit its Web site at www.99only.com to see whether a store is opening near you. Other dollar stores are probably in your area. Pull out the phone book (or bother the 411 operator) and see what you can find.

It's not unusual for dollar store warehouses to sell direct to a retailer (that's you!). Find out where the distribution warehouse is for your local dollar store chain and make contact. The 99¢ Only stores have a wholesale unit called Bargain Wholesale that started in their City of Commerce California offices. They sell directly to retailers, distributors, and exporters.

If you live in Los Angeles, Houston, or Chicago, you can visit one of their showrooms. If not, you can purchase merchandise online on their Web site at www.bargainw.com and shop for your business. To be able to buy at the site, you must have a business license or a resale number from your state. They also have a minimum order; if it's too high for you, why not split an order with another seller?

Big Lots

Another super selling chain is the Big Lots company, which encompasses the Pic N Save, Mac Frugal's, Big Lots, and Odd Lots stores. They may have items priced at more than a dollar, but they specialize in closeout merchandise. All their merchandise sells for well under what most discounters charge and at deep discounts to retailers. This is a great place to find toys, household goods — almost anything. Troll their aisles at least once a month to find items that you can resell on eBay. The Big Lots company has stores in forty-six states; check its Web site at www.biglots.com for store locations near you.

When you get your state's seller's permit (see Chapter 15), you can take advantage of the Big Lots Wholesale Web site at www.biglotswholesale.com. If you think that Big Lots regular prices are low, you should see their wholesale prices! The minimum order from the Web site is $500, which will get you a lot of merchandise. Before placing an order, be sure to check and see whether the item is selling on eBay. If many eBay sellers are trying to sell the item now, why not place an order and sell when the other sellers have exhausted their stock? When fewer sellers are selling, the price usually goes up. Supply and demand is the name of the game.

Tuesday Morning

One of my editors is going to kill me for mentioning one of her favorite eBay merchandise sources — but here it is. Tuesday Morning has more than five hundred stores scattered over the United States. They sell first-quality designer and brand-name closeout merchandise at deep-deep discounts, 50 percent to 80 percent below retail.

The key here is that the store sells recognizable brand names, the kind of items that eBay shoppers look for. I've seem items at their store from Samsonite, Thomas Kincade, Limoges, Wedgwood, Royal Doulton, Madame Alexander, and even Barbie!

Find your local store at their Web site, www.tuesdaymorning.com. If you sign up for their eTreasures newsletter, you'll get advance notice of when the really good stuff arrives at the store. (Sometimes they have only a dozen of a particular item per store, so you have to be there when the doors open.)

Discount Club Stores

Warehouse stores made their mark by selling items in bulk to large families, clubs, and small businesses. In case you haven't noticed, these stores have recently upscaled and sell just about anything you could want. Their shelves are brimming with current merchandise ripe for the picking.

Sam's Club

In addition to shopping for bargains at the Sam's Club in your neighborhood, you can now visit their wholesale auctions at auctions.samsclub.com. What a fantastic place to find merchandise to sell on eBay. The closeouts on the auction site can sell at a fraction of the retail price.

Costco

Believe it or not, one day I was wheeling my cart around Costco (to buy my monthly ration of meat) and right in front of me was a huge display with women jumping and grabbing at the merchandise. I glanced above to read the sign: Fendi Baugette Handbags $199.99. My daughter and I elbowed our way (in a not-too-ladylike fashion, I might add) through the crowd and saw the regularly $450.00 purses stacked like lunchmeat. In those days, the Baugette was new and sold on eBay for around $350.00. Needless to say, we bought all that our credit cards could handle.

In the first edition of this book, I talked about a special on the Costco Web site, www.costco.com, for a new *Snow White & the Seven Dwarfs* DVD. For $18.49, you could pre-order the Snow White DVD and get a second Disney DVD for *free*. When there's an offer like this, you can sell two items on eBay for the price of one. If I had followed my own advice and bought a case of this deal and held some for future sales, I'd be in the money today. It seems that Disney movies are released for a limited time only. Now, that original DVD set sells on eBay for around $40.00.

When an item is new but has some collectibility, I suggest you buy in bulk, sell some of the item to make up your investment, and save the balance for later. This has paid off for me a good many times with Disney films, Barbies, and Andy Warhol dinnerware.

Garage Sales

What can be better than getting up at 6 a.m. to troll the local garage sales? I say nothing — if you're motivated to find lots of good eBay merchandise and prepared for the garage sales. Buy the newspaper or check your local newspaper's classified ads online (just run a Google search for your local newspaper's name), and print maps of the sale locations from MapQuest or Yahoo! You know the neighborhoods, so you can make a route that makes sense from one sale to the next — and figure in bathroom stops and coffee breaks.

Neighbors often take advantage of an advertised sale and put out some stuff of their own. Bring a friend; you can cover more ground faster if two of you are attacking the sales.

A few tips on shopping garage sales:

- Fancier neighborhoods have better stuff than poor or middle class ones. I know that sounds unfair, but I know for sure that rich folks' trash is better than mine.

- Look for sales that say "Early Birds Welcome," and make them the first on your list so you can get them out of the way. It seems like a universal bell goes off somewhere and all garage sales start at 8 a.m. *sharp!*

- The stuff you find at estate sales is often of a higher quality. These sales feature things that have been collected over many, many years.

- Keep an eye out for "moving to a smaller house" sales. These are usually people who have raised children, accumulated a houseful of stuff (collectibles? old toys? designer vintage clothes?), and want to shed it all so that they can move to a condo in Palm Springs.

  Any toys people are selling while downsizing are usually good ones.

- I usually put sales that feature "kids' items and toys" on the end of my list, and I go only if I'm not too tired. These are generally young couples (with young children) who are trying to raise money or are moving. More often than not, they're keeping the good stuff and are simply shedding the excess.

Going-Out-of-Business Sales

Going-out-of-business sales can be a bonanza, but be careful and don't be misled. Many states require businesses that are putting on a going-out-of-business sale to purchase a special license that identifies the business as *really* going out of business. Some store ads may read "Going Out for Business" or some similar play on words, so you need to be sure that you're going to the real thing. When a retailer is liquidating its own stock, you're going to get the best buys. A retailer will often run the sale week by week, offering bigger discounts as time goes by. If a company is really going out of business, don't be afraid to make an offer on a quantity of items.

Another benefit of going-out-of-business sales is that many times the stores are selling their fixtures for rock-bottom prices. If you're looking for a mannequin to model your fashions or display pieces for your photographs, run, don't walk, to that sale.

A chain of children's wear went out of business here in Southern California a while back. This chain also carried a smattering of popular dolls. A seller I know made an offer for all remaining dolls and subsequently purchased them at a great price. Throughout the following year, she sold them on eBay for three to four times what she had paid.

Auctions

Two types of auctions where you can pick up bargains are liquidation and estate auctions. (I also discuss charity auctions, where you may be able to find bargains while donating to a good cause.) You'll find perfectly salable and profitable items, but each type of auction has its idiosyncrasies. Before you go to any auction, double-check payment terms and find out if you must bring cash or can pay by credit card. Also, before you bid on anything, find out the *hammer fee,* or *buyer's premium.* These fees are a percentage that auction houses add to the winner's bid; the buyer has the responsibility of paying this fee.

Liquidation auctions

When a company gets into serious financial trouble, its debtors (the people to whom the company owes money) obtain a court order to liquidate the company to pay the bills. The liquidated company then sells its stock, fixtures, and even real estate. Items sell for just cents on the dollar, and you can easily resell many of these items on eBay. A special kind of auctioneer handles these auctions. Look in the phone book under Auctioneers: Liquidators and call local auctioneers' offices to get on mailing lists. This way, you'll always know when something good comes up for sale.

Estate auctions

Estate auctions are the higher level of estate garage sales. Here you can find fine art, antiques, ephemera, rare books, and collectibles of all kinds. Aside from the large estate auctions, most auction houses have monthly estate auctions in which they put together groups of merchandise from various small estates. Find out when these auctions are being held and mark them on your calendar.

These auctions are attended mostly by dealers, who know the local going prices for the items they bid on. But because they're buying to sell in a retail environment, their high bids will generally be the wholesale price for your area. If a particular item is flooding your market, the high bid may be low. I've seen some incredible bargains at Bonham's estate auctions here in Los Angeles. When you're in a room full of local dealers, they're buying what's hot to resell in your city — not what's going to sell across the country. That entire market will be yours.

Charity silent auctions

I'm sure you've been to your share of silent auctions for charity. A school or an organization will get everyone from major corporations to the local gift shop to donate items. The items are then auctioned off to the highest bidder, usually in a silent format.

You can find many a great item at these auctions. Aside from new merchandise, collectors may feel good about donating some collection overflow to a charity. I purchased the keystone of my Star Trek action figure collection at a charity auction: the very rare tri-fold Borg (one of perhaps only fifty in existence). This figure has sold for as high as $1000 on eBay, and I paid just $60, all while donating to a charity. (Okay, now it's selling for only about $400 on eBay — but heck, it was *still* a deal!)

Have you seen this headline before?

"Make Hundred$ of thou$ands in profits by reselling items from Government Foreclosure auctions!" Yes, I've seen this headline too. You send someone money, and they let you in on the big "secret." Here's the secret: You can find out about many government auctions at these sites:

- ✔ **www.ustreas.gov/auctions/:** This site gives information on seized Department of the Treasury property auctions held in New Jersey, California, Florida, Texas, Arizona, and other locations. The lists of the lots for sale are posted about a month before the auctions. You can also call the hot line at 703-273-7373 for up-to-date information. They also post the bid results for previous auctions, so you can get an idea about the selling price of various lots.

- ✔ **www.ustreas.gov/auctions/irs/:** Our buddies at the Internal Revenue Service have their own auction site. Here you can find a wide assortment of real property: patents, livestock, vehicles, planes, boats, business equipment, household goods, and real estate. They sell just about everything. (These guys are serious about collecting their tax money!)

- ✔ **gsaauctions.gov/gsaauctions/ gsaauctions:** This is the official link to the General Services Administrations surplus, seized, and forfeited property auctions. These are electronic bidding online auctions that are held daily. You can even find used crash test vehicles here (good for selling the undamaged parts on eBay).

- ✔ **eBay seller ID usps-al-pmsc/:** Got a hankering to be tooling around town in a modified postal truck? Well, here's your chance! The USPS sells all kinds of vehicles on eBay.

- ✔ **www.usps.com/auctions:** Ever wonder where all the post office's lost packages go? Check this site for auction locations and times. Also search Google for *mail recovery centers.*

- ✔ **www.govliquidation.com:** This is a private company specializing in government liquidation auctions.

For other sites, run a Google search for *state surplus* (results include tons of links to individual state-seized property auctions), *seized property, tax sales, confiscated property,* and *state auction.* Remember, if you're asked for payment to get the information, it's not an official site.

Goodwill, Salvation Army, and Resale Shops

Participating in a charity such as Goodwill or the Salvation Army is a powerful thing with many benefits. You don't have to worry about having a garage sale to get rid of unwanted stuff (no need to have strangers trodding all over the lawn, crunching the daisy borders while sniffing around at the stuff for sale), and you can pretty much write off many items as a charity tax deduction. And it's simple: You just load the goods into your car and take 'em to the store. It's a win-win-win situation. The extra win is that you can also acquire valuable pieces at bargain-basement prices.

At resale stores, such as Goodwill and the Salvation Army, you'll sometimes uncover treasures while other times you'll find only junk. I recommend befriending the manager who sees the merchandise as it comes in, will know just what you're looking for (because you said so in a friendly conversation), and will call you before the items hit the floor. This type of relationship can save you from making fruitless trips.

Some stores receive merchandise from a central warehouse, where donations are first sent for minor rehabilitation and cleaning. Other, smaller operations process items in-house, with the store manager supervising. The resale store is a business that runs on a schedule. Ask the manager (whom you've befriended) when the truck regularly comes in. Being there when the truck arrives enables you to view items before the general public.

A sharp seller I know is always at his local Salvation Army when the trucks come in. One day as workers unloaded the truck, he saw a plaque-mounted baseball bat. Withholding his excitement, he picked it up and found that it was a signed Ty Cobb bat with a presentation plaque. Although he didn't know exactly what it was, he took a gamble and brought it to the cash register, where he paid $33 minus the senior citizen discount. He took the bat to his office and made a few phone calls, later discovering that the bat was indeed a rare Louisville Slugger bat that had been presented to the Georgia Peach, Ty Cobb. But he'll never sell it because it's his good luck bat, which now hangs above the desk in his warehouse.

Goodwill Industries is definitely gearing up for the twenty-first century. You can shop at its online auctions and get super values on the best of their merchandise. Don't forget to check the going prices on eBay before you buy. Have fun at www.shopgoodwill.com.

Freebies

Freebies come in all shapes and sizes and — best of all — they're free, of course. Freebies are usually samples or promotion pieces that companies give away to introduce a new product, service, or, best of all, media event. Even carefully trimmed ads from magazines can fetch high prices from collectors.

When you go to the cosmetic counter and buy a way-too-expensive item, be sure to ask for tester-sized samples. Name-brand cosmetic and perfume samples of high-priced items sell very well on eBay. Also, look for *gift with purchase* deals. If it's a specialty item, you can usually sell it on its own to someone who'd like to try a sample themselves rather than plunge headlong into a large purchase. Less special items can be grouped together as lots. Be sure to put the brand names in the title.

Remember the talking Taco Bell Chihuahua giveaway? Those cute little dogs were all the rage and sold for big money on eBay. It almost seems foolish to remind you of the McDonald's Teenie Beanie Baby giveaways; moms, dads, and dealers were driving in circles through the drive-thru, purchasing as many of the Happy Meals as each store would allow. They'd then drive to the next McDonald's to purchase a different toy. In my house alone, we had frozen hamburgers for three months!

When *Return of the Jedi* was re-released in 1997, the first one hundred people to enter each theater got a Special Edition Luke Skywalker figure. These figures are still highly prized by collectors, and when the next part of the Star Wars saga is released, you can bet the prices on this figure will rise yet again.

In 1995, Paramount network premiered a new show, *Star Trek Voyager*. In selected markets, Paramount sent a promotional microwave popcorn packet as a Sunday newspaper insert. These are still selling well (when you can find them), although the value rises and falls according to current interest in Star Trek.

Before you pass by a freebie, reconsider its possible future resale value.

Salvage: Liquidation Items, Unclaimed Freight, and Returns

The easiest buys of all, *salvage merchandise* is retail merchandise that has been returned, exchanged, or shelf-pulled for some reason. Generally, this merchandise is sold as-is and where-is and may be in new condition. To buy this merchandise, you must have your resale (sales tax number) permit and be prepared to pay the shipping to your location — unless you're buying the merchandise on eBay.

Available all over the country, the liquidation business has been thriving as a well-kept secret for years. As long as you have space to store salvage merchandise and a way to sell it, you can acquire it for as low as 10 cents on the dollar. When I say you need storage space, I mean lots of space. To buy this type of merchandise at bottom-of-the-barrel prices, you must be willing to accept truckloads — 40- to 53-foot eighteen-wheelers, loaded with approximately twenty-two to twenty-four 4-x-4-x-6-foot (or 7-foot) pallets — of merchandise at a time. Often these truckloads have manifests listing the retail and wholesale price of each item on the truck. If you have access to the more than 10,000 square feet of warehouse that you'll need to unpack and process this amount of merchandise, you're in business.

Several types of salvage merchandise are available:

- **Unclaimed freight:** When a trucking company delivers merchandise, a *manifest* (a document containing the contents of the shipment) accompanies the freight. If, for some reason, a portion of the shipment arrives incomplete, contains the wrong items, or is damaged, the entire shipment may be refused by the merchant. The trucking company is now stuck with as much as a truckload of freight. The original seller may not want to pay the freight charges to return the merchandise to his or her warehouse (or accept blame for an incorrect shipment), and so the freight becomes the trucker's problem. The trucking companies arrive at agreements with liquidators to buy this freight in the various areas that the liquidators serve. This way, truckers are never far from a location where they can dump, er, drop off merchandise.

- **Returns:** Did you know that after you buy something and decide that you don't want it and return it to the store or mail-order house, it can never be sold as new again (in most states anyway)? The merchandise is generally sent to a liquidator who agrees in advance to pay a flat percentage for goods. The liquidator must move the merchandise to someone else. All major retailers liquidate returns, and much of this merchandise ends up on eBay or in closeout stores.

    If you're handy at repairing electronics or computers, you'd probably do very well with a specialized lot. You may easily be able to revitalize damaged merchandise, often using parts from two unsalable items to come up with one that you can sell in like-new working condition.

- **Liquidations:** Similar to the liquidation auctions that I mention in a previous section on auctions, these liquidators buy liquidation merchandise by truckloads and sell it in smaller lots. The merchandise comes from financially stressed or bankrupt companies that need to raise cash quickly.

- **Seasonal overstocks:** Remember my motto? "Buy off-season, sell on-season"? At the end of the season, a store may find its shelves overloaded with seasonal merchandise (such as swimsuits in August) that it must get rid of to make room for the fall and winter stock. These brand-new items become salvage merchandise because they're seasonal overstocks.

- **Shelf-pulls:** Have you ever passed up one item in the store for the one behind it in the display because its box was in better condition? Sometimes the plastic bubble or the package is dented, and you'd rather have a pristine one. That box you just passed up may be destined to become a *shelf-pull*. The item inside may be in perfect condition, but it's cosmetically unsalable in the retail store environment.

Drop-shipping to your customers

Some middlemen, wholesalers, and liquidators specialize in selling to online auctioneers through drop-ship services or warehouses. Some crafty eBay sellers make lots of money selling lists of drop-shipping sources to eBay sellers — I hope not to you. Dealing with a drop-shipper means that you don't ever have to take possession of (or pay for) the merchandise. You're given a photo and, after you sell the item, you give the vendor the address of the buyer. They charge your credit card for the item plus shipping, and they ship the item to your customer for you.

This way of doing business costs *you* more and lowers your profits. If you're in business, your goal is to make as much money as you can. Because the drop-shipper is in business too, they'll mark up the merchandise they sell to you (and the shipping cost) so they can make their profit. Drop-shipping can work as a *supplement* to your basic eBay business.

Be careful when using a drop-shipper. Ask for references. Don't give them your credit card number with carte blanche to keep charging your account month by month if you're not benefiting from their services. See whether a zillion sellers are selling the same merchandise on eBay — and not getting any bites. Check, too, that the price you will pay for the item leaves you room for profit. I've researched some of these items on eBay and noted that many inexperienced sellers only mark up drop-ship goods by a fraction. They seem to be happy making $5 a sale; they don't take into consideration how much the listing fees for other, unsold items cost them. That's just not smart business on their part, hence they can ruin the market for such items for everyone else.

Also, what happens if the drop-shipper runs out of an item that you've just sold? You can't just say oops to your buyer without getting some nasty feedback. It's your online reputation at stake. If you find a solid source and believe in the product, order a quantity and have it shipped to your door. Don't pay for someone else's mark-up for the privilege of shipping to your customers.

WARNING! A proportion of liquidation items, unclaimed freight, and returns may not be salable for the reasons that I discuss in the rest of this section. Although you'll acquire many gems that stand to bring you profit, you'll also be left with a varying percentage of useless items. Read on carefully.

Items by the pallet

Some suppliers take the risk and purchase salvaged merchandise by the truckload. They then break up each truckload and sell the merchandise to you a pallet at a time. You'll probably find some local liquidators who offer this service, or you can go online to find one. Here's the rub: finding the right person to buy from.

As in any business, you'll find both good-guy liquidators and bad-guy liquidators. As you know, the world is full of e-mail scammers and multilevel marketers who are in business to take your money. No one trying to sell you merchandise can possibly *guarantee* that you'll make money, so beware of liquidators who offer this kind of promise. I don't care who they are or what they say. Carefully research whomever you choose to buy from. Use an Internet search engine and search for the words *salvage, liquidation,* and *pallet merchandise.*

Some liquidation sellers sell their merchandise in the same condition that it ships in to their location, so what you get is a crapshoot. You may lose money on some items while making back your money on others. Other sellers who charge a bit more will remove less desirable merchandise from the pallets. Some may even make up deluxe pallets with better-quality merchandise. These loads cost more, but if they're filled with the type of merchandise that you're interested in selling, you'll probably write better descriptions and subsequently do a better job selling them.

Getting a pallet of merchandise shipped to you can cost a bundle, so finding a source for your liquidation merchandise that's close to your base of operations is a good idea. You'll notice that many liquidation sites have several warehouses, which translates to lower shipping costs for the buyer. (They can then also accept merchandise from places close to the various warehouses.) You might see FOB (freight on board) and a city name, which means that when you buy the merchandise, you own it in the city listed. You're responsible for whatever it costs to ship the merchandise to your door. Search around; you may have to go through many sources before you find the right one for you.

When you find a source from which you want to buy merchandise by the pallet, check out a few things before spending your hard-earned cash:

- ✔ Do they sell mostly to flea marketers (you might not want that kind of merchandise because you're looking for *quality* at a low price) or closeout stores (more retail oriented)?
- ✔ Did you get a reply within 24 hours after calling or e-mailing?
- ✔ Does anyone you speak to appear to care about what you want to sell?
- ✔ Are the available lots within your budget?
- ✔ Are the lots general or have they been sorted to include only the type of merchandise that you want to sell?
- ✔ How long has this liquidator been in business and where does its merchandise come from?

- ✔ Does the source guarantee that you *will* make money or that you *can* make money by buying the right merchandise? ***Remember:*** No one can guarantee that you'll make money.

- ✔ Does the supplier offer on its Web site references that you can contact to find out some usable information on this seller's items and the percentage of unsalable goods in a box or pallet?

- ✔ Is a hard sell involved? Or is it a matter-of-fact deal?

Before you get dazzled by a low, low price on a huge lot and click the Buy It Now button, check the shipping cost. Many so-called wholesalers will lure you in with bargain-basement prices, only to charge you three times the normal shipping costs. Do your homework before you buy!

Job lots

Manufacturers often have to get rid of merchandise, too. Perhaps a particular manufacturer made five million bobbing-head dolls and then sold only four million to retailers. It has to quickly unload this merchandise (known as *job lots*) so that it'll have the cash to invest in next season's array of items. Job lots often consist of hundreds or thousands of a single item. You'd best enjoy what you're selling because you'll be looking at the stuff for a while.

Remember supply and demand — don't ever flood the eBay market. Otherwise, your item will become valueless.

Many Web sites specialize in job lots, but you have to visit them often because the deals are constantly changing. One worth checking out is Liquidation.com, shown in Figure 6-1. Visit them at `www.liquidation.com`.

Figure 6-1: Liquidation.com has desirable lots of liquidation merchandise.

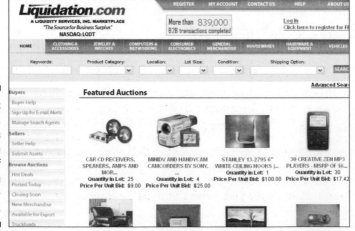

True Wholesale Merchandise

Purchasing wholesale merchandise may require that you have your state's resale license, which identifies you as being in the business. Be sure that you have one before you try to purchase merchandise direct from another business. Also, when you have a resale number and purchase merchandise from another business — known as a business to business (B2B) transaction — you probably won't be charged tax when you purchase your stock because you'll be paying sales tax when you sell the items. Go to Chapter 15 to find out how to get that magic resale number.

When you have your resale number, you can go anywhere you want to buy merchandise. If you want to buy direct from a manufacturer, you can. Unfortunately, manufacturers often have a monetary minimum for the amount of your order, which may be more than you want to spend (and you'd get more of a particular item than you'd ever want at once). To remedy that, see whether you can find some independent retailers who buy in quantity and who perhaps will let you in on some quantity buys with manufacturers.

To find wholesalers on the Internet, try Google.com. Refine your search to your favorite categories: golf, jewelry, skateboards — get the idea? Then run the following searches (inserting your choice of merchandise as indicated): *Dealer login jewelry; Wholesale login jewelry; Member login jewelry; Distributor login jewelry; Licensed retailers only.*

Sometimes the liquidators that I discuss in the preceding section get cases of perfectly salable goods in their loads. Pallets break up into many cases, and liquidators will often sell these cases individually on eBay. What a great way to acquire goods for your eBay business; I know of several eBay sellers who buy their merchandise this way.

Resale Items on eBay

I'll keep this eBay buying technique short and sweet: Use the magic search engine! But be careful; many a get-rich-quick schemer will use boldface keywords in their auctions to attract your attention. Look only for good-quality merchandise to resell. Remember that the only way to make a living on eBay is to sell quality items to happy customers so that they'll come back and buy from you again. Be sure to search eBay auction titles for the following keywords: *resale, resell,* "*case of*" (see Figure 6-2), "*case quantity,*" "*lot of,*" "*pallet of*" (see Figure 6-3), *closeout,* and *surplus.* Be sure to use the quotes anywhere that I've included them here because this forces the search engine to find the words in the exact order you write them inside the quotes.

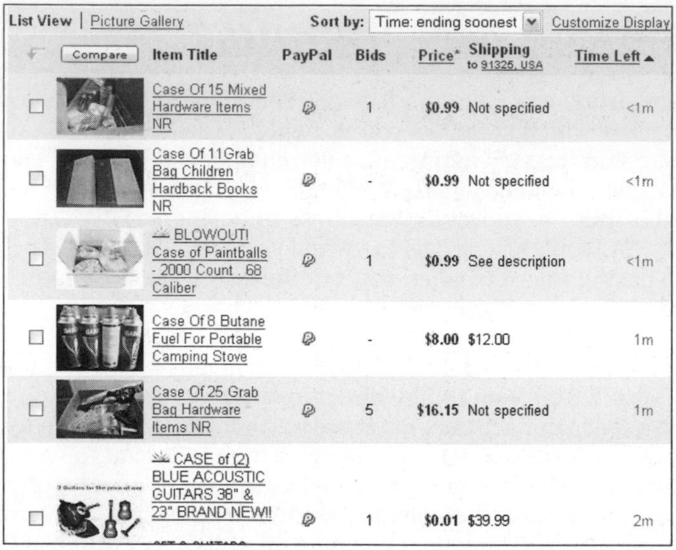

List View	Picture Gallery		Sort by:	Time: ending soonest		Customize Display

	Compare	Item Title	PayPal	Bids	Price*	Shipping to 91325, USA	Time Left ▲
☐		Case Of 15 Mixed Hardware Items NR	🅿	1	$0.99	Not specified	<1m
☐		Case Of 11Grab Bag Children Hardback Books NR	🅿	-	$0.99	Not specified	<1m
☐		BLOWOUT! Case of Paintballs - 2000 Count . 68 Caliber	🅿	1	$0.99	See description	<1m
☐		Case Of 8 Butane Fuel For Portable Camping Stove	🅿	-	$8.00	$12.00	1m
☐		Case Of 25 Grab Bag Hardware Items NR	🅿	5	$16.15	Not specified	1m
☐		CASE of (2) BLUE ACOUSTIC GUITARS 38" & 23" BRAND NEW!!	🅿	1	$0.01	$39.99	2m

Figure 6-2: Results of a "case of" search on eBay.

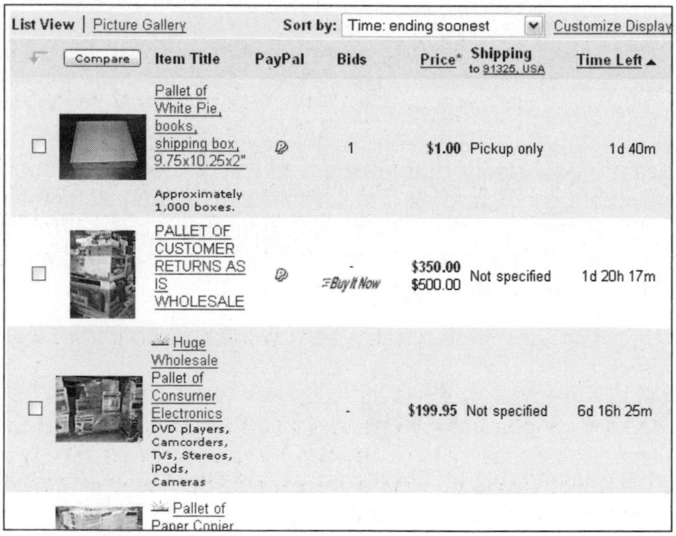

List View	Picture Gallery		Sort by:	Time: ending soonest		Customize Display

	Compare	Item Title	PayPal	Bids	Price*	Shipping to 91325, USA	Time Left ▲
☐		Pallet of White Pie, books, shipping box, 9.75x10.25x2" Approximately 1,000 boxes.	🅿	1	$1.00	Pickup only	1d 40m
☐		PALLET OF CUSTOMER RETURNS AS IS WHOLESALE	🅿	≡Buy It Now	$350.00 $500.00	Not specified	1d 20h 17m
☐		Huge Wholesale Pallet of Consumer Electronics DVD players, Camcorders, TVs, Stereos, iPods, Cameras		-	$199.95	Not specified	6d 16h 25m
☐		Pallet of Paper Copier					

Figure 6-3: Results of a "pallet of" search.

Also be sure you check out the wholesale categories on eBay. After noticing how many sellers were buying from other sellers, eBay set up wholesale sub-categories for almost every type of item. You can find the wholesale items in the category list on the left side of the page after performing a search, or just go to the eBay home page, scroll down the list of categories, and click Wholesale. You'll be brought to the Wholesale Lots hub page, as shown in Figure 6-4. Just click the category of your choice to find some great deals.

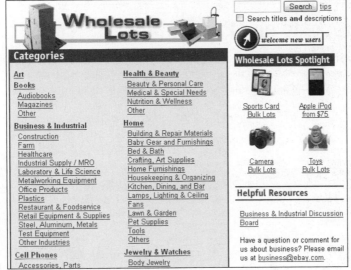

Figure 6-4:
eBay's
Wholesale
Lots hub
page.

Consignment Selling

Consignment sales are the up-and-coming way for you to help newbies by selling their items on eBay. Lots of sellers do it, and several retail locations base their business on it. You take possession of the item from the owner and sell it on eBay. You're responsible for taking photos and marketing the auction on eBay — for a fee. In addition to the money you earn selling on consignment, you also get excellent experience for future auctions of your own merchandise.

To set up your business for consignment sales, you should follow a few guidelines:

1. Design a consignment agreement (a contract), and send it to the owners of the merchandise before they send you their items. Doing so ensures that all policies are set up in advance and that no questions will arise after the transaction has begun.

2. Have the owners sign and send the agreement to you (the consignor) along with the item.

3. Research the item based on past sales so that you can give the owners an estimated price range of what the item might sell for on eBay.

4. Photograph the item carefully (see Chapter 11 for some hints) and write a thoughtful, selling description.

5. Handle all e-mail inquiries as though the item were your own; after all, your fee is generally based on a percentage of the final sale.

Become an eBay Trading Assistant

After you have fifty feedbacks under your belt on eBay (and have sold at least four items in the past thirty days), you can become a registered eBay Trading Assistant. Check out `pages. ebay.com/tahubn` (shown in the figure) to get all the details.

eBay publishes a directory of consignment sellers that you can search by inserting your address. Check out who in your area is a registered Trading Assistant. Read their terms and fees. Consignment sellers charge varied amounts based on their geographic location (some areas can bear higher fees than others).

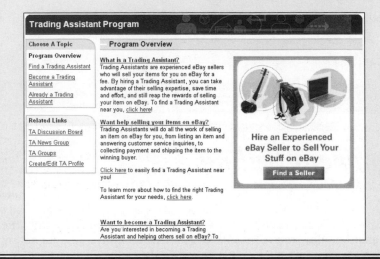

What do you charge for all your work? I can't give you a stock answer for that one. Many sellers charge a flat fee for photographing, listing, and shipping that ranges from $5–$10 plus as much as a 30 percent commission on the final auction total (to absorb eBay fees). Other sellers base their fees solely on the final sale amount and charge on a sliding scale, beginning at 50 percent of the total sale, less eBay and payment service fees. You must decide how much you think you can make on an item.

Traditional auction houses handle consignment sales in a similar fashion.

When you've reached the next level of your eBay enterprise and are looking to spend some serious money on your merchandise, check out my book, *eBay Timesaving Techniques For Dummies.* In that book I delve into the type of wholesale-buying secrets normally reserved for the big-time retailers.

Chapter 7

Pricing Your Items to Sell

. . . .

In This Chapter

▶ Searching eBay

▶ Finding publications in your area of interest

▶ Using online appraisal services

▶ Authenticating your merchandise

. . . .

*I*f you don't know what your item is worth, you may not get the highest price in any market. If you don't know how to make your item easy to find, it may not be noticed by even the hardiest of collectors. If you don't know the facts or what to say, your well-written title and detailed description (combined with a fabulous picture) may still not be enough to get the highest price for your item.

Knowing your item is a crucial part of successful selling at eBay. This is why I suggest in Chapter 1 that you specialize in a small group of items in the beginning so that you can stay on top of ever-changing trends. An item may be appraised or listed in a book for a high value, but what you care about is the price at which the item will actually sell. Imagine someone uncovering a hoard of your item and, not knowing the value of it, dumping them on eBay with low Buy It Now prices. This frequent scenario drives down the value of the item within a couple of weeks.

The values of collectibles go up and down. *Star Wars* items are a perfect example; values skyrocketed during the release of the latest movie, but now prices have settled to a considerably lower level. A printed book of value listings is valid only for the *moment* the book is written. If you stay on top of your market in a few specialties, you'll be aware of these market fluctuations. If you're looking for the highest price instead of looking to liquidate excess inventory, I'd hold any special *Star Wars* items until the buzz starts up again.

You no doubt *will* purchase the occasional gem and will want to make the most money possible, so in this chapter I examine the different ways you can find out just how much something is worth. I start with the easiest and most accurate method, and end with the most laborious. I hope you can get your answer the easy way.

The Easy Way: eBay Search

Who woulda thunk it? The best tool for evaluating your items is right under your nose. The eBay search tool is the best and quickest link to finding your pricing information. To see how items like yours have been selling, search the completed auctions. You can search these results also to see in which categories to list your item.

Every type of item has a different type of bidder. This makes sense, right? Would a person searching for collectible dolls have the same shopping habits as a coin collector? Probably not; coins tend to be more expensive than collectible dolls. Although generalities can be dangerous, *profiling* your item's buyer is worthwhile. After you check out the completed auctions for items like yours, you'll be amazed at how the buying patterns of shoppers in different categories become crystal clear. After you arm yourself with this knowledge, you'll know not only how much your items should go for but also the best time to end the auction.

If you're selling a common item, it's also important to check to see how many other sellers are selling the same item — and when their auctions close. Nothing can kill your profits like being the second or third auction closing with the same piece of merchandise. You have to space your auctions apart from the others, or the law of supply and demand will kick in — and kick you in the wallet.

The way the search system works has changed drastically over the years, so be sure that you know how to use this valuable tool. Almost every eBay page has a small box for searching. Initially you may find it easier to go to the search page, but if you know the search engine *syntax,* or shorthand, you can pinpoint your items with amazing accuracy.

Here are some pointers to help you get the most out of the eBay search engine:

- The search engine isn't case sensitive, so you don't have to worry about using capitalization in your search.
- To find more needles in the haystack, be sure to select the Search Titles and Descriptions option.

✔ To find historical pricing (what the item has sold for in the past two weeks), be sure to select the box to search Completed listings as well as current.

✔ If you're using common search terms, don't search only auction titles and descriptions; search by category, too. For example, suppose that you're searching for a Winnie the Pooh baby outfit. Type *Pooh outfit* and you'll get a bunch of results. Look to the left of the page, and see the category that more closely matches your search. In Figure 7-1, the matching category is Clothing, Shoes & Accessories. Click the link below for the Infants & Toddlers subcategory. Now you'll see the search results in the appropriate category — I guarantee you'll find exactly what you're looking for.

Figure 7-1:
The eBay search results with the Matching Categories refinement box.

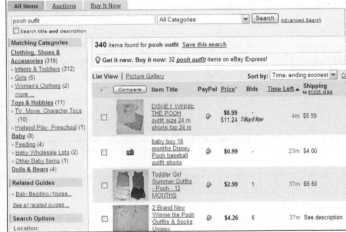

✔ Don't use conjunctions *(or, and)* or articles *(a, an, the)* in your search; the search engine might misconstrue these *noise* words as part of your search. Some sellers use the ampersand (&) in place of the word *and,* so if you include *and* in your search, you won't find auctions that use the ampersand. In addition, some sellers, due to the fifty-five-character limit, may not place *the* in their title; the same goes for *a, or,* and *and.*

Advanced searching methods

If you need to pinpoint a particular item or just want to weed out bogus responses, you can try a variety of advanced search methods, shown in Table 7-1. You can use these shortcuts in any of eBay's search windows.

Table 7-1	Advanced Search Syntax	
Symbol	*Effect*	*Example*
Quotes (",")	Limits search to the exact phrase in the quotes	**"American Staffordshire"** yields auctions relating only to this breed of dog
Asterisk (*)	Works like a wild card in poker	**196* fashion** displays auctions that relate to 1960s fashion
Parentheses (()) and comma (,)	Finds items related to either word	**(shipperke,schipperke)** finds items spelled both ways
Minus sign (–)	Excludes words	**watch –digital** gets you a lovely analog watch
Minus sign (–), parentheses (()), and comma (,)	Excludes more than one word	**Packard –(hewlett,bell)** finds those rare Packard auto collectibles
At (@) and number 1	Searches two out of three words	**@1 new purse shoes dress** gets you a nice new outfit

Now that you know how to finesse the search engine, head to the search page and see if you can work some magic.

If you have the item number, you can type or paste it into any of the eBay search boxes to get to that item.

Using eBay Advanced Search

By clicking the Advanced Search link just to the right of the Search button at the top of most eBay pages, you can access eBay's advanced search options. With the advanced search, you can narrow your search to check out the competition (who's selling your items). The Advanced Search area has many options; here are a few of the more important:

- ✔ **View results:** You can choose whether you want to see a mini-gallery of photos or see your results by item number. Although this may not ordinarily help when you're doing research, information is key; you might just see a variation of the item in photos that you didn't know about.

✔ **Search in categories:** You can narrow your search to one of the thirty-four major categories at eBay. If your product is made for men, women, or children, you may get more efficient results by looking in the category that applies directly to your item. Strangely, when searching for a ladies watch, I found the following synonyms and abbreviations for *ladies: lady's, ladys, lds,* and *femmes.*

✔ **Completed listings only:** Select this check box to go directly to completed listings for your item research.

✔ **Sort by:** You can find items by auctions that end first (default), newly listed items first, lowest prices first, or highest prices first.

✔ **Payment:** You can isolate your search to only those sellers who accept PayPal. This may enlighten you as to whether buyers of this product pay higher prices if they have the option to pay with credit cards. (Although the PayPal exclusion will not include other methods of credit card payments, it still speaks strongly for credit card users.)

✔ **Locate items near you:** If you're selling something big that you can't (or don't want to) ship, you want to deliver it or have the buyer pick it up. This option allows you to check out the competition only in your closest major metropolitan eBay trading area.

✔ **Multiple item listings:** This option lets you search by quantity or lot.

So how can you search completed auctions to find bidding patterns on items like yours? Here's a way to dig out all the details you need: Perform a search on the item for which you want information using the search box you see on every eBay page. When the results appear (see Figure 7-2), you'll see how many other sellers are selling your same item. That way, you can determine whether it's the right time to sell. (If all active auctions for your items have high bids, its time to sell — just be sure not to list your auction to end at a similar time as another one.)

To dig into the details for historic pricing, you can scroll down (on the left side of any search results page) to the Search Options area:

1. **Select the Completed Listings check box in the Show Only area of the page.**

2. **Click the Show Items button below the list of options.**

   You are presented with the search results of completed listings for the past two weeks.

3. **To sort by price, go to the Sort By drop-down box at the top of the listings and select the Price, Highest First option.**

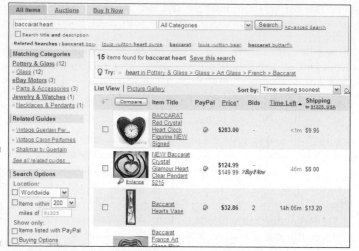

Figure 7-2:
Results
of an
investiga-
tory search.

The results of completed auctions of your particular item for the last fourteen days appear sorted by highest prices first. Now you're at the heart of
the matter (see Figure 7-3). Pull out your calendar and make note of what
days your item landed the highest bids. More often than not, you'll find that a
pattern appears. Your item may see more action on Sunday or Monday or
Thursday or whenever. After you figure out the days that your item gets the
highest bids, pull out a copy of the eBay time chart, which appears on the
Cheat Sheet (at the front of this book), and evaluate what time of day your
high bidders like to bid.

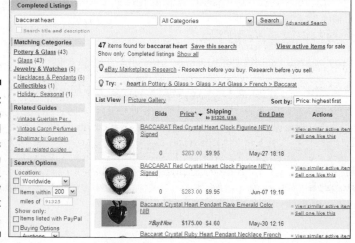

Figure 7-3:
The
Completed
Listings
search
results,
sorted by
highest
prices first.

There you have it: the method that will get you the most information that eBay can give you on the sales trends on your item. It's money in the bank. Use it!

If you can't find any auctions for your item, you have a few more options. You're not gonna believe I'm saying this, but try searching `auctions.amazon.com`. At least you'll see whether someone else in the world is selling one of your items. None of the cool search features that I previously discuss will work — hey, they ain't eBay.

eBay also has a superior tool for checking your competitor's auctions. After a while, you will identify the sellers who frequently sell items similar to yours. Aside from keeping them in your favorite sellers list on your My eBay page (for more on that, see Chapter 3), here's a way to see whether one of your competing sellers has an item like yours up for sale:

1. **Go to the Advanced Search area, and click the Items By Seller link on the left.**

2. **Enter the seller's user ID in the box provided.**

   a. **If you're not sure of the spelling of the seller's ID, select the Show Close and Exact User ID Matches option.**

   b. **To search completed listings, select the option to Include Completed Listings. From the drop-down menu, select the time frame in which you want to search.**

   You may go back as far as thirty days.

3. **Go to the bottom and click the Search button.**

Useful Publications

So what if your item isn't for sale on eBay and hasn't been for thirty days? What's the first thing to do? Check out your local newsstand for one of the many publications devoted to collecting. Go over to Yahoo! Yellow Pages at `yp.yahoo.com`. Type your ZIP code to limit the search to your part of the country, and type a search for *newsstand* and *news stand.* You can also search for *Magazines — Dealers* in your area. Let your fingers do the walking and call the newsstands in your area and ask whether they have publications in your area of interest. If no newsstands are listed in your area, visit the local bookstore.

Here's a list of some popular reference publications:

- ✔ *Action Figure Digest:* Find out who's hot in the action figure biz in this monthly magazine. Its Web site sells back issues; go to www.tomart.com.

- ✔ *Antique Trader:* This magazine has been the bible of the antique collecting industry for more than forty years. Visit its online home on the Collect.com Web site at www.antiquetrader.com for more articles and subscription information.

- ✔ *Autograph Collector:* This magazine gives the lowdown on the autograph business as well as samples of many autographs for identification. Its Web site, www.autographcollector.com, features links to price guides that it publishes.

- ✔ *Collector Editions:* You'll find information on plates, figurines, glass, prints, cottages, ornaments, and dozens of other contemporary decorative collectibles in this monthly magazine.

- ✔ *Doll Reader:* The *Ultimate Authority Doll Reader* has been dishing out the scoop on collectible dolls of all sorts for more than twenty-five years. It's the place to go to catch the trends on the latest in doll collecting. At www.dollreader.com, you'll get an idea of what's in this informative magazine. They even have a newsletter.

- ✔ *Goldmine:* The magazine for CD and record collecting. The Web site, www.goldminemag.com, has many sample articles and information from its issues.

- ✔ *Haute Doll:* *Haute Doll* magazine covers vintage and contemporary dolls and is geared to the adult collector. They cover trends in collecting dolls such as artist dolls, Alex, Barbie, Betsy McCall, Blythe, Brenda Starr, celebrity dolls, Cissette, Cissy, Coco, Coty Girl, Dawn, Elise, Gene, Ginny, Ginger, Jenny, Jill & Jan, Kitty Collier, Little Miss Revlon, Miss Seventeen, Momoko, Somers & Field, Tammy, Tiny Kitty, Tressy, Tyler, Sydney, Vivian, and more! Visit the site at www.hautedoll.com for subscriptions and news.

- ✔ *Linn's Stamp News:* I subscribed to this magazine when I was in grade school, and it's still around. Actually it's been around a lot longer, since 1931. (Hey, I'm not that old!) They too have an informative Web site; go to www.linns.com or their online magazine at www.linns online.com.

- ✔ *Numismatic News:* Another standard, *Numismatic News* has been around for more than fifty years. The first issue each month includes a pull-out guide to retail U.S. coin prices. Every three months, it also includes a U.S. paper money price guide. Check out *Numismatic News* on the Web at www.numismaticnews.net.

✔ *Sports Collectors Digest:* Takes sports collectibles to the highest level. Visit its Web site at www.sportscollectorsdigest.com/ and sign up for a free e-mail newsletter.

✔ *Teddy Bear Review:* Since 1986, this review has offered pages of information on bear collecting. For a free sample issue, go to www.teddy bearreview.com.

It seems that every leading magazine has its own Web site. In the next section, I mention some useful Web sites for pricing references.

Online Sources of Information

Because you're all so Internet savvy (what's better than getting the information you want at a millisecond's notice?), I assume you plan to visit the magazine Web sites that I mention in the preceding section. In this section, I give you a few more fun online sources where you might be able to get more insight about your items.

Web sites

Many Web sites devoted to different collectible areas list prices at recently completed auctions. These auctions are the best evaluation of an item's value because they're usually directed towards specialists in the specific collectible category. Most of the participants in these auctions *really* know their stuff.

You may have to poke around the following Web sites to find the prices realized at auction, but once you do, you'll have the holy grail of estimated values. Look for links that point to auction archives. Many of these sites will consign your item from you as well and sell it to their audience:

✔ Antiques, art, all kinds of rare stuff: www.sothebys.com

✔ Art auctions: www.artprice.com charges for its searches by artist, but has an immense database

✔ Autographs, movie posters, and comic books: www.autographs.com

✔ Coins and sports memorabilia: www.collectors.com and www.superiorsports.com

✔ Collectible advertising glasses: www.pgcaglassclub.com (you have to see this stuff!)

- ✔ United States coin price guide: `www.pcgs.com/prices/`
- ✔ Currency auctions: `www.lynknight.com`
- ✔ Rare coins: `www.bowersandmerena.com`

Online appraisals

I've had a bit of personal experience with online appraisals, which seem quite tempting at first glance. At second glance, though, I realized that unless the person doing the appraisal could actually *see* and *feel* the item, an accurate appraisal couldn't be performed. Also, you have no guarantee that the person at the other end is really an expert in the field that relates to your item.

I had a few items *e-appraised* by a prestigious (and now defunct) online appraisal company, and the appraisals seemed a bit off. Then I took one, a painting, to Butterfields (now Bonhams) in Los Angeles and found that the value of the painting was ten times what my e-appraisal read.

The bottom line here is that if it's an item of real value and it's worth apprais-ing, it's worth getting appraised in person. Most large cities have auction houses, and many of those auction houses have monthly *consignment clinics* (a way for auction houses to get merchandise for their future auctions). If you bring an item to the auction house, you aren't legally bound to have it sell your item for you, but it may not be a bad idea. All you'll get is a free verbal appraisal; the auction house won't fill out any official paperwork or anything, but at least you'll get an idea of what your item is worth. Real appraisals are expensive, are performed by licensed professionals, and come with a formal appraisal document.

Authentication Services

Some companies provide the service of *authenticating* (verifying that it's the real deal) or authenticating and *grading* (determining a value based on the item's condition and legitimacy). To have these services performed on your items, you'll have to send them to the service and pay a fee.

Following are a few excellent sites for grading coins:

✔ Professional Coin Grading Service (PCGS): www.pcgs.com.

✔ American Numismatic Association Certification Service (AMNACS) — sold to Amos Press in 1990: www.anacs.com.

✔ Numismatic Guaranty Corporation of America (NGCA): www.ngccoin. com/ebay_ngcvalue.cfm. The site offers eBay users a discount and features a mail-in grading and certification service for your coins.

✔ PCI Coin Grading Service (PCI): www.pcicoins.com.

Stamp collectors (or those who have just inherited a collection from Uncle Steve) can get their stamps "expertized" (authenticated) by the American Philatelic Society. Visit www.stamps.org/services/ser_ aboutexpertizing.htm for more information.

For comic books, Comics Guaranty, LLC (CGC), https://www.cgccomics. com/ebay_comic_book_grading.cfm, will seal (enclose in plastic to preserve the quality) and grade at a discount for eBay users.

You can find more links and some authentication discounts for eBay users at pages.ebay.com/help/community/auth-overview.html.

Sports cards and sports memorabilia have a bunch of authentication services. If you received your autograph or memorabilia direct from the player or team, you can assure its authenticity. Having the item authenticated may or may not get you a higher price at eBay. Try these sites:

✔ **Professional Sports Authenticator (PSA):** Offers eBay users a discount at www.psacard.com/cobrands/submit.chtml?cobrandid=23.

✔ **Online Authentics:** Reviews autographs by scans online or by physical review. Look at its services at www.onlineauthentics.com.

The best way to find a good authenticator in your field is to search the items at eBay and find the most prominent authenticator listed in the descriptions. For example, note in the coins area that certain grading services' coins get higher bids than other services. You can also go to an Internet search engine (Google or Yahoo!) and type the keywords **coin grading** (for coins). You'll come up with a host of choices; use your good sense to see which one suits your needs.

Remember that not all items need to be officially authenticated. Official authentication does add value to the item, but if you're an expert on your items, you can comfortably rate them on your own in your auctions. People will know from your description whether you're a specialist. Your feedback will also work for you by letting the prospective bidder or buyer know that your merchandise from past sales has been top-drawer.

Chapter 8

Establishing a Base of Operations: Your Web Site

*S*uccess in e-commerce follows a natural progression. There isn't a quick fix. All business expansion will cost you time *and* money. When you're rushing to make the big bucks — listing items so fast you can't count them — you can't possibly learn from your mistakes. Also, expansion costs money, so it only makes sense to *make* some profit before you spend it.

The progression goes like this. One, get started on eBay and get the hang of it (make money). Two, open an eBay store and stock it (make more money). Keep in mind that no one can learn the intricacies of running an online business in a month or two. That said, here's number three: After you've shown some healthy profit, it's time to expand and invest in your own e-commerce enabled Web site.

Your eBay store is important to your business, but it doesn't replace an e-commerce Web site. Yes, eBay is an important site (duh) for your sales and store, but so is your own business Web site. You should establish your own presence on the Web. And although you can — and should — link your site to eBay, don't miss out on the rest of the Internet population.

You don't have a Web site yet? The Web has so many sites with pictures of people's dogs and kids that I just assumed you had your own site, too. The space for a Web site comes *free* from your ISP. (I even have an embarrassing one with family pictures.) One of these sites can be the practice site for your business. Take down pictures of the baby, and post pictures of items you're selling — or at the very least, install the eBay-To-Go package (see Chapter 2).

You do have a Web site? Have you taken a good look at it lately to see whether it's up to date? Does it link to your eBay auctions or eBay store?

Most small and medium businesses are increasing their online revenue. In a recent survey of small online businesses, 63 percent of respondents have five or fewer employees — does that sound like you?

Whether or not you have a Web site, this chapter has something for you. I provide a lot of detail about Web sites, from thinking up a name to choosing a host. If you don't have a site, I get you started on launching one. If you already have a site, I give you some pointers about finding the best host. For the serious-minded Web-based entrepreneur (that's you), I also include some ever-important marketing tips.

Free Web Space — a Good Place to Start

Although I love the word *free,* in real life it seems like nothing is *really* free. *Free* generally means something won't cost you too much money — but may cost you a bit more in time. When your site is free, you aren't able to have your own direct URL (Universal Resource Locator) or domain name. Most likely, a free Web site has an address such as one of the following:

```
www.netcom.com/~marshac
home.socal.rr.com/marshac
www.geocities.com/marshac_1998
members.aol.com/ebaygal
```

Having some kind of site at least gives you the experience in setting up the site. When you're ready to jump in for real, you can always use your free site as an extension of your main business site.

To access the Internet, you had to sign on with an Internet service provider (ISP), which means you more than likely already have your own Web space. Most ISPs allow you to have more than one e-mail address per account. Each e-mail address is entitled to a certain amount of free Web space. Through the use of *hyperlinks* (small pieces of HTML code that, when clicked, route the clicker from one place to another on the page or on other Web site), you can combine all the free Web space from each e-mail address into one giant Web site. Take a look at Table 8-1, where I compare some popular ISPs.

Table 8-1	ISPs That Give You Free Web Space	
ISP	*Number of E-Mail Addresses*	*Total Space per Account*
America Online (AOL)	7	2MB per e-mail address (14MB)
AT&T WorldNet	6	10MB per e-mail address (60MB)
Earthlink	8	10MB
MSN (using Explorer 6.1)	10	30MB
Road Runner	5	5MB and $0.99 per extra MB per month
msnTV	6	3MB
Yahoo! GeoCities*	1	15MB

*Yahoo! GeoCities isn't an ISP, but it is a reliable online community that gives each member online Web space. Membership is free. Extra megabyte space is available for purchase.

If America Online (AOL) is your Internet service provider, you may already know that AOL often has some serious issues regarding its users getting e-mail from the rest of the Internet. You can't afford to run a business in an area that has e-mail issues. Your AOL account gives each of your seven screen names 2MB of online storage space (refer to Table 8-1). You can best utilize this space by using it to store images for eBay, not to run a business site. Each screen name, at 2MB, can store fifty 40K images. (For more information on how to use this space for your extra images, see Chapter 11.)

Many ISPs have their own page-builder (HTML-generating) program that's free to their users.

Poke around your ISP's home page for a Community or Your Web Space link. For example, after looking around the Road Runner ISP's home page (www.rr.com), I found and clicked the Member Services link, which led me to a page offering various options. I finally found a Personal Home Page link, which took me to a page that would walk me through setting up my own home page. After agreeing to the Terms of Service, I can simply log on and set up my home page. Road Runner offered me the option of using Microsoft FrontPage, which is considered to be one of the best and easiest Web site–building programs around.

Why learn HTML when Web page editors can do it for you?

If you need some help designing those first pages (I *never* became proficient in HTML and still depend somewhat on software to design my site), try looking for inexpensive HTML Web software. I just checked eBay, and searched *web design* in the Software category. Plenty of software is available for as little as $9.99. The key is to find one that includes a graphical (WYSIWYG, or what-you-see-is-what-you-get) interface that allows you to preview your pages as you design them. Some have predesigned templates. You can also use an older version of Microsoft FrontPage (without the extensions) to design simple Web pages.

Then again, the longer you're on the Internet and the more you study, the more you'll learn about HTML. It's often just easier to type out HTML code yourself once you get the hang of it. That's why Patti Louise Ruby and I wrote the book, *eBay Listings That Sell For Dummies.* Only two subjects are covered in the book: HTML and photography for your online business. (Patti covered HTML, and I covered the photography portion.) It also has several HTML templates that you might like to use as your own.

I've used Microsoft's FrontPage in the past, and if you want all its benefits, you need a site that uses FrontPage *extensions* (portions of the FrontPage program that reside on the server and enable all the HTML magic to happen automatically — you don't have to write in the code). Save the use of FrontPage extensions for *hosted* Web sites (the ones you pay for) when you have a good deal of allotted space. Installing Microsoft FrontPage extensions on a small Web site like the one that Road Runner provides will take up too many of your precious megabytes. (Yahoo!, however, has them installed for the GeoCities sites, and doesn't count them as part of your allotted megabyte count.)

Paying for Your Web Space

If you've been on the Internet for any length of time, daily spam has bombarded you with hosting offers. A Web-hosting company houses your Web site code and electronically doles out your pages and images to Web page visitors.

If you take advantage of PayPal's free Pay Now buttons or Shopping Cart, you can turn a basic-level hosted site into a full-on e-commerce store without paying additional fees to your hosting company. The PayPal tools are easily inserted into your pages with a snippet of code provided by PayPal.

Before deciding to spend good money on a Web-hosting company, thoroughly check it out. Go to that company's site to find a list of features they offer. If you still have questions after perusing the Web site, look for a toll-free number to call. You won't find any feedback ratings like you find on eBay, but the following are a few questions to ask (don't hang up until you're satisfied with the answers):

- **How long have they been in business?** You don't want a Web host that has been in business only a few months and operates out of their basement. Deal with someone who's been around the Internet for a while and, hence, knows what they're doing. Is the company's Web site professional looking? Or does it look like your neighbor's kid designed it? Does the company look like it has enough money to stay in business? You wouldn't want it disappearing mysteriously with your money.

- **Who are some of their other clients?** Poke around to see whether you can find links to sites of other clients. Take a look at who else is doing business with them and analyze the sites. Visit several of their client sites. Do the pages and links come up quickly? Do all the images appear in a timely manner? Web sites that load quickly are a good sign.

- **What is their downtime-to-uptime ratio?** Does the Web host guarantee _uptime_ (the span of time its servers stay operational without going down and denying access to your site)? Expecting a 99 percent uptime guarantee is not unreasonable; you're open for business — and your Web host needs to keep it that way.

- **How much Web space do you get for your money?** MSN (Microsoft Network Internet access service) gives you 30MB for free; you'd better be getting a whole lot more if you're paying for it!

- **What's their data transfer limit?** _Data transfer_ is a measurement of the amount of bytes transferred from your site on the server to the Internet. In July 2001, my site had 93,000 hits; in July 2004, it had more than 500,000. Each hit transfers a certain amount of bytes (kilobytes, megabytes) from your host's servers to the viewer's computer.

- **Do they offer toll-free technical support?** When something goes wrong with your Web site, you need it fixed immediately. You must be able to reach tech support quickly without hanging around on the phone for hours. Does the Web host have a technical support area on its Web site where you can troubleshoot your own problems (in the middle of the night)?

Whenever you're deciding on any kind of provider for your business, take a moment to call their tech support team with a question about the services. Take note of how long you were on hold and how courteous the tech was. Before plunking down your hard-earned money, you should be sure that the provider's customer service claims aren't merely that — just claims.

✔ **What's the policy on shopping carts?** In time, you're probably going to need a shopping cart interface on your site. Does your provider charge extra for that? If so, how much? In the beginning, a convenient and professional-looking way to sell items on your site is to set up PayPal Shopping Cart or PayPal Pay Now button. When you're running your business full-time, however, a shopping cart or a way to accept credit cards is a must.

✔ **What kind of statistics will you get?** Visitors who go to your Web site leave a bread-crumb trail. Your host collects these statistics, so you'll be able to know which are your most and least popular pages. You can know how long people linger on each page, where they come from, and what browsers they're using. How your host supplies these stats to you is important. One popular reporting format is provided from a company called WebTrends (`www.webtrends.com`).

✔ **Are there any hidden fees?** Are they charging exorbitant fees for setup? Charging extra for statistics? Imposing higher charges if your bandwidth suddenly increases?

✔ **How often will the Web host back up your site?** No matter how redundant a host's servers are, a disaster may strike; you need to know that your Web site won't vaporize. *Redundancy* is the safety net for your site. You may be interested in how many power backups a company has for the main system. Perhaps it has generators (more than one is good) and more.

What's in a Web Site Name: Naming Your Baby

What to name the baby, er, Web site? It's almost as much of a dilemma as deciding on your eBay user ID or eBay store name. If you don't have an existing company name that you want to use, why not use the same name as your eBay store? (Check out Chapter 5 for details about eBay Stores.) Lock it up now so that you can keep your brand forever.

Name your site with a name that identifies what you do, what you sell, or who you are. And be sure you like it, because once its yours and you begin operating under it and establishing a reputation, it'll be with you twenty years from now when you're still selling online! (I know, it should only happen!)

A few Web sites offer wizards to help you decide your domain name. A particularly intuitive one can be found at `www.snapitnow.com`. In a small, Web-based form, you input your primary business type and keywords that describe your business. The wizard then displays a large number of options and also lets you know whether the options are available. Very convenient.

Before you attempt to register a name, you should check to be sure it isn't anyone else's trademark. To search an updated list of registered U.S. trademarks, go to the following and use the electronic trademark search system: www.trademarksearchforfree.com.

Registering Your Domain Name (Before Someone Else Takes It)

Talk about your junk e-mail. I get daily e-mails advising me to *Lose 40 pounds in 40 days, accept credit cards now,* and of course *REGISTER MY NAME NOW!* The last scam seems to be geared to obtaining my e-mail address for other junk mail lists rather than trying to help me register my Web site. Choosing a *registrar* (the company that handles the registering of your site name) is as important as choosing the right Web host. You must remember that the Internet is still a little like the Wild West, and that the James gang might be waiting to relieve you of your hard-earned cash. One of the ways to protect yourself is to understand how the registry works (knowledge *is* power), so read on.

In October of 1998, U.S. government officials decided to expand the domain registration business by breaking up the Network Solutions site (previously the only place that you could register your Web site). This opened up the Web to all kinds of people selling domain names.

Before you decide on a registrar for your domain name, take a minute to see whether the registrar is accredited by ICANN (Internet Corporation for Assigned Names and Numbers — the international governing body for domain names) or is reselling for an official ICANN-accredited registrar. (You'll have to ask who they register with.) The Accredited Registrar Directory is updated constantly, so check the following for the most recent list: www.internic.com/regist.html.

Domain parking

Suppose that you've come up with a brilliant name for your site and you get really big and famous. Then someone else uses your Web site name but registers it as a .net — while yours is a .com. To avoid this situation, when you're ready to register your site, make sure you register both domains (.com and .net) and park them with your registrar. For example, www.ebay.net and ebay org are registered to (guess who?) ebay.com. You can check the owner of any domain name at any of the Web-hosting or registrar sites.

Making your personal information private

ICANN requires every registrar to maintain a publicly accessible WHOIS database displaying all contact information for all domain names registered. Interested parties (or fraudsters) can find out the name, street address, e-mail address, and phone number of the owner of the site by running a *whois* search on the domain name. You can run a whois search by going to `www.whois.net` and typing the domain name in question.

This information can be useful to spammers who spoof your e-mail address as their return address to cloak their identity, identity thieves, stalkers, and just about anyone up to no good. To see the difference between private and public registrations, run a whois search on my Web site, `www.coolebaytools.com`, and `www.yahoo.com`.

Registrars such as Network Solutions offer private registration for an additional $9 a year. Check to see whether your registrar offers this service and how much they charge.

You'll usually get a substantial discount from the more expensive registrars when you register your domain name for multiple years — a good idea if you plan on staying in business. Also, if you register your name through your hosting service, you might be able to cut the price in half! The only drawback is that your prepaid registration might go out the window if you choose to change hosting companies.

If you're registering a new domain name but already have a site set up with your ISP, you need a feature called URL forwarding. This feature directs any hits to your new domain name from your existing long URL address. Some registrars offer this service, but watch out for hidden surprises, such as a free offer of the service, which means they will probably smack a big fat banner at the bottom of your home page. Your registrar should also have some available tech support. Trying to troubleshoot DNS issues is a job for those who know what they're doing! Remember, sometimes you get what you pay for.

Marketing Your Web Site (More Visitors = More Business)

After you set up your Web site, it's time to let the world know about it. Having spent many years in the advertising business, I can spot businesses that *want* to fail. They open their doors and expect the world to beat a path to them and make them rich. This doesn't happen — ever.

You must take an active approach to letting the world in on the goodies you have for sale. This means spending a good deal of time promoting your site by running banner ads and getting your URL into a search engine. There are no shortcuts.

About a trillion people out there want to take your money for advertising your Web site. As with all transactions regarding your Web site, knowing who you're dealing with is key. If you want to run your banner on someone else's site, don't spend money; ask to do an exchange. The more advertising that you can get for free, the better. If you decide that you want to pay for advertising, I recommend that you wait until after you've made a profit selling merchandise from your site.

A simple link to your Web site from your eBay About Me page will draw people to your site initially. You'll be pleasantly surprised.

Getting your URL into a search engine

For people to find your site (and what you're selling), they must be able to locate you. A popular way that people do this is by searching with a search engine. So you should submit your site to search engines. Go to the search engines that interest you and look for a link or a help area that will enable you to submit your site. Be sure to follow any specific instructions on the site; some may limit the amount of keywords and the characters allowed in your description.

To submit your URL to search engines, you need to do a little work. (Nothing's easy, is it?) Write down twenty-five to fifty words or phrases that describe your Web site; these are your *keywords.* Now, using as many of the words you came up with, write a description of your site. With the remaining words, create a list of keywords, separating each word or short phrase by a comma. You can use these keywords to add metatags to the header in your HTML document for your home page. *Metatags* are identifiers used by search engine *spiders,* robots that troll the Internet looking for new sites to classify on search engines. Metatags are used like this:

```
<META NAME = "insert your keywords here separated by
         commas" CONTENT = "short description of your
         site">
```

If you have a problem coming up with metatags, check out the free Yahoo! GeoCities handy metatag generator at `http://geocities.yahoo.com/v/res/meg.html`.

Google

Google crawls the Internet regularly with its spider, Googlebot, looking for new sites to index on Google Search. If Googlebot has missed your site, go to the following and let Google know that you're site is ready for listing: `www.google.com/addurl.html`. Google doesn't guarantee that your site will be listed, but the process takes less than a minute. What could it hurt?

Yahoo!

Yahoo! is one of the more difficult sites to list with, although you *can* get a free listing if you fill out all the forms correctly and wait six to eight weeks. Instructions for the free listing are at `http://docs.yahoo.com/info/suggest/`. Yahoo! guarantees that you'll be reviewed in just seven business days.

You'll hear a lot about search engine optimization (SEO) when getting your Web site set up. This basically means that you want to use the right keywords in your metatags to get the spiders to see your site.

Paid search advertising

Paid search advertising helps you get visitors to your site. When you go to a search engine, you'll see several searches on the right side of the page (Google) or on the top of the search results (Yahoo!); these are the paid listings that match your search. Each time you click one of these links, the site owners pay a fee for directing a new visitor to their site.

The two major players in the field are Google Adwords (`adwords.com`) and Yahoo! (`/smallbusiness.yahoo.com/marketing/`).

In my book, *eBay Powerseller Practices For Dummies,* I go into far more detail on how to take advantage of this service.

Part III

Business Is Business — Time to Get Serious

The 5th Wave   By Rich Tennant

In this part . . .

*L*et's delve into the dollars and sense of your eBay business. In this part, I discuss automating your business by using online and offline tools, sprucing up your listings, setting up your home photo studio, and handling shipping (the bane of most businesses). I also give you the lowdown on two other important aspects of your business: working with customers and collecting payments.

Chapter 9

Software Built for Online Auctions

. . . .

In This Chapter

▶ Figuring out what tasks you can automate

▶ Finding online auction management services

▶ Exploring auction management software

. . . .

*N*ow that eBay has become a world marketplace, a single-page auction or item listing is becoming an increasingly valuable piece of real estate. Millions view your sale, and the more auctions and fixed-price items that you can list, the better your chance to make a good living. Time is money: You need to post your auctions quickly and accurately.

Auction posting, record keeping, inventory cataloging, photo managing, and statistic gathering are all tasks that you can automate. The more your business grows, the more confusing things can become. Automated tools can help you keep it all straight. But remember that the more tools you use, the more expense you may be adding to your business. Always keep your bottom line in mind when evaluating whether to use fee-based software and services.

In this chapter, I discuss how to automate different tasks, software that you can use to automate, and Web sites that offer services to make your daily chores considerably more bearable. After you read this chapter, you'll be well equipped to decide whether or not you want to automate your business.

Considering Tasks for Automation

You'll have to perform certain office tasks, no matter how few or how many auctions you're running. Depending on your personal business style, you may want to automate any or all of the following tasks. You may choose to use a single program, a manual method, or some features from one program and some from others. For those who aren't ready for the automated plunge, I offer alternatives. Where appropriate, I insert references guiding you to where in this book or on the Web you can find more information about the automated services I discuss.

Setting up images for automatic FTP upload

You have several ways to store the images in your auctions. If you're using an auction management service or software (such as Marketworks.com or Channel Advisor, both of which I discuss later in this chapter), an *uploader* is usually included as a part of the software. Many online services merely fetch the photos from your hard drive without the need for additional FTP (File Transfer Protocol) image uploading software.

With this format, you merely click the Browse button to access the Open File window, and then find the location of the images on your hard drive. When you've located the images that you want to upload (one per line), click the Upload button and the images will be on their way to the service's servers.

If you choose to keep images on your own Web site (which makes the images available for your Web site, too), you'll have to use some sort of FTP software. You probably aren't using close to the total space that your hosting service allots for your Web site, whicl leaves plenty of room to store a separate folder of eBay images. ISPs often also give you several megabytes of storage space (see Chapter 8).

The Mozilla Firefox 2 Internet browser includes a free FTP program called FireFTP. Just go to the Tools drop-down menu at the top of the Firefox window and click FireFTP. It's a straightforward FTP software program that should be part of your auction arsenal, even if you use a service or other software. You can download a free version of Firefox at `www.mozilla.com/en-US/firefox`.

Sorting auction e-mail

A vital function of any auction software or system is the ability to customize and send e-mails to your winners. Many sellers use the default letters in these programs, which tend to be a bit — no, incredibly — impersonal and uncaring. (To see some examples of customer-friendly e-mails and tips on drafting your own, head to Chapter 12.) You must decide whether you want the program to receive e-mail as well.

Most computer-resident auction management programs have their own built-in e-mail software as part of the program. When you download your winner information from eBay, the program automatically generates invoices and congratulatory e-mails.

How to handle your auction-related e-mail is a personal choice. Although I currently use eBay's Selling Manager to send auction-related e-mails, I receive auction e-mail through Outlook, using a separate folder titled Auctions that contains subfolders for eBay Buy and eBay Sell.

Automating end-of-auction e-mail

If you want to set up e-mails to be sent automatically after an auction ends, you must use a software application to do so. (I use Selling Manager Pro.) The software should download your final auction results, generate the e-mail, and let you preview the e-mail before sending it out. Many online sites that I discuss later in this chapter (see the section "Online auction management sites") send out winner confirmation e-mails automatically when an auction is over; be sure that you set your preferences to Preview the e-mail before sending if you want to use this option.

eBay sends an end-of-auction (transaction) e-mail as part of its standard procedure. What many sellers don't know is that you can customize these e-mails through your PayPal account. As long as you indicate PayPal as a payment option in your listings, you can add your logo and a personalized message. To sign up for this, log on to your PayPal account and then follow these steps:

1. **Click the My Account tab, and then click the Profile tab.**

2. **In the Selling Preferences column, click the Auctions link.**

3. **Change the Off radio button to On and type your personalized message.**

4. **Click Submit.**

Keeping inventory

Many eBay PowerSellers depend on the old clipboard or notebook method — crossing off items as they sell them. If that works for you, great. Others prefer to use an Excel spreadsheet to keep track of inventory.

Most of the auction management packages that I detail later in this chapter (see the section "Auction management software") handle inventory for you. Some automatically deduct an item from inventory when you launch an auction. You have a choice of handling inventory directly on your hard drive or keeping your inventory online with a service that's accessible from any computer, wherever you are.

I handle my inventory on my desktop through QuickBooks. When I buy merchandise to sell, and post the bill to QuickBooks, it automatically puts the merchandise into inventory. When I input my sale, it deducts the items sold from standing inventory. I can print a status report whenever I want to see how much I have left — or have to order.

Generating HTML

Fancy auctions are nice, but fancy doesn't make the item sell any better. Competitive pricing and low shipping rates work in your favor — especially with eBay's Compare Items feature in Search. Also, a clean listing with as many photos as necessary goes a long way to sell your product. Some software and services offer a large selection of templates to gussy up your auctions. But you must think of your customers; many of them are still logging on with dial-up connections, which are notoriously slow. The use of simple HTML doesn't slow the loading of your page, but the addition of miscellaneous images (decorative backgrounds and animations) definitely makes viewing your auction a chore for those dialing up. And forget the background music — it *really* slows things down!

Don't fret; you can make do by repeatedly incorporating two or three simple HTML templates, cutting and pasting new text as necessary. Most auction management programs offer you several choices of templates. I recommend that you stick with a couple that are similar, giving a standardized look to your listings, the way major companies give a standardized look to their advertising and identity. Your customers will get used to the look of your auctions and feel comfortable each time they open one.

Inserting your hosted pictures in your description

An important line of code that everyone seems to forget is the one that inserts a picture into your auction description. On the Sell Your Item page, click the tab to view in HTML mode, and insert the following line below where you'd like your image to appear in your description:

```
<img src="http://www.your
     server.com/imagename
     .jpg" />
```

Be sure to substitute your own server and image name. If you want to put one picture on top of another, just type <P> between the lines of code — repeat the HTML line with a different image name for each image that you want to display.

One-click relisting and selling similar items

Using auction software or an auction service speeds up the process of posting or relisting items. After you input your inventory into the software, posting or relisting your auctions is a mouse click away. All the auction management software packages that I detail later in this chapter include this feature.

If you buy your items in bulk, you might want to take advantage of eBay's free relisting tool. By clicking the Sell Similar link on any ended listing, you can automatically relist your items. Sell Similar starts the listing as new, so if your item doesn't sell, you can avail yourself of the Relist feature. This way, if the item sells the second time, your listing (insertion) fees for the first listing will be credited.

Although eBay says that Sell Similar is for relisting items, it also works when listing a duplicate of an item that has sold successfully. The only difference is that you aren't credited for the unsold listing fee.

Scheduling your listings for bulk upload

If you want to schedule the unattended launch of your auctions without incurring eBay's 10-cent fee, you must use an online management service (check out the "Online auction management sites" section, later in this chapter). If you can be at your computer to send your auctions to eBay singly or in bulk, you can use the Turbo Lister application, which eBay offers at no charge. (For details, see the "Turbo Lister" section, later in the chapter.)

Researching your statistics

There are so many questions when you're selling on eBay. What is the best time to end my auction? What day should I start my listing? Is it better to run a five-day or a seven-day auction? Now an online service can help you separate the rumors from the facts.

Lots of eBay *experts* out there will give you hard-and-fast rules to guarantee success with your listings. It's a lot of bunk. Every category and every type of item may draw shoppers at different times of the day and different days of the week. The best experts are those who are selling every day on eBay, day in and day out. They are usually PowerSellers and do their own research for their listings. They don't have the time to spout off and give you secrets. I'm a regular seller on eBay (a PowerSeller too), and I've noticed distinct variations in my sales through a fantastic online service called ViewTracker from Sellathon. It's really one of a kind.

Sellathon tracks your listings using a small piece of code that you insert in your auctions. The site gives you loads of information about your visitors, without violating anyone's privacy. Here are some of the things you can find out:

- How many times someone has visited your auction
- The date and time the visitor arrived at your auction, and what city, state, and country your visitor is from
- Whether the reserve price was met when the visitor arrived
- When the item received a bid (and how many bids had been placed up to that moment)
- Whether the visitor had chosen to watch this listing in his or her My eBay page
- Whether the visitor browsed a category, searched a category, searched all of eBay, used eBay's Product Finder utility, or came from the See Seller's Other Items page or some other page and what category he or she was browsing
- If the visitor was searching, what search terms he or she used to find your item and whether the search was for Titles Only or Titles and Descriptions
- Whether the user elected to view Auctions Only, Buy it Now, or both

You get all this information and more. Sellathon offers a thirty-day free trial at www.sellathon.com. After that, the service is $4.95 a month.

To end an old wives' tale about what days and times your listings get the highest hits, Figure 9-1 shows you some charts from my Sellathon account, showing how many visits my listings got each day. Verrry interesting.

Automating other tasks

That's not all! You can automate a few more tasks. Having so many options is like being in a candy store: You may want it all, but that might not be good for you. For example, if you use online postage, you may not want to print your labels because that would be doubling your work. Take a serious look at the options you're offered and see whether they fit into your particular work style.

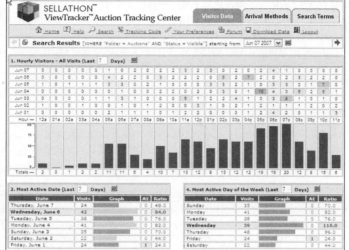

Figure 9-1: Seems like a very unlikely Wednesday wins the race.

Checking out

When someone wins or buys an item, eBay's checkout integrates directly with PayPal and will also indicate your other preferred forms of payment. If you're closing less than a hundred auctions a day, that's all you need. eBay and PayPal will also send an e-mail to you and the buyer so that you can arrange for payment.

Some online auction management services offer your own private checkout area, which will cost you a percentage of your sale, so you must decide whether your business warrants this option. A personalized winner's notification e-mail can easily contain a link to your PayPal payment area, making a checkout service unnecessary.

Printing shipping labels

Printing shipping labels without printing postage can be the beginning of a laborious two-step process. Two companies, Endicia.com and Stamps.com, print your labels and postage all in one step. Check out Chapter 17 for information on how this works.

Some sites print your winners' address labels without postage, as does eBay's Selling Manager. That works well if you don't mind carrying your packages to the post office for postage. (Why would you do that? A burning need to stand in line, I guess!)

Tracking buyer information

Keeping track of your winners isn't rocket science. You can do it in an Excel spreadsheet by downloading the information from PayPal. If you choose to have an online management service do this for you, be sure that you can download the information to your computer (in case you and the online service part ways someday).

Generating customized reports

Sales reports, ledgers, and tax information are all important reports that you should have in your business. Online services and software supply different flavors of these reports.

PayPal allows you to download your sales data into a format compatible with QuickBooks, a highly respected and popular bookkeeping program. You can also choose to download your data to an Excel spreadsheet. PayPal reports are chock-full of intensely detailed information about your sales and deposits. Putting this information in a standard accounting software program on a regular basis makes your year-end calculations easier to bear. (In Chapter 16, I detail what else you might need for this task.)

Submitting feedback

If you're running a lot of auctions, leaving feedback can be a chore. One solution is to automate the submission of feedback through an online service or software. But timing the automation of this task can be tricky.

Don't leave feedback for an eBay transaction until after you've heard from the buyer that the purchase is satisfactory. Leaving positive feedback immediately after you've received payment from the buyer is too soon. After you receive an e-mail assuring you that the customer is satisfied, manually leaving feedback by going to the feedback forum (or the item page) can be just as easy — if not easier — as bulk-loading feedback. The Selling Manager Pro program on eBay has a setting that will automatically post positive feedback for a buyer, after they've left positive feedback for you.

Managing Your Business with Online Resources and Software

If you searched the Internet for auction management services and software, you'd come up with a bunch. For simplicity's sake, I've chosen to examine just a few of these services in this chapter. After speaking to many sellers,

I've found online services that offer uptime reliability (uptime is key here; you don't want the server that holds your photos going down or mislaunching your auctions) and software that's continually updated to match eBay changes.

Using a site or software to run your auctions takes practice, so I suggest that you try any that appeal to you and that offer free preview trials. As I describe these different applications, I include a link so that you can check them out further. Table 9-1 compares the costs of many auction management and online services.

Table 9-1	Cost Comparisons for Auction Management Services and Software
Site Services or Software	*Entry-Level Cost*
AAASeller.com	$9.95/month
Auction Wizard 2000 (`auctionwizard2000.com`)	$100.00 (first year) and $50.00 renewal
ChannelAdvisor.com	$29.95/month ($299.00/year)
eBay Blackthorne Basic	$9.99/month
eBay Blackthorne Pro	$24.99/month
eBay's Selling Manager	$4.99/month
eBay's Selling Manager Pro	$15.99/month
InkFrog.com	$9.95/month
Marketworks.com	$29.95/month
Shooting Star (`www. foodogsoftware.com`)	$120.00 flat fee
Vendio Pay As You Go (`www. vendio.com`)	$0.10 per listing, 1.25% FVF ($4.95 maximum per item)

Some software and services work on a monthly fee, whereas others work on a one-time-purchase fee. For a one-time-purchase software application to truly benefit you, it *must* have the reputation for updating its software each time eBay makes a change in its system. The programs that I discuss in this chapter have been upgraded continually to date.

Most services have a free trial period. Be sure that you don't spend a bunch of your precious time inputting your entire inventory, only to discover you don't like the way the service works. Instead, input a few items to give the service a whirl.

Online auction management sites

Auction management Web sites handle almost everything, from inventory management to label printing. Some sellers prefer online (or hosted) management sites because you can access your information from any computer. You might use every feature a site offers, or you might choose a bit from column A and a bit from column B and perform the more personalized tasks manually. Read on to determine what service might best suit your needs.

Although quite a few excellent online services for automating sales are available, I have room here to show you only a few. Remember that by using an online service, your information resides on a server out there in cyberspace; if you're a control freak, it may be a bit much to bear. Many services are similar in format, so in the following sections I point out some of the highlights of a few representative systems.

When selecting a service, look for a logo or text indicating that the service is an eBay Certified Developer, Preferred Solution Provider, or API licensee. These people have first access to eBay's system changes and can implement them immediately. Others may have a day or so lag time to update their software. Note that these logos do not guarantee the quality of their service — only that they subscribe (pay money) to eBay for the logo and use of the API.

ChannelAdvisor

ChannelAdvisor's founder Scot Wingo got into the auction business around the turn of the century. His first foray into the eBay world was AuctionRover, a site that had tools to perform an extensive eBay search, list auctions, and check pricing trends. The company's old Rover logo was fashioned after Wingo's Border Collie, Mack.

Fast forward to today. ChannelAdvisor is a highly popular management service for all levels of eBay sellers. They supply listing and management services to everyone from Fortune 1000 companies to the little old lady next door.

How? They offer three levels of software: Enterprise for large businesses that want to outsource their online business, Merchant for midsized businesses and higher-level PowerSellers, and Pro for small businesses and individuals. The powerful software suites help eBay sellers successfully manage and automate the sale of their merchandise.

Starting at the entry level, you can get the Pro version of ChannelAdvisor. Here's what they offer the beginner-level seller:

- ✔ **Listing design and launching:** Create your listings with their standard templates or use your own HTML to design auction descriptions. List your items immediately or schedule a listing. ChannelAdvisor will launch the auction when you tell them to.

- ✔ **Item and inventory management:** If you want to keep your inventory online, you can create it on their system. If you want to input your inventory offline, you can import it from their Excel template. You can also import open auctions or store listings to your ChannelAdvisor account for relisting or servicing.

- ✔ **Image hosting:** You get 250MB of space to host your images. You can upload images to the site four at a time, or use FTP to upload a large quantity of images.

- ✔ **Post-auction management:** This function merges your winning auction information and generates customized e-mails and invoices to your buyers. You can print mailing labels too.

To tour the various offerings of ChannelAdvisor and find out about their free trial period, visit www.channeladvisor.com.

Marketworks (previously AuctionWorks)

A group of collectors who saw the need for power tools for PowerSellers developed this highly graphical site (www.Marketworks.com). I think they've succeeded. (They were known in the eBay community as AuctionWorks but changed their name in June 2004.) A high percentage of eBay PowerSellers use the site. They launch approximately six million listings on eBay every month. Marketworks offers help links at every turn, a first-rate online tutorial, free toll-free support (that's a free phone call and free support), and free interactive training classes for registered users. The site integration is broad; here are just a few of their features:

- ✔ **Item and inventory management:** Features the ClickLaunch Single Step Launcher, which launches individual items to auction while adding them to inventory. (The site also has a bulk item-launching capability.) LaunchBots provides automated launching of your listings. With their Bulk Inventory Upload form, you can import existing auctions from eBay into Excel and MS Access.

- ✔ **Image hosting:** Enables you to bulk upload fifteen images at a time to their servers. The basic account allows 100MB of storage. If your images average 30K each, you should be able to upload almost 3500 images into the 100MB image-hosting space.

eBay's Selling Manager

eBay replaced the All Selling tab of your My eBay page with Selling Manager, which displays a summary of your current transactions. Many sellers (even some PowerSellers) rely on Selling Manager to handle their eBay management chores.

From Selling Manager, you can

- ✔ **View listing status:** You can see which sales activities you've completed and what you still have to do.

- ✔ **Send custom e-mail and post feedback:** Customize your e-mail templates and set up stored feedback comments to help you run through the post-sales process quickly.

- ✔ **Relist in bulk:** Relist multiple sold and unsold listings at once.

- ✔ **Maintain sales records:** See individual sales records for every transaction, including a history of the transaction status.

- ✔ **Print invoices and shipping labels:** Print labels and invoices directly from sales records.

- ✔ **Download sales history:** Export your sales records to keep files on your computer.

- ✔ **Keep track of NPB and FVF:** File nonpaying bidder alerts and final value fee requests.

The fee to use Selling Manager is $4.99 a month. (It's free when you have a basic eBay store.) They also offer a Pro version that incorporates inventory management and more for $15.99 a month. Many sellers (myself included) love the Pro version. The figure shows a Pro summary page.

- ✔ **Auction reporting:** Generates accounts receivable, item history, and post-sales reports from the Reports area. Marketworks has its own Traction System for sales and item tracking. The reporting feature offers customizable views of your sales data, item and auction data, accounts receivable, and sales tax by state!

✔ **Templates and listing:** Marketworks uses their own trademarked Ballista template listing system. You can use their predefined color templates or use their macros with your own predefined HTML template, substituting the macros for stock areas in your template. By using their custom ad template option and well-thought-out macros, you can take your own HTML and make a Marketworks template.

✔ **Post-auction management:** Sends out automated e-mail to your winners, linking them back to your own branded checkout page. If customers want to pay with PayPal or through your own Merchant Account, they have to link from there. Marketworks combines multiple wins for shipping and invoicing. You have the option to set six different feedback comments, which you choose at the time of posting.

Marketworks offers all their users a StoreFront with its own URL at no additional charge. If an item sells from your StoreFront, you pay the usual 2 percent commission. When you load items into inventory, you have the choice of immediately listing them in your StoreFront. All your items are seamlessly integrated. To get current information and sign up for a free trial, go to www.Marketworks.com.

Auction management software

Many sellers prefer to run their auction businesses from their own hard drives. I happen to like the option of being able to reference my old auctions on my backups. Luckily, some valuable auction software programs are available to perform all the same tasks you get from the online services.

To those who would rather have the software at home, there are some solid choices other than the ones I examine in the next section. You might also want to visit these other sites for their quality auction management software:

✔ Auction Tamer (auctiontamer.com)

✔ Shooting Star (foodogsoftware.com)

✔ SpoonFeeder (www.spoonfeeder.com)

You can accomplish almost all the same tasks on your own computer as you can with online services — except online auction checkout. You can always use eBay's checkout as your final stop or include a link in your end-of-auction e-mails. And if you want, you can set up a checkout page on your own Web site that gathers your auction information.

Most of the software packages will perform the following operations:

- ✔ Maintain inventory
- ✔ Prepare and list auctions
- ✔ Manage e-mail
- ✔ Automate feedback
- ✔ Provide HTML templates
- ✔ Track income and expenses

Auction Wizard 2000

Way back in 1999, Standing Wave Software developed a product that would handle large inventories and meet the needs of the growing eBay population. Enter Auction Wizard. In 2000, the company introduced a more robust version, Auction Wizard 2000, to meet the challenges presented by changes on eBay.

This software is a tour-de-force of auction management programs whose pieces are integrated into one program. Aside from the processes just described, you can also

- ✔ Keep track of consignment sales by consignees, including all fees.
- ✔ Import your images, and crop, rotate, or resize them before uploading.
- ✔ Upload your pictures with built-in FTP software while you're working on your auctions, eliminating the need for another piece of auction business software.

The program interface is straightforward. I always plunge into new programs without reading the instructions, and I was able to use the program right off the bat. I'm still not an expert, but that's probably because Auction Wizard 2000 has so many features that I haven't had the time to study them all.

To begin using the software, simply download your current eBay auctions directly into the program. When your auctions close, send customized e-mails (the program fills in the auction information) and manage all your end-of-auction business. Some sellers launch their auctions using Turbo Lister (see the "Turbo Lister" section at the end of this chapter), and then retrieve them and handle the end-of-auction management with Auction Wizard 2000. For a sixty-day free trial, go to their site at www.auction wizard2000.com.

Blackthorne Basic and Pro

Of the two versions of Blackthorne Basic and Pro, the professional version is what you're going to need for your eBay business (but it's also the toughest to learn). Because the software is owned by eBay, it's the first to have updates for eBay's latest changes.

eBay's Blackthorne Basic is a solid listing program, offering a variety of templates. Blackthorne automatically inputs your standard shipping information and auction messages into your auctions so you don't have to retype them every time. You can customize your e-mail correspondence, and Blackthorne will generate the appropriate e-mail messages after retrieving your completed auction information from the site. The program is available as a monthly subscription fee charged to your regular eBay bill.

The Pro version (which supports multiple user IDs) takes things up a notch, handling your auction listings as well as automating bulk listing and end-of-auction business. For example, the Pro version will

- ✔ Spell check your auction listings
- ✔ Schedule your auction launches for a later posting (see the following tip)
- ✔ Keep track of your inventory
- ✔ Launch items directly from stock at hand
- ✔ Automate bulk-feedback postings
- ✔ Print shipping labels
- ✔ Create sales reports

One of the finer points of the Pro edition is that you can schedule your auction listings for a particular time and space out your auctions (within a group of items to be listed) by a set number of minutes. (You can also do this in eBay's free Turbo Lister.) This is valuable because so many bidders bid during the last few minutes of an auction, when the highest bidding takes place.

To check out the latest changes and upgrades, and to compare all of eBay's selling program versions, visit pages.ebay.com/selling_manager/comparison.html.

Turbo Lister

I like Turbo Lister because it's simple and easy to use. It has a built-in WYSIWYG (what you see is what you get) HTML editor and makes preparing my listings offline easy. When I'm ready, I just click a button and they're all listed at once. You can also stagger listings and schedule them for a later date for a fee.

Using Turbo Lister is as simple and straightforward as posting a listing using the Sell Your Item page on the eBay site. One of the benefits of Turbo Lister is that it allows you to prepare auctions while offline and group them for launching all at once to eBay. You can also keep listings in the program for relisting in the future.

Using the program is a two-step process. First, you download the application from eBay at `pages.ebay.com/turbo_lister/download.html`. Next, you install Turbo Lister on your computer. What could be simpler?

Chapter 10

Dollars and Sense: Budgeting and Marketing Your Sales

• •

In This Chapter

▶ Marketing your listings by choosing the right category

▶ Using promotional options to your advantage

▶ Paying eBay: The lowdown on basic fees

• •

*Y*our entire online business is just that: a business. In every business, decisions are made regarding how much money is spent for each division of the company. Because you're the head of your company, you must make these decisions. Even if you're selling on eBay on a part-time basis, you still have to address budget concerns. The one area in which you don't have to set aside money is shipping and fulfillment; in the eBay business model, the buyer pays your shipping and handling costs. (See Chapter 14 for more on shipping.)

When you list an item for sale on eBay, you must consider what the item will sell for, in what category to list it, and whether to add any eBay listing options. Establish a minimum percentage that you assign as your profit so that you can determine how much to spend on your advertising (marketing) budget. If your item has a considerable amount of competition in its category, you may want to add some of the options eBay offers to make folks notice it and want to buy it. The cost of these options (or advertising) needs to fit into your established budget for the particular item.

In this chapter, I give you a preview of the various options eBay offers its users, highlighting the cost of these options along the way and the pros and cons of each. I also detail the basic eBay fees. When you've finished reading this chapter, you should be well on your way to establishing a working budget and have a handle on marketing your items.

Listing Your Items

With tens of thousands of categories, finding the right place for your item can be daunting. (For more on eBay categories, see Chapter 2.) You need to apply some marketing techniques when deciding where to place your auctions. You should always also be thinking about your budget; you can list an item in two separate categories, but you have to pay double for that. Does your budget allow for it? Will the added expense really bring in more customers? Figure 10-1 shows you how eBay lists the categories where your searched items appear. It helps you hone your choice of popular category.

Figure 10-1:
Results of the category item search, showing the categories in which the item is listed (on the left).

To find where other sellers have listed items that are similar to yours, perform a completed item search for your item in the Advanced Search page. In the Search box, type your item keywords and click the option to search Completed Listings Only. When you get the results, indicate that you want them sorted by highest prices first by using the drop-down menu.

After you have your results, click the completed listings with the highest bids. At the top of the auction page, you'll see the listed category. You may find that your item is listed successfully in more than one category.

Check the active listings; are lots of people selling your item? If you see that you're one of forty or fifty selling the item, you need to get creative as to where to list your item. Evaluate the item and its potential buyers. In what categories would someone shopping for your item search?

Over my eBay career, I have sold several things in "iffy" categories. My catnip cigars come to mind. I was selling these adorable seven-inch cigars filled with organic catnip and was being blown away by the zillions of listings in the *Cat Toys* category. So I got a little creative. It is a cigar, and one of eBay's popular categories is Tobacciana, so I listed it there. If someone is a cigar buff, they may be browsing that category. And perhaps they just may happen to own a cat they'd like to share a cigar with! I'm just stretching the category rules a tad. I normally list the cigars solely in my store, but at other times (like holidays), I list them for auction.

Suppose you've found two perfect categories in which to list your item. eBay allows you to list an item in two categories (see Figure 10-2), but does that mean it's the best marketing decision for your listing? That depends. When you list an item in two categories, you must pay two listing fees. Depending on the time, the season, the availability of your item, and how much you paid for it, you probably don't have the money to budget for paying double listing fees (and double any options you use). In addition, most eBay buyers (busy people that they are) use the search engine because they can find what they're looking for quickly. If they search for your item using the search engine rather than by browsing the categories, listing the item in two categories is a needless expense.

Figure 10-2: You can list an item in two categories.

You can change your category midauction, starting it in one category and ending it in another, as long as your listing has no bids. And at the end of an auction in which your item doesn't sell, you can use the relisting feature to run the auction again in another category.

eBay's Optional Listing Features

When you're listing an item for sale, you'll no doubt be presented with eBay's recommendations to improve your listing. This usually consists of recommending that you add one of the options that (according to eBay's research) will improve your final selling price. Sounds pretty good, doesn't it? But getting carried away with these options is easy and can lead to spending all your profits before you earn them.

In the eBay University classes, instructors quote auction success rates for the various features, but in the real life of your business, success varies from listing to listing and category to category. If you take the boldface option and then your listing appears in a category full of boldface titles, the bold just doesn't have the punch you expected to get (and paid for). Your item would stand out more without the bold option. It's the same with highlighting. Certain categories are loaded with sellers that go overboard in the use of this feature — all the auction titles appear in a big lavender blur.

You need to weigh the pros and cons in terms of how these options affect your eBay business. Will spending a little extra money enhance your item enough to justify the cost? Will you be able to make the money back in profits? You must have a good understanding of what the options are and when and how you can use them to their fullest advantage.

For every item you put up for sale, you have to pay a minimum of two fees: an insertion fee for listing the item *and* a final value fee. (I discuss these two fees in the "eBay's Cut of the Action" section, later in this chapter.) If you accept credit card payments through PayPal, you must also pay a fee to the payment service. Estimate your expenses from these basics before you consider spending money for advertising.

When I get a new product, I put together a chart like the following to calculate my fees *before* I list the item. I run it through once or twice with my expected sales figures to get an idea of the costs for listing the item. There is a free widget on the Web at `http://www.sellathon.com/ebay_calculator.html` that can help you calculate your eBay fees.

Starting bid	$29.99
Insertion fee	$1.20
Gallery option	$0.35
Item sells for	$78.00 + $8.95 shipping = $86.95
Listing fee	$1.55
Final value fee on $78.00	$3.04 ($25 @ 5.25% + $53 @ 3.25%)
PayPal fee on total of $86.95	$2.82
Total fees	**$7.41**

Home-page Featured auctions

A new user going to visit eBay for the first time arrives at the eBay home page, www.ebay.com. A Featured Items area appears in the middle of the home page; below this area are links to six home-page Featured auctions. When the user clicks the See All Featured Items link (see Figure 10-3), the home-page Featured Items page appears (see Figure 10-4). Most of these items are fixed-price listings that feature hundreds of items at a time. Many also feature specialty items that list for tens of thousands of dollars.

Figure 10-3: The Featured Items area on the eBay home page.

Featured Items	Learn how
1.51 PRINCESS SQUARE ENHANCED DIAMO...	
40 Acre Arizona Ranch on the Colora...	
Costa Rica Cattle farm 99+ acres Mo...	
SYMETRIX SYMNET AUDIO MATRIX 8X8 PR...	
1893 Great Lakes Freighter Anchor ,...	
196A: Federico Maldarelli (1826-189...	
See all featured items...	

Figure 10-4: The home-page Featured Items page.

1697 items found Save this search				Back to all items			
List View	Picture Gallery			Sort by: Time: newly listed ▾		Customize Display	
☐ Compare	Item Title	PayPal	Price*	Bids	Time Listed ▾	Shipping to 91325, USA	Item #
Featured Items							
☐ MUST SEE	Darkness Volume 1 #6 Mint Cond Image Comics Comic Book	⊘	$9.99	Buy It Now	Jun-05 18:21	See description	290125980495
☐ Enlarge	Knife Website, proof of traffic & income, $500/month!!! 1000+ mailing list,9000+ uniques/mo.,3x traffic of 2006		$12,000.00 $18,000.00	Buy It Now	Jun-05 18:19	Not specified	170119357117
☐ Enlarge	$43,000-77ct Aquamarine 14KT Pendant-Sapphire Necklace ROYAL STYLE! VERY SENSATIONAL NECKLACE! BID NOW AT$1/HR	⊘	$1.00 $19,000.00	Buy It Now	Jun-05 18:16	$20.00	130121831916
☐ Enlarge	$85,750-8ct Top Fine Ceylon Sapphire& Diamond 18KT Ring EXCELLENT QUALITY RARE AND VALUABLE RING..WOW!	⊘	$1.00	1	Jun-05 18:15	$20.00	130121749193

If you want the opportunity to have your listing title link occupy this very special piece of real estate, the home-page Featured auction option will set you back $39.95 for a single item. If you have two or hundreds of widgets to sell, it'll cost $79.95. For big-ticket items, you've found the perfect location to draw an audience that may easily earn back your $39.95. People who are new to eBay come in through the front page; this is prime real estate. The six auctions

190 **Part III: Business is Business — Time to Get Serious**

featured on the home page rotate randomly throughout the day. There's no guarantee that your item will be featured as one of the six home page links — but it will appear in the home-page featured category linked from the home page.

Another benefit of this option is that if someone searches your keywords or browses through your category, auctions featured on the front page appear at the top of the page (along with Featured Plus auctions, which I describe next). But you must keep in mind how much you're paying for this option. Unless your auction will bring you more than several hundred dollars, this feature probably isn't worth the additional cost.

Featured Plus

Featured Plus is an option I've used with much success. When you choose the Featured Plus option, your listing is listed at the top of the page when a shopper searches for keywords or browses the category. Although your item doesn't appear on the eBay home page (see the preceding section), it will appear at the top of your selected *category* home page (see Figure 10-5).

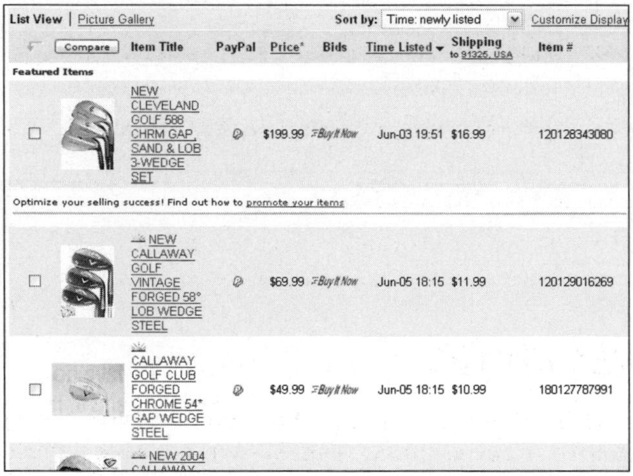

Figure 10-5: A category page showing the premier position for Featured Plus listings.

You get extra exposure for just $19.95, but you must still consider your auction budget. How much do you expect your item to sell for? Will the $19.95 expense benefit your auction enough to justify the expenditure? Be sure that your item will bring you more than a few hundred dollars before choosing this option.

Subtitle

You may use fifty-five characters for you item's title. Title search is the de facto, number-one way people search on eBay. From the statistics I've seen of my own items, 90 percent of searches were made for title only, versus title and description. But how can you make your item stand out when it shows up with hundreds of other items that look the same? Use the subtitle option! This can be a great marketing tool when you offer something special or have a little more information to give those who are searching or browsing.

When your item has something special about it or could use some extra punch, the subtitle option allows you more space to catch the eye of the prospective buyer. Take a look at my example in Figure 10-6.

Figure 10-6: Here, aunt*patti makes good use of the subtitle option by adding pertinent information to make her items stand out.

Picture hide	Item Title	Price	Bids	Time (Ends PDT)
	VHS Columbia House THUNDERBIRDS CE TV Series Video Tape Collector's Edition - Edge of Impact - Security Hazard	$8.00	Buy It Now	May-15-04 08:33:46 PDT
	VHS Bill THE COSBY SHOW CE PILOT EPISODE Series Video Here We Go Columbia House Collector's Edition 4 Episode	$8.00	Buy It Now	May-15-04 08:35:54 PDT
	VHS Illinois Basketball Symphony Video Tape Illini Gill Lou Henson and the 1989 NCAA Final Four Season	$8.00	Buy It Now	May-15-04 08:38:18 PDT
	VHS Moby Dick NEW Read Aloud Learn ESL Video Animated Learn to Read - English as a Second Language	$8.00	Buy It Now	May-20-04 09:54:10 PDT

Items for Sale by aunt*patti (871 ☆)

4 items found.

All items | Auctions | Buy It Now

Find more great stuff at my eBay store
View text-only format

Highlight option

I was excited when eBay first announced the highlight option. I'm a big fan of highlighting books, reports, and the like. Ever since college, I can't read a book without my trusty neon-yellow highlighter. Highlighting makes anything stand out on a white page of text. This works on eBay, except eBay uses a lavender-colored highlighter — ick!

Unfortunately, as with anything in life, less is more. If you choose to list your auction in a category where all the sellers decide to use the highlight option, the only listings that will stand out will be the ones *without* highlighting.

The highlight feature will set you back just $5. Does your budget allow for that? To give your auction title a punch for a smaller amount of money, consider the Border option.

Outline border

I like the outline border option. For only $3 your listing is outlined in a clean, neat bold border that really draws the eyes! When looking at a page where a listing is outlined with this option, the item immediately stands out. For $2 less than the highlight, I think it's a much better way to go. It's a low-price option (when your item will sell for a couple of hundred dollars) that will really pay back in page views — and, hopefully, in big bids.

Listing Designer

eBay comes up with options to fill the needs (or wants in this case) of users. Sellers enjoy putting colorful graphics around their descriptions. It will also help you design your description, placing pictures in different places on the page. But if you have a good description (creatively done with HTML color and emphasis) plus a good picture (inserted with the HTML code I gave you), your item will draw bids just the same as if you spent $0.10 extra (per listing) for the Listing Designer option.

If you want your descriptions surrounded by graphics, make sure the graphics aren't too intensive. Otherwise, the pages will load too slowly for dial-up users. Also, take a look at *eBay Listings That Sell For Dummies,* a book I wrote with eBay guru Patti Louise Ruby. It's a comprehensive book that covers eBay photography and HTML for listings. After you've set up your own templates from the easy samples in the book, you'll never have to lay out another penny for more. In Chapter 9, I show you how you can buy reasonably priced templates from savvy eBay graphics experts.

You can use a graphics template to "brand" your listings on eBay, giving them a uniform look. If you want to use a template, decide on one and make it your trademark.

Boldface option

The boldface option is probably the most used option in the eBay stable. An auction title in boldface type stands out in a crowd, unless . . . you got it, unless it's in a category loaded with boldface auction titles. If the $1 that eBay charges for this benefit is in your auction budget, odds are it will get you a good deal more views than if you don't use it.

eBay's special combo deals

Any restaurant that serves up a menu of tempting treats will usually offer combo deals. Surprise — so does eBay. They can be a great way to save money while combining options:

Value Pack: I use the Value Pack all the time. It's only $0.65 and combines some of eBay's best features at a bargain-basement price:

- Gallery: You have to have a Gallery picture to make your item stand out (regularly $0.35).

- Subtitle: Give your item some extra selling power with the extra information you put in your subtitle (regularly $0.50).

- Listing Designer: This can be a little iffy. Choose from one of the many colorful graphics eBay has to offer if one appeals to you. But you may have your own template, or you may just not want to use one of the kitschy graphics. That's okay too. You don't *have* to use Listing Designer to get this deal; just leave the Listing Designer box empty when you get to that part on the Sell Your Item form (regularly $0.10).

So, you actually get $0.95 worth of options for $0.65. Even if you don't use the Listing Designer, you're saving money.

Pro Pack: Whether the Pro Pack at $29.95 is a good deal is a good question. You get several *big* options here:

- Featured Plus!: I'm a big fan of this (it really works), but it's only $19.95 by itself.

- Gallery Featured: In this book, Gallery Featured doesn't even get its own heading because I think it's redundant. You get the same push for your item by using Featured Plus, but you get a slightly larger gallery picture and your link is laid out differently. I doubt I'd ever use these two options together; it's an either/or proposition (regularly $19.95).

- Border: Yep, a great option, but it only costs $3.00 on its own.

- Highlight: $5.00 by itself; can be overkill when combined with the Border option.

- Bold: Yep, a good option, but it's regularly $1.00.

Because you're not an amateur (you know the ropes of eBay), you don't need to spend extra for this package. You can simply put together your own "pro" stand-out option package for only $24.30 by using Featured Plus!, Border, Bold, and a $0.35 gallery picture.

To recap your title option costs, see the "Insertion (listing) fees" section later in this chapter.

View counter

Counters have become a popular free option in the online world. Placed on your listing in the Sell Your Item form, the numeric view counter ticks up each time someone loads your page from eBay. This can add up to numbers that impress bidders (convincing them they're viewing a hot deal) or impress other sellers to run out and sell the identical item at eBay.

A counter is a terrific tool for marketing your auctions — sometimes. If you have an auction with no bids and a counter that reads a high number, newbie bidders may be dissuaded from taking a flyer and bidding on your auction. Their thinking is, if that many people looked at this listing and didn't bid, something must be wrong with the item. They'll tend to doubt their own instincts as to what is and isn't a good deal. In a situation such as this, however, what might be going on is that savvy bidders are just watching your auction, waiting to bid at the last minute.

Also offered by eBay is a *hidden counter* that shields the numbers from the eyes of casual lookie-loos. The figures are available only to you, after you sign on to eBay and click the item in your My eBay page. The number of page views appears at the top of the page.

Professional counters can be more sophisticated and can give you valuable marketing data about your items. Smart counters offer a breakdown of visitors hour by hour. Others can let you know where your customers have come from and what keywords they used to find your item. The specialized type of counter that I use is ViewTracker from Sellathon.com (see Figure 10-7 — more information on how to get it is in Chapter 9). eBay offers you a free counter, but it's not a very smart one. By the way, readers of this book can get a thirty-day free trial of ViewTracker by going to www.sellathon.com?af=0-186.

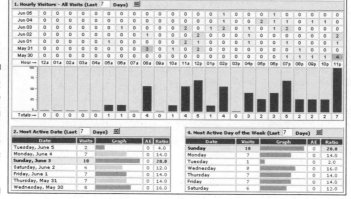

Figure 10-7: A ViewTracker 3.0 marketing counter for one of my items.

The gallery

Let me start by saying that a gallery picture is an absolute *must* for most listings. eBay bills the gallery as its "miniature picture showcase," and indeed it is. By adding a gallery photo, a thumbnail image (96 x 96 pixels) of your item appears next to your listing when the user browses the category view or search results, which can reap you many benefits. When someone runs a search, eBay defaults to showing all items, and that includes a gallery preview, as shown in Figure 10-8.

☐		NIB Ballet Pink BEAR FEET Flower Mary Janes Sandals 9	📷	$48.33	3	1m $4.60	140123936627
☐	📷	3-Pack Designer Pink Foil Scrapbook Paper Ballet/Dance	📷	$0.99	1	37m $1.00	190118988634
☐	📷	NEW BLOCH pink leather FS ballet shoes Adult 9.5 NM	📷	$9.99	-	39m $3.50	230137063527
☐	📷	NEW! pink leather split sole ballet shoes adult 8 N	📷	$8.99 $9.99 ⌐Buy It Now	-	39m $3.50	230137063636
☐		DIESEL Obi Flats Women Shoes Sz 10 Ballet Pink	📷	$17.50	10	42m $8.00	260124688603
☐	📷	NEW! pink FS leather ballet slippers / shoes Adult 6 N	📷	$8.99	1	42m $3.50	230137064234
☐		Darling Ballerina Ballet Polka Dot Flat Shoe 9 Pink	📷	$8.99 $11.99 ⌐Buy It Now		42m $10.99	130119848329

Figure 10-8: Note how the gallery photos draw your attention.

If you don't use the gallery image, but still have a picture in your description, your listing features only a sad little green camera icon in the gallery space ina search. This makes choosing the 35¢ option a worthwhile expenditure. If your item will sell for less than $10, however, I recommend that you reconsider the extra charge and simply rely on the lowly green camera icon to let the folks know you have a picture in your description.

Nothing draws the eye better than the gallery photo next to a listing in a search with hundreds of results. Which auction would you check out? The one with the tiny camera icon, or the one with the crisp clear gallery picture tempting you to open the listing? Pictures are the key to all quality advertising. Don't miss an opportunity to add this extra little "billboard" to your listings.

eBay also offers to feature your gallery photo on the top of search and category pages for $19.95. These photos run three across the top of the page versus five across for regular gallery pictures. These featured gallery pictures are also larger (140 x 140 pixels) than the regular gallery pictures.

When you take advantage of the gallery, be sure to crop your photo tight to the subject. For more help with your images, see Chapter 11.

Buy It Now

The Buy It Now feature, shown in Figure 10-9, has many significant benefits. If you have a target price for the item you're listing, make that your Buy It Now price. You can also use this option during frenzied holiday shopping times or with very hot items. Try posting a slightly higher than normal price and perhaps you'll get a bite, er, sale.

Figure 10-9:
The Buy
It Now
feature.

The Buy It Now feature disappears when someone bids on the item or, if you've placed a reserve on the auction, when a bidder meets your reserve price. You can't use Buy It Now with a Multiple Item (or Dutch) auction.

To use this feature, you must have a feedback rating of at least 10, or be ID verified. (ID Verify is eBay's secondary form of identification, permitting you to participate in the site without submitting a credit card. See Chapter 3 for more info.)

Buy It Now adds costs to your listing on a graduated scale based on your selling price, as shown in Table 10-1. If your item will sell for a low price, remember my golden rule: Before paying for a feature, ask yourself whether it's in your listing budget.

Table 10-1	Buy It Now Fees
Buy It Now Price	*Fee*
$0.01 to $9.99	$0.05
$10.00 to $24.99	$0.10
$25.00 to $49.99	$0.20
$50.00 or more	$0.25

eBay's Cut of the Action

Becoming complacent and blithely ignoring your eBay costs as you list items for sale is easy to do. As sellers, we easily can fall into the habit of listing and relisting without reevaluating the profitability of our final sales. As a person in business for yourself, you must always take into account outgoing costs as well as incoming profits. The cost of your initial listing is just the beginning of your advertising budget for that item; you have to factor in the cost of all the options and features you use as well. Then, when the item sells, you pay eBay an additional final value fee. (For fees regarding your eBay store, check out Chapter 5.) In this section, I review the costs for listing an auction and for a fixed-price listing on eBay.

The fees I detail here aren't the end of your fees. If you use a credit card payment service like PayPal, they will also charge you a fee. In Chapter 13, I examine the costs of the most popular credit card payment services.

Insertion (listing) fees

Your insertion fee is based on the highest dollar amount of two things: your minimum opening bid or the dollar amount of your reserve price. If you start your auction at $0.99 and have no reserve, the listing fee is $0.20. (By the way, if you start your listing at $1.00, your fee is $0.40 — why double your fees for just a penny more start price?) But if you start your auction at $0.99 and set an undisclosed reserve price of $50.00, your auction costs $4.40 to post. When you place a reserve on your item, you're charged an insertion fee based on the amount of the reserve — plus the reserve auction charge.

The reserve auction charge is automatically refunded if the reserve price is met and your item sells.

For a summary of eBay insertion fees, see Table 10-2. (The fees for eBay Motors are in Chapter 2.)

Table 10-2 eBay Listing Fees for Fixed-Price Single Item or Auction	
Opening Bid or Reserve Price	*Insertion Fee*
$0.01 to $0.99	$0.20
$1.00 to $9.99	$0.40

(continued)

Table 10-2 *(continued)*

Opening Bid or Reserve Price	Insertion Fee
$10.00 to $24.99	$0.60
$25.00 to $49.99	$1.20
$50.00 to $199.99	$2.40
$200.00 to $499.00	$3.60
$500.00 and more	$4.80

If your item doesn't sell, don't think you can get your insertion fees back. They are nonrefundable. You do have the option of relisting your unsuccessful item without being charged a second listing fee, but *only* if your item sells with the second listing. If it doesn't sell the second time, the charge for the second listing will stand. Writing a better title, starting with a lower opening bid, or adding a snappier description will help in selling the item. Maybe you should think about changing the category as well.

Whether you're listing one item with a starting bid of $1000.00 or one hundred items for $5.00 each in a Multiple Item (Dutch) auction, your insertion cost per auction is never more than $4.80.

I recap the cost of the valuable eBay listing options in Table 10-3. Note that eBay will no doubt come up with other tasty add-ons for your listings. One that I'll never figure out is their little blue gift box, which you can add to your listing for $0.25. Who clicks something just because it has a gift box?

Table 10-3   Listing Option Fees

Option	Fee
Home page featured	$39.95 (single item); $79.95 (multiple items)
Featured Plus	$19.95
Highlight	$5.00
Border	$3.00
Subtitle	$0.50
Bold	$1.00

Option	*Fee*
Listing Designer	$0.10
Gallery	$0.35
Gallery featured	$19.95
Scheduled listing	$0.10
List in two categories	Double fees
Ten-day listing	$0.40

eBay final value fees

eBay's version of the Hollywood back-end deal is the final value fee. Big stars get a bonus when their movies do well at the box office; eBay gets a cut when your auction sells. After your auction ends, eBay charges the final value fee to your account in a matter of minutes.

An auction in the Real Estate category (Classified Ad) is *not* charged a final value fee. Successful auctions in the eBay Motors category, however, are charged a flat final value fee. (See Chapter 2 for information on fees in both categories.)

Even a rocket scientist would have trouble figuring out exactly how much eBay receives at the end of your auction. To help you calculate how much you'll owe eBay, see Table 10-4.

Table 10-4	Final Value Fees
If Your Item Sells For	*You Pay a Final Value Fee Of*
$0.01 to $25.00	5.25% of the selling price
$25.01 to $1000.00	5.25% on the first $25.00 plus 3.25% of the remainder of the selling price from $25.01 to $1000.00
$1000.01 and up	5.25% on the first $25.00 plus 3.25% of the next $975.00 plus 1.5% of the remainder on selling prices over $1000.00

Here are some sample prices and commissions:

Closing bid	What you owe eBay
$10.00	5.25% of $10.00 = $.53
$256.00	5.25% of $25.00 ($1.31) plus 3.25% of $231.00 ($7.51) = $8.82
$1248.00	5.25% of $25.00 ($1.31) plus 3.25% of $975.00 ($31.69) plus 1.5% of $248.00 ($3.72) = $36.72
$1,000,000.00	5.25% of $25 ($1.31) plus 3.25% of $975.00 ($31.69) plus 1.5% of $999,000.00 ($14,985.00) = $15,018.00

To save yourself brain-drain, use an eBay fee calculator to check your fees before you set prices. See Chapter 9 for software that will do this for you.

Chapter 11

Setting Up Listings That Sell

· ·

· ·

Rule #1: A good photograph and a concisely written description should be the goal for all your auctions. My years of advertising and marketing experience have proven this to me repeatedly in almost every type of media. If you're trying to fetch the highest possible price for an item, keep your listings simple and professional: no dancing clowns (unless you're selling clowns), no overdone graphics, and no difficult-to-read typefaces. Less is more.

In this chapter, you find out how to write eye-catching descriptions and improve the visual elements of your listings. Once you have some solid recommendations, you can make your own decisions regarding what you want to do and how to best accomplish your goals.

Writing Winning Text

When you write descriptions for your listings, be sure that you describe your items clearly and completely. Mention everything about the article; if the item is used or damaged, be sure to describe the flaws. When you're honest up front, you'll have a happy buyer. Remember to include your terms of sale and specify the types of payment and credit cards you accept. Be sure to include appropriate shipping charges, too. Following is a checklist of some of the things to mention:

- Size, style, color (garment measurements in inches are also valuable because sizes aren't universal across brands)
- Condition (new, new with tags, used, gently used, well-worn)
- Manufacturer's name
- Year of manufacture (if vintage, it's always good to mention an era at least)
- Fabric or material
- Any damage to the item
- Special features
- That you've stored it in a clean, dry place (if you have)

After you list all the facts, get excited and add a little showmanship in your description. Think *infomercial!* Think *Shopping Channel!* Whoopee! These people know how to make things sound so good that you feel that you *must* have whatever item they're selling. You can do the same, if you just get those creative juices flowing. In Chapter 12, I give you some more pointers on how to write the best descriptions possible.

Your eBay Photo Studio

Taking pictures? No problem! You have a digital camera, and you know how to use it. Just snap away and upload that picture, right? Sorry, but no. There's a good way and a bad way to take photos for eBay and, believe it or not, the professional way isn't necessarily the most expensive way.

I recommend that you have a mini photo studio for taking your eBay pictures. That way, you won't have to clean off your kitchen counter every time you want to take pictures.

If you must use the kitchen counter or a desktop, be sure to use a solid color, inexpensive photo stage, which you can find on — where else — eBay.

Beware of following instructions in books about digital photography. In most cases, their instructions are valid for pictures that you want to print. Online images are a horse of a different color (oooh, did I really say that?). Be sure you follow instructions that are written for Web images, such as in the steps in my *eBay Listings That Sell For Dummies.*

You need several basic things in your photo studio; the extras you should have are based on the type of merchandise you're selling. An eBay *generalist,* someone who will sell almost anything online — like me! — should have quite a few extras for taking quality photos. Check out a portion of my home photo studio in Figure 11-1. The setup packs up neatly into a bag when I'm not using it.

Figure 11-1:
My eBay
photo setup.

What you find in this section might be more than you thought you'd need to take good pictures. But quality photographs will sell your merchandise, so you need to take this technical part of your business seriously. Of course, if you sell only one type of item, you won't need such a varied selection, but you should have the basic photo setup. Go into it slowly, spending only as much as is prudent at the time. Also check my Web site (`www.coolebay tools.com`) for more ideas.

For the best images of your item, be sure to zoom in on it. No one needs to see the background — they want to see the merchandise up close and personal. Also, when it comes to the background, be sure it is solid and preferably a neutral color.

Digital camera

Digital cameras are mysterious things. You may read about *mega pixels* (a million pixels) and think that more is supposed to be better, but that doesn't apply to eBay applications or to Web images. Mega pixels measure the image resolution that the camera is capable of recording. For online use, all you need from a camera is 800 x 600 pixels (or at most 1024 x 600) because the majority of computer screens are incapable of taking advantage of more pixels. If you use a higher resolution picture, all you'll do is produce a pixel-bloated picture that can take a looooong time to load online.

You don't need a million pixels, but you do need the following:

- **Quality lens:** I'm sure anyone who has worn glasses can tell the difference between good lenses and cheap ones. Really cheap cameras have really cheap plastic lenses, and the quality of the resulting picture is accordingly lousy. Your camera will be your workhorse, so be sure to buy a well-known brand from a manufacturer known for making quality products.

- **Removable media:** Taking the camera to your computer and using cables and extra software to download pictures to your hard drive is old-fashioned and annoying. Removable media eliminates this annoyance. The most popular are Smart Media cards (wafer-thin cards), Secure Digital (even tinier than Smart Media cards), Compact Flash cards (in a plastic shell), and Sony Memory Sticks; all are no larger than a matchbook. You insert one of these cards into your computer, if your computer has a port for it, or you can get an adapter that connects to your computer through a USB port. You can get an adapter on eBay for a few dollars.

- **Tripod and tripod mount:** Have you ever had a camera hanging around your neck while you're trying to repackage some eBay merchandise that you've just photographed, and the camera is banging into everything? Or perhaps you've set down the camera for a minute (in a safe place) and then can't find it? Avoid all this by using a tripod to hold your camera. Tripods also help you avoid blurry pictures from shaking hands — and when you're shooting in macro mode, shaking comes with the territory. To use a tripod, your camera needs to have a tripod mount, which is the little screw hole that you see on the bottom of most cameras. In the following section, I give you some tips on finding the right tripod.

- **Macro setting capability:** If you're ever going to photograph coins, jewelry, or small detailed items, you must have a macro setting on your camera (usually symbolized by a little flower icon). This setting enables you to get in really close to items while keeping them in focus.

- **White balance setting:** Without getting into a long-winded discussion of measuring Kelvin and color rendering (I did this in another book), just know that good cameras have a sensor that ensures that colors are represented faithfully. It can be an automatic function of the camera, or you can select presets based on the type of light you are using: daylight, tungsten bulb, fluorescent bulb, and so on.

✔ **High optical zoom:** When you're shopping for a digital camera, you'll see optical zoom and digital zoom. Optical zoom enlarges the pictures through traditional quality lenses. The digital version pseudo-enlarges your images with a software interface within the camera. If you've ever enlarged a low-resolution photo and found that it got grainy and out of focus, you have an idea of what happens with digital zoom. The quality just isn't there.

✔ **Autofocus:** This option just makes life easier when you want to take pictures.

The bottom line here is to buy a brand-name camera. I use a Sony; a fancy Cybershot DSC-H1 (with a 12x optical zoom with image stabilization to overcome shaky hands — available on eBay for under $200), and an old, outdated Mavica FD92 (with a 10x optical zoom — available for around $60). Although the FD92 is pretty much an antique, it has all I need for eBay photos. They both store images on a Sony Memory Stick, which I just pop out and insert in either of my computers.

I bet you could find a camera that fits your needs right now on eBay for less than $150. Remember that many digital camera users buy the newest camera available and sell their older, lower-megapixel cameras on eBay for a pittance. Don't forget that many brick-and-mortar camera stores also sell used equipment.

Other studio equipment

Certain endeavors seem to be open pits that you throw money into. I promise that your eBay photo studio will not be one of these pits — now or later.

Tripod

A tripod is an extendable aluminum stand with three legs (get it? tripod?) that holds your camera steady for shooting pictures. You should look for one that has a quick release so that if you want to take the camera off the tripod for a close-up, you don't have to unscrew it from the base and then screw it back on for the next picture.

The tripod can be a tabletop version or one with extendable legs. The legs should extend to your desired height, should lock in place with clamp-type locks, and should have a crank-style geared center column so that you can raise your camera up and down for different shots. Most tripods also have a panning head for shooting from different angles. You can purchase a tripod from a camera store or on eBay for as low as $25.

Power supplies

If you've ever used digital cameras, you know that they can blast through batteries faster than sugar through a five year old. A reliable power supply is a must. You can accomplish this in a couple of ways:

- **Rechargeable batteries:** Many specialists on eBay sell rechargeable batteries and chargers. Pick up quality Ni-MH (nickel metal hydride) batteries because this kind, unlike Ni-Cad (nickel cadmium) batteries, has no memory effect. That means you don't have to totally use them up before you put them back in the recharger.

- **CR-V3 lithium ion batteries:** This is a new kind of battery that takes the place of two standard AA batteries. Lithium batteries are the longest lasting and lightest batteries available, but they're also expensive. Then some smart guy figured out a way to put the equivalent of two batteries into one unit; considerably cutting the price. The CR-V3 can average 650 photos before you have to change it. The CR-V3 is available also in a rechargeable form, thereby extending its life even further (and reducing your battery budget significantly). Some cameras can use them; some cannot. Check out yours before making the purchase.

If your eBay photo studio includes a camera on a tripod (and it should), you can use a good, old-fashioned AC adapter (you know, the one that plugs into the wall). As long as you pay your electric bill, you're going to have power to your camera.

Lighting

Trying to take good pictures of your merchandise can be frustrating. If you don't have enough light and use the camera's flash, the image might be washed out. If you take the item outside, the sun might cast a shadow.

In the early (stone-age) days of eBay, I used my camera's flash and had my daughter shine a flashlight on the item as I took pictures from different angles — all the while hoping that the color wasn't wiped out. Also, the autofocus feature on many digital cameras doesn't work well in low light.

After consulting specialists in the photo business to solve the digital camera lighting problem, I put together an inexpensive studio lighting set for online auction photography. Please check my Web site (www.coolebaytools.com) for information on how to obtain this package. It's the same one I successfully use in my home photo studio (refer to Figure 11-1). Or if you prefer, search eBay for studio lighting; I'm sure you'll find a good deal.

To eliminate shadows, it's best to have at least two lights, one for either side of the item.

Professional studio lights bulbs aren't necessary. Although they do the trick, professional lights are very expensive and short lived.

Cloud Dome

If you're going to attempt to photograph jewelry, collectible coins, or other metallic items, you'll quickly become frustrated at the quality of your pictures. (Touching up the pictures in PhotoShop is a time-wasting option.) Metallic objects pick up random color from any kind of light (other than true color) you shine on them for picture taking. Gold jewelry will also photograph with a silver tone and silver will look goldish!

After much experimentation, I learned the secret of getting crisp, clear, close-up pictures: Use a Cloud Dome. It stabilizes your camera (just as if you were using a tripod) and filters out all unwanted color tones, resulting in image colors that actually look like your item.

The Cloud Dome is a large plastic bowl on which you mount your camera. You take pictures through a hole in the top of the dome. The translucent white plastic diffuses the light so that your item is lit evenly from all sides, eliminating glare and bad shadows. Check out the manufacturer's Web site at www.clouddome.com to see some amazing before and after pictures.

The Cloud Dome also manages to get the best images from gems. You can actually capture the light in the facets! Pearls, too, will show their luster. Several eBay members (including yours truly) sell the Cloud Dome; I highly recommend it!

Cloud Cube Tent

Cloud Cube Tent is an ingenious product that replaces the traditional (and expensive) photographer's tent. Professional product photography requires pictures with no glare, no harsh shadows, and no burnout of item details. The Cloud Cube Tents are made of translucent white fabric that diffuses the light and provides a perfect lighting condition for many objects. There are plenty for sale on eBay, and most sellers include wrinkle-free backgrounds. The Cubes are also combined in kits along with floodlights, as in my own photo studio.

Props

To take good photos, you need some props. Although you may think it strange that a line item in your accounting program will read "Props," they do qualify as a business expense. (Okay, you can put it under photography expense; *props* just sounds so Hollywood!)

How often have you seen some clothing on eBay from a quality manufacturer, but you just couldn't bring yourself to bid more than $10 because it looked like it had been dragged behind a car and then hung on a hanger over the bathroom door to be photographed? Could you see how the fabric would hang on a body? Of course not. Take a look at Figure 11-2; that dress looks simply fantastic, darling!

Diane Von Furstenberg BRAND NEW with tags!

100% Silk Jersey dress
Fits Size 6 or 8

This lovely silk number is THE sexiest dress! It's by hot designer Diane Von Furstenberg (who is featured in the new issue of Vogue). It's a fabulous silk jersey spaghetti strap dress, with a sexy cowl neckline. The original price of the dress is $220, and it can be yours for the highest bid. Draping beautifully on the body, it's got a sexy below the knee length and a very flattering cut.

Bid with confidence and bid whatever you feel this great dress is worth to you as it is selling with NO RESERVE! Winning bidder to pay shipping & handling of $5.25, and must submit payment within a week of winning the auction. Credit cards are accepted through Billpoint and PayPal.

GOOD LUCK, HAPPY BIDDING!

Click below to...
View my other auctions - Win more than one and $AVE on shipping!

Figure 11-2: Midge, the mannequin, modeling one of my eBay successes.

Mannequin

I hate to even say it, but if you're selling clothing, you'll get higher prices for your apparel if you photograph your items on a mannequin. If you don't want to dive right in and buy a mannequin, at least get a body form to wear the outfit. Just search eBay for *mannequin* to find hundreds of mannequin forms selling for less than $20. I've seen the quality store kind on eBay for a low as $75. If you sell children's clothing, get a child's mannequin form as well. The same goes for men's clothes. If worse comes to worst, find a friend to model the clothes. There's just no excuse for hanger-displayed merchandise in your auctions.

I got my mannequin (Midge) at a department store liquidation sale here in Los Angeles. I paid $25 for her. She's showing her age and her face paint is a little creepy, so I often crop her head out of the photos. She has a great body and everything she wears sells at a healthy profit. Many stores upgrade their mannequins every few years. If you know people who work at a retail store, ask when they plan to sell their old mannequins; you may be able to pick one up at a reasonable price.

Steamer

Clothing is usually desperately wrinkled when it comes out of a shipping box. It may also get crumpled lying around, waiting for you to photograph it and sell it on eBay. If the clothing isn't new, but is clean, run it through your dryer with Dryel (the home dry-cleaning product) to take out any musty smells and loosen the wrinkles. There's nothing like old, musty-smelling clothes to sour a potentially happy customer.

The clothes you want to sell may be wrinkled, but ironing is a bear (and may damage the fabric), so do what the retail professionals do: Use steamers to take the wrinkles out of freshly unpacked clothing. Get the type of steamer that you can use while the article of clothing is hanging up so you can just run the steamer up and down and get the wrinkles out. The gold standard of steamers is the Jiffy Steamer. It holds a large bottle of water (distilled only), rolls on the floor, and steams from a hose wand. Some models sell on eBay for under $100. Until you're ready to make an investment that big, at least get a small handheld version that removes wrinkles; search eBay for *(garment, clothes) steamer* to find some deals.

Display stands, risers, and more

Argh. I just browsed the jewelry category and saw some horrendous pictures. Many sellers use photos supplied from the manufacturer, and those are beautiful, but the majority of sellers either didn't zoom in on the piece or the colors were off. Jewelry does not photograph well on most people's hairy hands (that's why hand models make the big bucks). It looks a lot better when you display it on a stand or a jewelry display, or flat on a velvet pad. If you're selling a necklace, why not display it on a necklace stand. I bought my display stands from a manufacturer, but had to wait several months to receive them. These days, the manufacturers and sellers have moved to eBay with ready-made goods. Just search for *ring stand, necklace display,* and the like.

Risers can be almost anything you use to prop up your item to make it more attractive in a picture. Put riser pieces that aren't attractive under the cloth that you use as a background. (You can also find risers on eBay.)

You wouldn't believe what the back of some professional photo setups look like. Photographers and photo stylists think resourcefully when it comes to making the merchandise look good — from the front of the picture, anyway! Throughout my years of working with professional photographers, I've seen the most creative things used to prop up items for photography:

✔ **Small bottles of sand:** Use small bottles (prescription bottles work well) filled with very heavy sand to prop up small boxes and other items in a picture. (A photographer I once worked with used little bottles of mercury, which is a heavy liquid metal but is also a poison, so I don't recommend using it.)

✔ **Beeswax, putty, and clay:** To set up photos for catalogs, I've seen photographers prop up fine jewelry and collectible porcelain with beeswax (the kind you can get from the orthodontist works great) or clay. Beeswax is good because it's also a neutral color and doesn't usually show up in the photo. However, you must dispose of beeswax often because it gets filthy when it picks up dirt from your hands and fuzz from fabric.

✔ **Museum Putty and Quake Hold:** These two products are invaluable when you want to hold a small object at an unnatural angle for a photograph. (They're like beeswax and clay, but cleaner.) Neutral colored Museum Putty works very well — be careful not to use the clear version, because it's often difficult to get off the item. I discovered them after losing everything breakable in my home in the Northridge earthquake. Museums use these clay-like products to securely keep breakables in one place — even during an earthquake!

✔ **un-du and Goo Gone:** un-du is a clear liquid that will get sticky residue off almost anything. If your item has sticker residue on it, it's bound to show up in the picture. Squirt on a little un-du and use its scraper to remove the goo and bring back the shine. Goo Gone is another product useful for cleaning items. The product comes in several forms including a sticker lifter. Some sellers use lighter fluid when they can't find un-du. The problems of working with lighter fluid are obvious. I don't recommend it.

✔ **Clamps and duct tape:** These multipurpose items are used in many photo shoots in some of the strangest places. Your mannequin may be a few sizes too small for the dress you want to photograph. How do you fix that? Don't pad the mannequin; simply fold over the dress in the back and clamp the excess material with a metal clamp (even a heavy-duty plastic hair clamp), or use a small piece of duct tape in the back to hold the fabric taut.

Keep a collection of risers and propping materials in your photo area so they're always close at hand.

Backgrounds for your images

Backgrounds come in many shapes and sizes. You can use paper, fabric, or one of the portable photo stages for smallish items.

In professional photo-talk, *seamless* is a large roll of three-foot (and wider) paper that comes in various colors and is suspended and draped behind the model and over the floor. (Ever wonder why you never see the floor and wall come together in professional photos?) Photographers also drape the seamless over tabletop shots for an *infinity* look. Some people use fabrics such as muslin instead of seamless.

I keep several backgrounds on hand. (If you use velvet, be sure to clean it with sticky tape before you use it in a picture — lint appears huge in pictures.) I recommend using neutral fabrics, papers, or plastics, such as white, light gray (18%), natural, dark blue, and black, so that the color of the fabric doesn't clash with or distract from your items.

The Cloud Dome people have also invented a cool photo stage. I like it because it's portable (easy to store), nonbreakable, simple to clean, and inexpensive. It's sold on eBay and is pictured in Figure 11-3.

Figure 11-3: Cloud Dome's photo stage (seltzer bottle not included).

Taking Good Pictures

If you have a small photo studio setup (see the preceding section) with a quality camera, a tripod, props, and lights, you're well on your way to taking some quality shots for your auctions. A few things to remember:

✓ **Zoom in on your item:** Don't leave a bunch of extraneous distracting background in your pictures. Crop any extra background in your photo-editing program (see the "Image-Editing Software" section, a bit later in this chapter) before you upload the images to eBay or your image-hosting site.

✔ **Watch out for distracting backgrounds:** If you don't have a studio table-top, or if the item is something that won't fit on a table, try to make the background of the photo as simple as possible. If you're shooting the picture outside, shoot away from chairs, tables, hoses — you get the idea. If you're shooting in your home, move the laundry basket out of the picture.

One of my favorite eBay pictures featured a piece of fine silver taken by the husband of the lady selling the piece on eBay. Silver and reflective items are hard to photograph because they pick up everything in the room in their reflection. (This is when you need the Cloud Cube Tent). In her description, the lady explained that the man reflected in the silver coffeepot was her husband and not part of the final deal. She handled it with humor and her faux pas added to the listing!

✔ **Be sure the items are clean:** Cellophane on boxes can get nasty looking, clothing can get linty, and all merchandise can get dirt smudges. Not only will your items photograph better if they're clean, they'll sell better, too.

Clean plastic or cellophane with WD-40 (no kidding); it will take off any sticker residue and icky smudges. Un-Du or Goo Gone StickerLifter are the best adhesive removers for paper, cardboard, clothing, and more, plus they come with a handy plastic scraper. I also keep a kneaded rubber art eraser around to clean off small dirt smudges on paper items. Any cleaning solution helps your items (even a little Method or 409), but use these chemicals with care so that you don't destroy your items while cleaning them.

✔ **Check the camera's focus:** Just because a camera has an autofocus feature doesn't mean that pictures automatically come out crisp and clear. Low light, high moisture, and other things can contribute to a blurred image. Double-check the picture before you use it.

Using a Scanner

Scanners have come a long way in the past few years. A once expensive item can now be purchased new for a little more than a hundred dollars. If you sell books, autographs, stamps, or documents, a scanner may be all you need to shoot your images for eBay.

When shopping for a scanner, don't pay too much attention to the resolution. As with digital cameras, images for the Internet (JPEGs) needn't be any higher than 96 ppi (pixels per inch). Almost any scanner can get that resolution these days. Quality makes a difference in the manufacture of the scanner, so stick with brand names.

You should use a *flatbed* scanner, on which you lay out your items and scan away. I replaced my old scanner with an HP all-in-one product that combines a scanner, fax machine, copier, and printer in one handy little unit that saves me lots of space in my office. I've seen HP flatbed units, new in the box, sell on eBay (and even at Office Depot) for as low as $100.

There's an eBay store that sells Hewlett Packard authorized closeouts and refurbished items — cameras, scanners, and even computers for the lowest prices I've ever seen. Search eBay Stores for *HP Marketplace*.

A few tips on scanning images for eBay:

- ✔ If you're taking traditionally processed photographs and scanning them on a scanner, have them printed on glossy paper because they'll scan much better than those with a matte finish.

- ✔ You can scan 3-D items, such as a doll, on your flatbed scanner and get some respectable-looking images. To eliminate harsh shadows, lay a black or white t-shirt over the doll or her box so that it completely covers the glass. This way, you'll have a clean background and you'll get good light reflection from the scanner's light.

- ✔ If you want to scan an item that's too big for your scanner's glass, simply scan the item in pieces, and then reassemble it to a single image in your photo-editing program (see the following section).

- ✔ Boxed items are a natural for a flatbed scanner. Just set them on top of the glass and scan away. You can crop the shadowed background with your photo-editing software (see the following section).

Image-Editing Software

Lose the idea that the software that comes with your scanner is good enough. It may be just fine for some uses, but the kind of control that you need is only available in *real* image-editing software, not in a mere e-mail picture generator.

Because I have a graphics background, I've always been happy using Photoshop, but it's a large and expensive program. It's also overkill for eBay images. Most of the time I use Fast Photos by Pixby Software, a small but professional program at a fraction of the price of Photoshop, because it has just the tools that eBay sellers need for Web images, no more and no less. It's also one of the easiest-to-learn programs on the market because it works intuitively.

Fast Photos offers features that enable you to make a good picture out of a bad one. It also has an awesome export-to-Web feature that compresses the images so that they hold their quality while becoming smaller. Images compressed in this fashion download a lot faster. You can also touch up your family photos for Web albums in this easy-to-use (okay, very low learning curve) program.

And don't forget that you'll be working with images not only for eBay items but also for your Web site. (Check out Chapter 8 for more about putting together a Web site.) You can go to the manufacturer's Web site `http:// www.pixby.com/marshacollier` and download a twenty-one-day free trial for my readers.

A Home for Your Images

You need a safe place to store your pictures for eBay. If your images don't appear when someone clicks your auction, or if your images take too long to load, a user might click off your auction and go to the next one. If you have more than one option, test each with a few pictures because you want one that's reliable.

eBay's Picture Services are great for your initial and gallery pictures — and they're built directly into the Create Your Listing form. The only problem is that eBay charges $.15 for each additional photo you post using their service. By hosting your own pictures, you can insert additional images into your description without paying a penny more.

When you add your own photos, you may have to use an FTP (File Transfer Protocol) program to upload your pictures to a server. In the old days, this meant buying a program or getting shareware software. Now, if you use the free Firefox browser (I keep Firefox on my computer, right along with Microsoft's Internet Explorer, and often switch back and forth), you get a built-in FTP program. Firefox is stable and updated frequently, so there's no reason to fear installing it on your system. Just go to `www.firefox.com` for your free download and more information.

When you use auction management software to build your listings, you may not need an FTP program to upload your images. Most complete management programs integrate their own FTP program as part of the package and may also include image storage space on their server. Check out Chapter 9 for more about auction management software packages.

You should always put your eBay images in a separate directory — *not* in an active part of your e-commerce (if you have one) Web site. You may think that using your business Web site is a good place to store your images, but it isn't. If you want to keep track of your site statistics, such as the number of hits, hosting your own images may ruin the data. A call for one of your eBay images counts as a hit on your site, and you'll never get accurate Web site stats.

Free ISP space

Most ISPs (Internet service providers) give you at least 5MB of storage space for your personal home page. Although this space isn't appropriate for your final business site, it's a perfect place to host your pictures. Everyone has an ISP, and all ISPs give you space. You may have to use an FTP program to upload to your Web space, or your ISP may supply its own uploader. Go to the home pages for your ISP (the member area), and check out what it offers. Visit Chapter 8 for more information on ISP space.

If you use AOL software (which is free these days), you have a built-in Web service. AOL would like you to build an AOL Hometown page, but here's what to do instead: Go to the top of the AOL page frame and type *AOL Hometown* in the browser area. Then click the link to set up a blank Hometown page. Then (again in the browser address line) type *My FTP.* The window that opens, AOL My FTP Space, is the place where you can upload your photos for eBay.

From there you can upload all your files, up to a maximum of 20MB per screen name. (20MB is more than enough for your eBay images — and your personal Hometown page pictures.) Remember which photos are stored in each screen name FTP space because the URL locator address for each screen name is different.

To get the AOL browser, free e-mail addresses, and the FTP area, go to `free.aol.com/downloadaol`.

Auction management sites

If you're using one of the auction management Web sites that I discuss in Chapter 9, you're covered for most of your back office tasks. These Web sites supply enough Web space to hold all your eBay images. They also have a convenient one-click upload from your hard drive.

If you find that you truly have no place to host your images, take a look at some of the less expensive auction management sites. As of this writing, you can get image hosting *and* other auction utilities for around $10 a month at the following: `AAASeller.com`, `AuctionHawk.com`, `Inkfrog.com`, and `Auctiva.com` (Auctiva is free of charge).

eBay Picture Services

You can also use eBay Picture Services to host your photos for eBay, but the quality of your photos is better if you host them directly from a site. eBay recommends that the image you upload be 1024 x 768 pixels. Then eBay reformats your photo to fit in a layout 400 pixels wide by 300 pixels tall and then compresses the file for quick viewing. This process can destroy the quality of your carefully photographed images if you haven't saved them in a compatible size. You're running a business, so be businesslike and use the method that presents your photos in their best light.

To get the free top-of-page image that you see on many listings, you *must* use eBay Picture Services. I suggest that you use eBay for your primary image and also use secondary images of your items hosted elsewhere. If one of the picture servers goes down, at least your listing will have pictures. The first picture is free; all you have to do is click the Add Pictures box on the Create Your Listing page. This picture will also be the default picture for use as your all-important gallery image. (See Chapter 10 for more on using the gallery.)

eBay offers two versions of Picture Services. The basic version (see Figure 11-4) allows you to upload eBay-ready images as they appear on your computer. Click the Browse button to find pictures stored on your hard drive or media card.

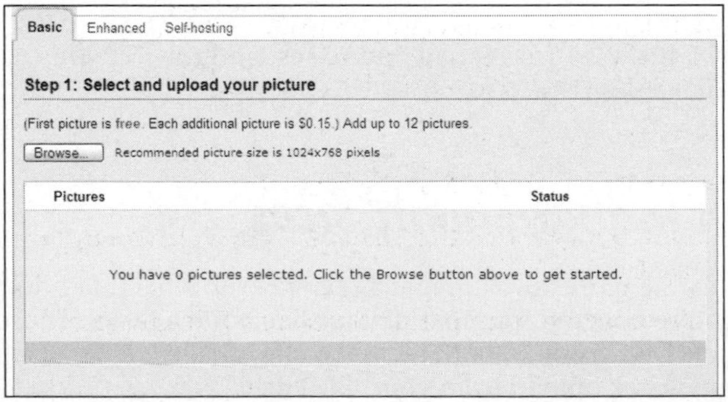

Figure 11-4:
The basic
Picture
Services
photo-
hosting
page.

Basic	Enhanced	Self-hosting

Step 1: Select and upload your picture

(First picture is free. Each additional picture is $0.15.) Add up to 12 pictures.

[Browse...]   Recommended picture size is 1024x768 pixels

Pictures	Status

You have 0 pictures selected. Click the Browse button above to get started.

If you want to rotate or crop the picture, you need to use the enhanced picture service. When you click the Add Picture link, a screen similar to Figure 11-5 appears. From there you can select Basic or Enhanced or a place to input the Web link to your image.

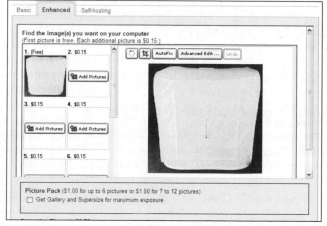

Figure 11-5:
eBay's
enhanced
Picture
Services.

To upload your pictures using the enhanced version, after clicking Add Pictures on the Create Your Listing page, you get a new window. Follow these steps:

1. **Click the Enhanced tab, which appears at the top of the window.**

2. **Click Add Pictures in the first box.**

   A browsing window appears.

3. **Locate the directory that holds your eBay images on your computer.**

4. **Click the image in the browsing window.**

   The image name appears in the filename box.

5. **Click the Open box.**

   The selected image appears in the picture frame.

6. **To rotate the image, click the circular arrow (at the upper-left of the main image box).**

7. **To crop the image to remove unnecessary background:**

   a. **Click the crop box in the right corner of the larger image.**

   Two squares appear at opposite corners of your main image.

   b. **Click the frame on the outside of your image,** and move the bar until the offensive area is cropped out. You can do this from all sides of the picture.

Sometimes Picture Services will shrink your image to a too-small size, but you can't do much about it. Just be sure to reload the image anytime you relist the item; otherwise, the gallery image may just get smaller and smaller. eBay continues to improve Picture Services, so don't give up on it. Use it for the free image, and be sure to upload secondary images from an outside site.

8. **To correct your image, do one of the following:**

   • You can automatically change the brightness, darkness, and contrast by clicking the AutoFix button. I don't recommend that you do that unless your picture is already a good one.

   • Try the Advanced Edit button next to AutoFix. In the Advance Edit area (see Figure 11-6) you can manually correct your image and see the results as you go.

9. **After you're happy with the results, click Save and the image appears as the default on the Create Your Listing page.**

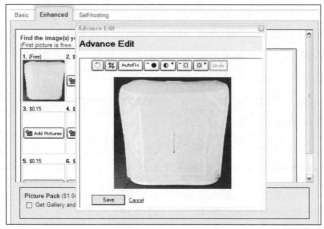

Figure 11-6:
eBay's
handy
Advance
Edit tool.

TIP

All store sellers receive 1MB of storage free through eBay's Picture Manager to host their store logo and store layout pictures, but that's enough to hold quite a few of your item's images as well.

HTML and You

My small grasp of HTML gets me only so far. I usually use a shareware program to produce code for my Web site or eBay listings. Luckily, you don't have to know a lot of code to produce eBay auctions.

The Create Your Listing form has an excellent, basic HTML generator that has a toolbar similar to the one in a word processor. As you can see in Figure 11-7, you can use the toolbar to change the size, font, or color of the text. You can also insert code by switching from the Standard design view to the HTML view of the description area to include your own hosted images in the listing description. (Check out Chapter 9 for some sample code to use to add images to your listings.)

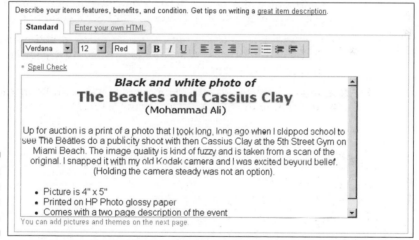

Describe your items features, benefits, and condition. Get tips on writing a great item description.

| Standard | Enter your own HTML |

Verdana | 12 | Red | **B** *I* <u>U</u>

• Spell Check

Black and white photo of
The Beatles and Cassius Clay
(Mohammad Ali)

Up for auction is a print of a photo that I took long, long ago when I skipped school to see The Beatles do a publicity shoot with then Cassius Clay at the 5th Street Gym on Miami Beach. The image quality is kind of fuzzy and is taken from a scan of the original. I snapped it with my old Kodak camera and I was excited beyond belief. (Holding the camera steady was not an option).

- Picture is 4" x 5"
- Printed on HP Photo glossy paper
- Comes with a two page description of the event

You can add pictures and themes on the next page.

Figure 11-7: eBay's HTML code generator.

For a quick and easy HTML fix, go to my Web site at `www.coolebaytools.com`. Then go to the Tools area and click Cool Free Ad Tool. You'll get a quick HTML generator; feel free to use it as often as you like. There's no charge. You can select border colors and include an image in your description area. Nothing fancy, mind you, just nice clean HTML. You type your information as indicated, and select colors, as shown in Figure 11-8.

When you're finished, click the View Ad button. On the next page, you'll see HTML code for your auction description that you can cut and paste into the auction description area of the Create Your Listing page.

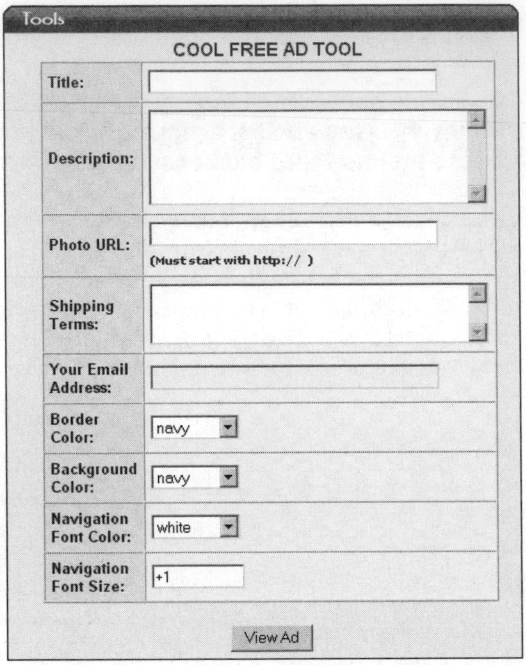

Figure 11-8: The Cool Free Ad Tool page.

Chapter 12

Providing Excellent Customer Service

- -

In This Chapter

▶ Making a good first impression

▶ Writing the perfect e-mail

- -

*e*Bay's supposed to be truckloads of fun! But if you're making money, you're in business. When you're in business, you must always deal with a few boring and un-fun details. First and foremost, you must remember that your customers are number one. Businesses become successful by providing fantastic customer service and selling quality merchandise. The image that you project through your e-mails and listings identifies you to the bidders as a good guy or a bad guy. No kidding. Your e-mails should be polite and professional. You shouldn't make prospective customers feel like you're hustling them, sneaking in hidden fees, or being pushy with overbearing rules for bidding.

You don't have to have the most beautiful listings on eBay to succeed. You need products that people want, and you need to take the time to build good customer relations. In this chapter, I cover some ways to let your customers know that they're number one in your book: from writing effective auction descriptions to sending cordial e-mails.

Meeting Your Customers

eBay is a person-to-person marketplace. Although many sellers are businesses (like you), the perception is that sellers on eBay are individuals earning a living (versus big business). The homespun personal approach goes a long way to being successful when selling on eBay. One of the reasons many buyers come to eBay is that they want to support individuals who have the gumption to start their own small enterprise on the site.

Telling your story

Being honest and forthright encourages customers to consider your offerings on eBay. Also, if you go the extra mile and give some bonus information, the customer will feel more at ease.

An excellent example comes from an eBay Motors seller, e.vehicles' John Rickmon. He throws in a few special touches to draw in the customer.

When you shop eBay Motors, a prospective buyer has the option of ordering a vehicle history report from the car's listing page. This costs the buyer $7.99 just to view the report. John orders a CarFax report himself and puts a link to a PDF version of it right into his auction descriptions. Saving the prospective buyer $7.99 doesn't seem like much, but its one of those simple touches that sets a customer at ease.

John also posts his business philosophy at the end of his auctions. Here's part of it:

"My dealership is entirely focused on the sales of vehicles via the eBay format. I make all purchasing and sales decisions and am 100% responsible for the content of my auctions, including all text and photography. I personally answer every email and conduct all business regarding the sale of this vehicle.

I buy and list approximately 5-10 units per month; I look at hundreds of vehicles each week that do not make the cut . . .

This is my living. *I do this full time. I do not have a "car lot." EBay has been my dealership for years and all operations are focused towards bringing you the best vehicle possible at the best price you will find. I am committed to this format and take your vehicle purchase very seriously. You are dealing with a secure seller."*

Wow, don't you just want to buy a car from this guy?

After you've written a brilliant title for your auction *(not IN ALL CAPITAL LETTERS please),* prospective buyers click your listing and scroll down to your description. Do they have to dodge through pointless verbiage, losing interest in your item along the way? Or do you get right down to business and state the facts about what you're selling?

Here are a few things to remember when writing your auction description (see Chapter 11 for more tips for your listings):

- ✔ **Write a factual description.** Do you carefully describe the item, stating every fact you know about it? Are you clear in your description and careful not to use any jargon? Finally, does it answer almost any question a potential buyer might ask? If not, do some revising.

- ✔ **Include some friendly banter.** You want to make the customer feel comfortable shopping with you. Don't be afraid to let your personality shine through!

- ✓ **Update your About Me page.** The small *me* icon that appears next to eBay usernames is an invitation to click. When viewers click the icon, they see a page that's all about you! Let people know who they're dealing with. When deciding between two people selling the same item and when all else is equal, buyers will place their bid with the seller who makes them feel secure. (Visit Chapter 3 for info on how to set up your About Me page.)

- ✓ **Limit the number of auction rules (or terms of sale).** Some sellers include a list of rules that's longer than the item's description. Nothing will turn off a prospective buyer more than paragraph after paragraph of rules and regulations. If you really *must* put in a litany of rules, use the following bit of HTML to make the size of the text smaller: `<font size=-1>`.

- ✓ **Choose a reasonable typeface size.** Many users are still looking at eBay on an 800 x 600 display. If you design your auctions at 1024 x 768, your typefaces may be way too large for the average user. Forcing a user to scroll and scroll to find the details only leads to frustrated customers.

- ✓ **Quote a flat shipping amount.** Many bidders pass up auctions that don't disclose shipping charges. Make use of eBay's shipping calculator to give your customers a fair shake at the shipping costs. But if many other sellers offer the same item, flat rates stand out in a search, and the lowest rate may help you reel in an undecided buyer.

   It's just plain bad taste to overcharge on shipping (and a violation of eBay's rules — you can be suspended for it). eBay buyers expect that you'll add up to a couple of dollars for handling costs, but adding more than that can make you look like you're trying to squeeze every penny out of your bidder . . . not a good feeling when you're on the other end!

- ✓ **Keep photos a practical size.** Some users still connect with a dial-up connection, and if they have to wait for your large pictures to load, they may go elsewhere. If your listing doesn't fully open within a few seconds, the person will simply back out and go on to another listing.

Communicating with Your Customers

Perhaps English class wasn't your favorite, but when it comes to being a professional, incorporating good grammar, proper spelling, and punctuation in your communications portray you as a pro. Before writing this book, even I hooked up with some grammar and punctuation sites to brush up on my writing skills. (Okay, I also have brilliant editors covering up my transgressions.)

Helping your buyers buy safely

When selling items of high value, you can attract new customers by bonding your eBay sales. Surety bonding has been used for about 5000 years to guarantee business transactions between buyers and sellers who don't know each other. It may be new to you and me, but lots of people know about it, and when someone looks at your listing and sees that the transaction is covered up to $25,000, they may be more likely to bid higher or pay more. BuySAFE is a service that bonds select sellers through various insurance companies. Shoppers like seeing a warranty; when they see a BuySAFE seal on your listings, they know they will get just what they want.

BuySAFE will bond your transactions on eBay or on your own Web site. To be eligible for the BuySAFE seal, you must pass a rigorous check, which proves to BuySAFE that you're a solid seller. After you get your seal and bond your transactions, you are charged 1 percent of your final selling price for the bonding. You don't have to bond all your listings. After you've been approved, you can bond just the ones you think will need the boost. I've found that the seal easily boosts the bids on my listings by 1 percent, so it works for me. For more details and an introductory offer for readers of this book, check out their site at `www.buysafe.com/coolebaytools`.

Throughout the rest of this section, I provide some examples of effective seller e-mails. Don't forget your good manners when writing, but don't be too formal — remain personable and polite.

The initial inquiry

The first written communication you may have with a prospective buyer is an inquiry e-mail. Buyers can ask you a question about your item by clicking the Ask Seller a Question link on the listing page, which automatically generates an e-mail addressed to you. Often these questions are brief.

At least 50 percent of the inquiries that I send to a seller don't get a response — guaranteeing that I won't be buying that product. Often, when I do get a response, it's a terse, brusquely written note. Many people choose not to use punctuation or capitalization in their e-mails. How professional looking is that? Not very. Sellers who take the time to write a short, considerate reply that includes a greeting and a thank you for writing will get my money.

To respond, use the Respond link by the listing in your my eBay Selling area or go directly to your My eBay Messages page. This way, you won't get sucked into responding to a spammer who's impersonating an eBay e-mail just to confirm that your e-mail address is live. That said, respond quickly, clearly, and politely — and with a sales pitch. Remind the soon-to-be buyer that you can package several items in one box to save on shipping costs. And by all means, use this opportunity to point out other listings you have that may also interest the writer. That's customer service.

Your note can be brief and straightforward. For example, I wrote the following note in response to a question regarding the condition of the Christmas tree in one of my auctions:

Hello,

Yes, the aluminum Christmas tree in my auction is in excellent condition. The 58 branches are full and lush and will look great for the holidays. Please write again if you have any more questions or concerns.

Don't forget to check my other auctions for a color wheel and a revolving tree stand. They would look great with this tree, and I can combine your wins so you can save on shipping.

Thank you for writing,

Marsha
www.coolebaytools.com

Isn't that nice? The note addresses the question in a respectful and personable manner. Writing a note like this doesn't take long. You should be doing it.

Also, putting your Web site or eBay store URL in your signature is a great way to get new customers to view your Web site or blog.

The winner's notification letter

Have you ever received a bulk-generated, boilerplate winner's confirmation letter? The seller hasn't bothered to fill in half the blanks, and you're almost insulted just by reading it? Receiving a note like this after you've requested that the seller combine purchases (and the letter pays no attention to your request) is especially annoying. E-mails can cross, but a personal approach goes a long way with customers.

I'm not saying you shouldn't automate your eBay business. I'm merely suggesting — strongly recommending — that you take the time to personalize even your canned e-mail responses. I admit that since I have my account set up to automatically send out invoices when someone purchases something, I do send out an automated e-mail. The following letter is just to let the customer know that there's a real person behind the automation:

Good news! You won eBay item #120089481873 Cloud Dome Photo Stage Studio.

Thank you for winning my eBay item. Buyers tend to go unrecognized on eBay a little too often, so I want you to know that your purchase is very much appreciated. If I can be of any assistance to you, please let me know. While this first e-mail is being generated automatically, I do welcome one-on-one contact with you. Just send a reply to this mail and I'll answer your inquiries directly.

I am serious about my business and look forward to the opportunity to serve you. I'd also like to invite you to check out my other items available on eBay.

marsha_c

Marsha Collier
Author, "eBay For Dummies" and "Starting an eBay Business For Dummies";
Host of the PBS program "Making Your Fortune Online"
www.coolebaytools.com

If you aren't selling many items at a time, I suggest a more personal approach. Here's the tried and true winner's notice that I have sent out:

Congratulations!

Yours was the winning bid on eBay item #122342911 for the Emilio Pucci book. You got a great deal! I am looking forward to a pleasant transaction and positive feedback for both of us.

You may pay by money order, with a personal check, or with a credit card through PayPal. If you are not set up with them, just e-mail me and I'll send you a PayPal invoice.

If mailing your payment, please include a copy of this e-mail with your name and shipping address along with your payment:

Winning Bid Amount	*$14.95*
Shipping and Handling	*$4.50*
TOTAL Amount Due	*$19.45*

A money order or online payment assures immediate shipping upon receipt of payment! If you pay by check, I will ship your item after a 14-day clearing period; be sure to include the item name and your e-mail address with payment. Please send your payment to the address shown below:

> *Marsha Collier*
> *1234 Anywhere Street*
> *Los Angeles, CA 91352*

Your payment is expected on or before Saturday, April 2, 2007. I look forward to receiving it. I will ship on receipt of payment in full, via USPS Priority mail with delivery confirmation.

Thank you for buying my item. I am delighted to be dealing with you and know you will enjoy your purchase.

Marsha_c

Marsha Collier
www.coolebaytools.com

The payment reminder

Writing a payment reminder can get sticky. You don't want to aggravate the buyer, but time is wasting and you could spend this time reposting your item. When writing a payment reminder, you need to be firm but pleasant. Real things can happen in people's lives. Family members get sick, and people just plain forget. Perhaps your payment fell between the seats of the winner's car on the way to the post office. (That's the excuse I use when I forget to mail a payment — feel free to use it yourself.)

When you honestly forget to send a payment, nothing is more humiliating than someone debasing you through e-mail. So remember that people do make mistakes, and check the winner's feedback before you send the letter. If you can garner from the feedback that this winner has a habit of not following through on bids, you can definitely be a bit firmer in your wording. Always set a clear deadline for receiving payment, as shown in the following letter:

Hello,

You won an auction of mine on eBay last week for the Emilio Pucci book. Your payment was due yesterday and it still has not arrived. Perhaps sending payment has slipped your mind considering your busy schedule. I know it can easily happen.

Please e-mail back within 48 hours and let me know whether you want to go through with our transaction. I'd like to put the item back up for sale if you don't want it.

Thank you for your bid,

Marsha Collier

How firm you choose to get with a nonpaying bidder is up to you. I've dealt with a few nonpaying bidders on eBay, but I've left only two negative feedbacks. Some people who tend to overbid are indeed violating the contract to buy, but legitimate reasons might explain why someone hasn't followed through on an auction. You must decide which method to take and how far you want to stretch your karma (what goes around comes around). Assess each case individually, and don't be hasty in leaving negative feedback until you know the whole story.

The payment received and shipping notice

I know that you probably aren't going to send out a payment received letter for every transaction, but it would surely be nice if you did. Staying in constant communication with your buyers will make them feel more secure with you and with buying on eBay. You want them to come back, don't you?

Leaving feedback for buyers

After you leave feedback, you can't rephrase or change an erroneous evaluation of another user. I *know* that it's easier to leave feedback once payment is received, but waiting to see how the transaction evolves afterwards is prudent — especially if the package gets lost in the mail, turning a previously kind and sweet buyer into an insane screaming nutcase. Same thing if the item is damaged. You should evaluate a buyer based on more than whether the person pays for an item. (Buyers are supposed to do that — it's a contract, remember?) When leaving feedback for buyers, consider the following:

✔ Did they return your communications quickly?

✔ Did they pay in a timely manner?

✔ If a problem occurred with the item or in shipping, did they handle it in a decent manner or did they try to make your life a living hell?

Remember that sellers are judged on communication, shipping time, the quality of packaging, and friendliness. As a seller, you have the duty of leaving quality feedback based on set guidelines that all sellers use to rate buyers.

When you receive payment and have shipped the item, sending a short note helps to instill loyalty in your customer. I always send out the automatic e-mail from UPS or FedEx announcing the shipment tracking number. You can additionally have PayPal send out an e-mail by inserting the tracking number into the PayPal payment record. Because PayPal e-mails aren't very personalized, I follow up with my own, more personal, note:

Subject: SHIPPED: eBay item: eBay Listings That Sell For Dummies

*Hi (*insert buyer's name*)!*

Thank you for buying my New 2006 eBay Listings That Sell For Dummies *and paying so promptly! I'm looking forward to a smooth transaction — and positive feedback for both of us.*

If you paid through PayPal, please check your PayPal account because I have posted your package's delivery confirmation number in our transaction record. Please note that if you purchased shipping insurance, you will not see the insurance reflected on the package. I insure my packages with a private insurance policy from U-Pic. (More information is on my Web site.)

If there is any question when the package arrives, PLEASE e-mail me immediately. Your satisfaction is my goal, and I'm sure any problem can be easily taken care of. Please let me know when the package arrives so that we can exchange some very positive feedback!

Marsha Collier
www.coolebaytools.com

Good customer service will get you many repeat customers and lots of positive feedback. Good communication will head off problems before they start. If your customers have received communications from you during the entire transaction, they'll be more likely to discuss a glitch with you rather than make a knee-jerk reaction and leave negative feedback.

Chapter 13

Working Your PayPal Account and Collecting Your Money

In This Chapter

▶ Finding the payment method that suits your needs

▶ Discovering the ins and outs of payment services

▶ Exploring merchant accounts

*T*he hours spent selecting your items, photographing them, touching up the pictures, and writing brilliant auction copy all come down to one thing: getting paid. At first thought, you might be happy to take any form of negotiable paper, bonds, and stocks (okay, not so much dotcom stock). As you become more experienced and collect for more auctions, however, you'll decide which payment methods you prefer and which are more heartache than they're worth.

Receiving and processing payments take time and patience. The more payment methods that you accept, the more methods you have to keep track of. Throughout this chapter, I detail some various payment options (including how to handle payments from international buyers) and how each affects your business.

It Doesn't Get Any Simpler: Money Orders

I begin my discussion of payments with money orders and cashier's checks because I think they're the greatest way to receive payment. Money orders and cashier's checks are fast, cheap, and negotiable (just like cash). Cashier's checks are purchased at a bank and are generally debited immediately from the winner's checking account at purchase. For some unknown reason, banks take it upon themselves to charge a minimum of $5.00 to issue a cashier's check. This is a pretty steep charge to the buyer, which is why I suggest money orders. Money orders are available almost anywhere. In my neighborhood, the stores I called charge from $0.50 to $1.29 for a money order up to $500.00.

There has been a spate of forged and counterfeit money orders. Beware of all money orders and delay shipping until the money order has cleared. If you have a U.S. post office money order, cash it at the post office. Postal counter workers will be able to identify counterfeit money orders immediately. Never accept a money order for more than the total price of the order, where the buyer asks for a refund for the excess amount tendered. A request like this should set off warning bells.

If you want to accept money orders, you should familiarize yourself with the various charges so that you can recommend to your auction winners the service with the most reasonable cost. Saving your customers money (especially when it's not going to you) is a sign of good customer service. Asking buyers to pay a large additional fee is unfair — unless the buyers are international. In that case, the best way for them to pay you is by money order through an issuer such as American Express (which has offices in most countries). International buyers deal in the currency of their own countries; when they purchase a money order and send it in dollars, you're paid with cash in good old American greenbacks.

7-Eleven (and other convenience stores)

There are more than twenty-one thousand 7-Eleven stores in the world. I'll bet there's one within driving distance of your house. For your customer, the best part about 7-Eleven is that each has an ATM to draw cash from credit cards with which to purchase a money order. At around $1, money orders from 7-Eleven are a bargain! If you don't know where the closest 7-Eleven is, go to www.7-eleven.com/storelocator/PrxInput.aspx.

You can also buy money orders from several other convenience store chains, such as Circle K, Dairy Mart, and AM/PM.

United States Postal Service

Most sellers love USPS money orders, which have all the benefits of a regular money order — plus, because the post office issues these money orders, the nice clerks at the post office will graciously cash them for you with proper identification. Postal money orders are safe, too, and acceptable everywhere. The post office goes to great pains to ensure authenticity by including a Benjamin Franklin watermark, a metal security thread, and a double imprint of the dollar amount on the money order. (No more fears that you've received a color copy of a money order.)

Both domestic and international (for sending U.S. dollars to foreign countries) money orders are available at post offices in amounts up to $1000 ($700 internationally). For a trace of a lost or stolen money order, buyers must present the receipt. For a small fee, buyers can also get a copy of a paid money order (as long as they have the receipt) for as long as two years after the date it has been paid.

Many sellers bring their money orders to the post office when they ship their packages and cash them for their petty cash fund — or to pay for outgoing postage.

Western Union

Western Union is the most popular money order seller, probably because it was the first or maybe because it promotes better than anyone else. Depending on the purchase location, they accept cash (duh), Visa, MasterCard, and Discover payments from your buyers (both in the United States and internationally).

To purchase a money order, go to the Western Union Web site, `www.westernunion.com/info/osMoneyOrder.asp`, and click the Find a Location link. Type in your ZIP code and you'll get a list (including phone numbers) of the various locations that sell money orders in your area. Give a few a call and find where you can get the best deal — different vendors charge different rates.

Pay Me When You Get This: Cash on Delivery

I can't say enough to discourage you from using C.O.D. as a payment method. But I'm gonna try! You give your package to the post office, UPS, or FedEx, which collects the payment after delivering the package. Sound straightforward and easy? What happens when the carrier tries to deliver the package and the recipient isn't home? Your items can sit for a week or two, during which time buyers may decide that they don't want to pick up the items from the shipper. If you're lucky, you'll get your items back in two to three weeks. Not only that, but it's also expensive. In addition to postage, the post office charges from $5.10 to $16.60 for C.O.D. services (based on the amount collected).

Another bad part of C.O.D.? You might wait a month to receive payment, even when the addressee is home the first time and accepts delivery. Do yourself a favor and don't offer it as a payment option. You're only asking for trouble. You're not a bank, and you're not in the finance business. Get your money up front.

Accepting cash payments

I'm sure you've received cash from some of your winners. I don't like cash. If the buyer doesn't send the exact amount due, you have to call the buyer, who may claim that the correct amount should be there. All of a sudden, *you* must have lost the difference — and you have no recourse with cash. Mail can be stolen, too. We had a rash of mail thievery where I live; people were stealing envelopes right out of mailboxes.

Postal inspectors are constantly battling this problem, but you won't know your mail is being stolen until you've missed enough mail — usually bills and outgoing checks. Explaining to a buyer that the money never arrived is difficult. The thief has the cash while your reputation may be shot. You can e-mail, phone, and talk and discuss, but the bottom line is that you haven't received your money and they insist you have it.

The Check's in the Mail: Personal Checks

Personal checks are the easiest way for buyers to make payments. They can just dash off a check, put it in the mail, and bam, you're paid. But it's not always as easy for the seller. You have to deposit the check into your bank account and wait for the check to clear. Believe it or not, in these days of electronic transfers, wiring funds, and international money transfers, you might wait more than two weeks for a check to clear.

Paper checks

After you deposit a check, your bank sends it to a central clearinghouse, which then sends it to the signatory's bank clearinghouse. Then the individual bank decides whether the check can be paid. You may think that a way around the system is to call the bank and see whether the account currently has sufficient money in it. The account may have sufficient funds when you call, but the depositor can withdraw money before the check gets through the system — and then the check bounces. And don't forget the 24-hour turnaround rule: Even if the bank has the money and you're standing there with the check, the bank can deny payment within 24 hours, leaving you with a bad check.

Even though everything seems to be electronic these days, the paper routing of old-fashioned checks can take two weeks or longer. I've received only one bad check as an eBay payment. I deposited the check, waited ten business days, and then shipped the item. On the eleventh business day, the bank sent me the bounced check. The buyer clearly knew that the check had bounced but didn't notify me. Luckily the buyer made good on the check.

TIP

If you find yourself with a check that's bouncing higher than a superball and an uncooperative buyer, remember that it's against the law to pass bad checks. To see a list of penalties, state by state, visit the National Check Fraud Center at the following address:

```
www.ckfraud.org/penalties.html
```

In many states, if a resident passes a bad check, you are legally able to collect three times the amount of the bad check!

Bottom line? I warn all my winners who pay with a personal check that I may hold the item for more than two weeks before I ship. I make exceptions for buyers who have an excellent feedback rating or who I've successfully done business with before. Dealing with personal checks isn't worth the potential grief they can cause. Try to get an e-check or an instant transfer through PayPal (see the following section), or have your winners pay with credit cards through a payment service. For more on payment services, see the "I Take Plastic: Credit Cards" section, later in this chapter.

Bank debits (e-checks and instant transfers)

Despite the attached fees and a *short* waiting period, accepting a PayPal e-check or an instant transfer is a nice, clean transaction because it's immediate cash in your account. After indicating that they want to pay with an e-check, buyers must register their bank account with PayPal and give them the information required, as shown in Figure 13-1

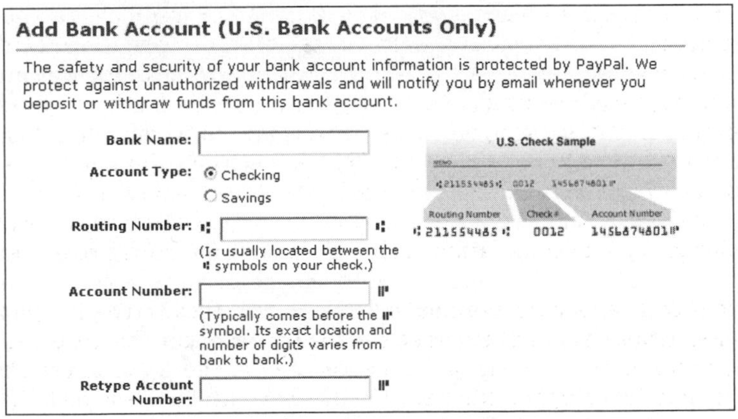

Add Bank Account (U.S. Bank Accounts Only)

The safety and security of your bank account information is protected by PayPal. We protect against unauthorized withdrawals and will notify you by email whenever you deposit or withdraw funds from this bank account.

Bank Name:

Account Type: ⦿ Checking
○ Savings

Routing Number: ⑈ [ ] ⑈
(Is usually located between the ⑈ symbols on your check.)

Account Number: [ ] ⑈
(Typically comes before the ⑈ symbol. Its exact location and number of digits varies from bank to bank.)

Retype Account Number: [ ] ⑈

U.S. Check Sample

MEMO
⑈211554485⑈ 0012 1456874801⑈

Routing Number   Check #   Account Number
⑈ 211554485 ⑈   0012   1456874801⑈

Figure 13-1: The bank information required to register your account with PayPal.

When a buyer pays with an electronic check, it will take as many as four days to clear. An instant transfer (on the other hand) credits your account immediately as long as the buyer has a credit card (or bank debit card) as a backup funding source — should your instant transfer fail. PayPal allows you to accept e-checks for up to $10,000 and will charge you the standard fees.

Hold This for Me: Escrow Service

Escrow.com (eBay's official escrow service) makes it more comfortable for a buyer to proceed with transactions of more than $500. By using escrow, buyers gain peace of mind because they know the transaction will be completed securely and easily. See Figure 13-2.

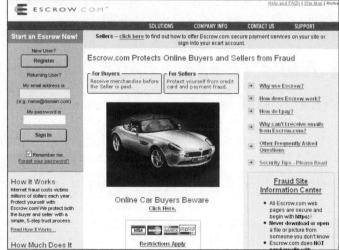

Figure 13-2:
Starting an escrow with Escrow.com for eBay services.

Another way to assure your buyer when participating in high-dollar transactions is to run a bonded auction. This type of service costs you far less time and money than an escrow service.

When you want to offer escrow as a payment option in one of your sales, be sure to indicate that you're willing to accept an escrow payment in the description area of the listing page. Be sure to clearly describe the terms. Are you willing to pay all the fees? Does the buyer pay fees?

International escrow services

Although Escrow.com is solely for United States and Canadian users, sellers in other countries can avail themselves of eBay-approved escrow sites:

Australia: `http://www.escrow australia.com.au/`

Europe, Italy, Spain: `http://www.escrow-europa.com/`

Germany: `http://www.iloxx.de/ebay/`

France, Belgium, Netherlands: `http://corporate.tripledeal.com/`

After you have a winning buyer, either you or the buyer should sign on to Escrow.com and create a transaction. If they are not a registered member of the site, they must register with Escrow.com. Registration is free.

To proceed with escrow, the buyer must send payment to Escrow.com. Escrow.com accepts all credit cards (including American Express and Discover), cashier's checks, money orders, wire transfers, and personal or business checks. A check is subject to a ten-day delay.

After the buyer makes the payment, Escrow.com asks the seller to ship the item to the buyer. When the buyer receives the merchandise, the inspection period begins promptly at 12:01 a.m. the next weekday and continues for a time previously set by the buyer and seller.

The buyer notifies Escrow.com that the merchandise is approved, and then Escrow.com releases payment to the seller. If the buyer doesn't feel that the merchandise is what he or she ordered, the buyer must return the item to the seller in its original condition, adhering to the Escrow.com shipping requirements. The buyer also must log on to the Web site to input return shipping information.

In the event of a return, the seller has the same inspection period to ensure that the item was returned in its original condition. After that is confirmed, Escrow.com will refund the buyer (less the escrow fee and, if agreed on ahead of time, the shipping fee). Either the buyer or the seller can pay the escrow fee; the two can even split the cost. But you need to decide who will pay the fee up front and indicate this in your auction listing. The buyer is responsible for paying the escrow fee for all returns, no matter who had initially agreed to pay the fees.

In Table 13-1, I include a listing of current escrow fees. (Credit cards or PayPal payments are not accepted for payments of more than $5000.)

Table 13-1	Escrow.com Standard Merchandise Escrow Fees
Transaction Amount	*Check or Money Order*
Up to $5,000.00	3.25% ($25.00 minimum)
$5,000.01 to $25,000.00	$162.50 plus 2% on the amount over $5000
$25,0000.01 and over	.89%

Sadly, escrow service has become one of the most highly publicized scams on the Internet. Unscrupulous sellers set up fake escrow sites, sell a bunch of high-dollar items on eBay to unsuspecting buyers, and then direct the buyers to the faux escrow Web site to set up their escrow. The buyers send their money (thinking the transaction is safe). After the fraudulent seller collects a bunch of money, he or she shuts down the Web site and absconds with the money! Many buyers are gun-shy of using escrow to pay for expensive items. Consider bonding your transactions to lure higher bids and confer a guarantee to the buyer.

If you're selling a vehicle, offering escrow can greatly enhance the activity of your sale. Escrow.com has a couple of useful services to encourage buyers and sellers to use their services:

- **Inspection service:** Following standard inspection procedures, trained inspection personnel go to the seller to inspect the vehicle and electronically record all information on handheld devices right in the field. Cost: $125.

- **Title transfer:** A real pain for those who buy vehicles online is getting the title transferred through their Department of Motor Vehicles. Vehicles sold within the fifty contiguous states can have their titles officially transferred and recorded for only $95.

Vehicle transactions come under a different fee schedule than regular merchandise. I've listed the fees in Table 13-2.

Table 13-2	Escrow.com Vehicle Transaction Fees
Transaction Amount	*Fee*
Up to $7,500	$125
$7,500.01 to $15,000	$170
$15,000.01 to $30,000	$200
$30,000.01 to $50,000	$275
$50,000 and over	0.6%

I Take Plastic: Credit Cards

As people become more comfortable with using credit cards on the Internet, credit cards become more popular for eBay payments. Plus, major credit card payment services have insured eBay payments to registered users, making credit cards safe for the buyer and easy for you. Credit card transactions are instantaneous; you don't have to wait for a piece of paper to travel cross-country.

For all this instantaneous money transfer, however, you pay a price. Whether you have your own *merchant account* (a credit card acceptance account in the name of your business) or take credit cards through a payment service (more on this in a minute), you pay a fee. Your fees can range from 2 to 7 percent, depending on how you plan to accept cards and which ones you accept. Unfortunately, many states have made it illegal to charge a credit card surcharge to make up this difference. You have to write off the expense of accepting credit cards as part of your business budget in the COGS (Cost of Good Sold, see Chapter 16 for an explanation).

The fees that brick-and-mortar stores pay for accepting credit cards are much less than those paid by online, mail, or phone orders. In most promotional material, the vendor usually quotes the "swiped card" rates. Because you won't have the buyer's card in hand to swipe, be sure to inquire with your provider for the proper rate before signing any papers.

I have to explain the downside of accepting credit cards for your online sales. To protect yourself, please be sure to check the bidders' feedback — both feedback they've received and feedback they've left — before accepting any form of credit card payment for a high-ticket item. Some buyers are chronic complainers and are rarely pleased with their purchases. They may not be satisfied with your item after it ships. In that case, they can simply call their credit card company and get credit for the payment; you'll be charged back (your account will be debited) the amount of the sale. (See the "Forget the buyer: Seller beware!" sidebar in this chapter.) PayPal protects sellers to an extent and is a safer way to accept credit cards for your sales.

Credit card payment services

Person-to-person payment systems, such as eBay's PayPal and BidPay, allow buyers to authorize payments from their credit cards or checking accounts directly to the seller. These services make money by charging percentages and fees for each transaction. It all happens electronically through an automated clearinghouse — no fuss, no muss. The payment service releases to the seller only the buyer's shipping information; all personal credit card information is kept private. This speeds up the time it takes the buyer to get merchandise because sellers are free to ship as soon as the service lets them know that the buyer has made payment and the payment has been processed.

From the seller's point of view, person-to-person payment service transaction fees are lower than the 2.5 to 3.5 percent (per transaction) that traditional credit card companies charge for merchant accounts. (Get the details in the "Your very own merchant account" section, coming up.) Even traditional retailers may switch their online business to these services to save money. In this section, I discuss the top payment services and how each works.

Forget the buyer: Seller beware!

When buyers dispute a sale, they can simply call PayPal or their credit card company and refuse to pay for the item. You lose the sale and possibly won't be able to retrieve your merchandise. A payment service or merchant account will then *chargeback* your account without contacting you and without negotiating. Technically, the buyer has made the purchase from the payment service — not from you — and the payment service won't defend you. I've heard of chargebacks occurring as long as six months after the transaction, although eBay says they can occur no later than two months after they sent you the first bill on which the transaction or error appeared. No one is forcing the buyer to ship the merchandise back to you. Just like eBay Fraud Protection (see Chapter 3), the credit card companies skew the rules to defend the consumer. As the seller, you have to fend for yourself. See Chapter 4 on how to report fraudulent buyers. You usually have no way to verify that the shipping address is the one the credit card bills to. So, to add to your problems, the card may actually be stolen.

PayPal confirms through AVS (Address Verification Service) that the buyer's credit card billing address matches the shipping address and gives you the option to not accept payments from buyers whose addresses don't match. PayPal offers seller protection against spurious chargebacks under the following circumstances:

- Fraudulent card use
- False claims of nondelivery

See the section on PayPal for more details on how to be covered by seller protection.

If the issuing bank resolves a chargeback in the buyer's favor, PayPal charges you $10 if you're determined to be at fault, but will waive the fee if you meet all the requirements of the PayPal Seller Protection policy.

Here's some good news: Major credit card companies are trying to curb online fraud for their merchant accounts. Visa has the new Verified by Visa acceptance, which takes buyers to a Visa screen (through software installed on the merchant's server) and verifies their identity through a Visa-only password. MasterCard uses SET (Secure Electronic Transactions), a similar encrypted, transaction-verification scheme. These systems are expected to substantially reduce fraud and chargebacks.

Before you decide which credit card payment service to use, get out your calculator and check their Web sites for current rates. Calculate your own estimates; don't rely on a site's advertised samples. I've found that the charts on the Web tend to leave out certain minor fees. I've also found that comparison charts quoting the competition's prices tend to include optional fees. Do your own math.

When you pay the fee to your payment service, realize that the total amount of your transaction — including shipping fees, handling charges, and any sales tax that you charge — incurs a fee. The payment service charges a percentage based on the total dollar amount that's run through its system.

BidPay

A respected name in the online payment provider service is BidPay, a division of CyberSource. BidPay was launched in 1999 and was one of the original payment options for online auctions offering money order payments. They perform a service similar to PayPal, accepting credit and debit cards (MasterCard and Visa). Isn't it nice to have an alternative? BidPay is easy to use and is an eBay Certified provider.

Once you join BidPay, you can indicate that you'd like their banners to appear in your listings, giving your buyer the opportunity to have an option to pay through a service other than PayPal.

To register with BidPay.com so that you can begin to accept them as a payment method for your sales, go to www.bidpay.com. Click Sign Up Now and provide some basic information. After BidPay.com processes your application, you will receive a confirmation.

BidPay is free for the buyer to use, but they will charge you, the seller, a transaction fee. Every payment you receive through BidPay is subject to a $0.50 transaction fee plus a percentage of the total amount sent. Their service is highly competitive with traditional merchant account fees. The charges for BidPay transactions are shown in Table 13-3.

Table 13-3	BidPay Transaction Fees
Transaction Amount	*Fee*
Domestic	2.5% plus $0.50
International payments	2.9% plus $0.50

Selling internationally through PayPal

PayPal operates in 190 markets and manages more than 133 million accounts. PayPal currently allows users to send, receive, and hold funds in sixteen currencies: Australian dollar, Canadian dollar, Czech koruna, Danish krone, euro, Hong Kong dollar, Hungarian forint, Japanese yen, New Zealand dollar, Norwegian krone, Polish zloty, pounds sterling, Singapore dollar, Swedish krona, Swiss franc, and U.S. dollar. PayPal operates locally in thirteen countries, and payments from international buyers are automatically converted to your desired currency.

There is a conversion fee for accepting foreign currencies from your buyers and having them converted to U.S. dollars. Because PayPal is not a currency dealer, they must purchase foreign currencies from a bank. PayPal receives a wholesale rate (twice a day) and adds an additional 2.5 percent above this rate to determine their retail foreign exchange rate. This 2.5 percent is added to PayPal fees as shown in the table.

PayPal Fees for Receiving Payments from Non-U.S. Buyers

Monthly Sales	Price per Transaction
$0.00 to $3,000.00	3.9% plus $0.30
$3,000.01 to $10,000.00	3.5% plus $0.30
$10,000.01 to $100,000.00	3.2% plus $0.30
$100,000.00 and over	2.9% plus $0.30

Residents in forty-eight new markets can now use PayPal in their local markets to send money online. These new markets include Indonesia, the Philippines, Croatia, Fiji, Vietnam, and Jordan. A complete list can be viewed at www.paypal.com/worldwide.

Warning! It is against policy for you to charge your buyers additional funds to cover this expense.

PayPal

PayPal is the largest of the online person-to-person payment services. Thankfully, eBay had the presence of mind to acquire this previously independent service in 2002, so it has now become the de facto standard for paying for items bought on eBay.

PayPal (see Figure 13-3) allows buyers to safely click and pay with a credit card, instant transfer, or e-check directly from eBay after they've won an auction or made a purchase. PayPal conveniently integrates into all eBay transactions. If your auction uses the Buy It Now feature or is a fixed-price listing, you can require buyers to pay for their purchases immediately with PayPal payments.

Figure 13-3:
The
PayPal.com
home page.

To accept credit card payments, you must have a premier or business account. Buyers may join when they win their first auction and want to pay with PayPal, or they can go to www.PayPal.com and sign up. The story's slightly different for the seller. You need to set up your PayPal account *before* you choose to accept it in your auctions or sales.

Here are more than a few particulars about PayPal accounts:

- ✔ Auction payments are deposited into your PayPal account. Choose one of several ways to get your money:

  - • Have the money transferred directly into your registered checking account.

  - • Receive payment by check (PayPal charges $1.50 for the check).

  - • Keep the money in your PayPal account for making payments to other sellers.

  - • Withdraw the cash from an ATM with a PayPal debit card and get back 1.5 percent of the money spent on purchases.

  - • Shop online with a virtual credit card that carries your balance to any Web site that accepts MasterCard.

- ✔ PayPal has its own feedback system (actually called a reputation number). The number after a username reflects the number of unique PayPal Verified users with whom this user has conducted business. Buyers will see a link to your Member Information box on the Send Money Confirmation page. The higher the reputation number, the more likely the user is experienced and trustworthy. Clicking the number produces a report, like the one shown in Figure 13-4, giving information on the seller.

Member Information

About **The Collier Company, Inc:**

To protect your security, PayPal offers information on the status of this member.

Seller Reputation:	(3295) Verified Buyers
Account Status:	Verified
Account Type:	US Business
Account Creation Date:	Feb. 2, 2000
PayPal Member For:	7 years 4 months 3 days

- Member accepts all payments

Business URL: http://www.coolebaytools.com

Cust. Service Email: mcollier@coolebaytools.com

Seller Reputation
The Seller Reputation Number measures how many Verified PayPal members have paid that seller. New transactions are added 30 days after they occur, to ensure that the Reputation Number reflects successful exchanges.

Account Status
U.S. Users are considered "Verified" if they have confirmed the bank account they have added to their PayPal account. Verification is a positive signal to the Community that a user has complied with Community security measures.

Account Type
Accounts can be Personal, Premier, or Business. Active sellers are required to have a Premier or Business account.

Figure 13-4:
My PayPal Member Information box.

✔ As a seller with a premier or business account, you can choose to accept or deny a payment without a confirmed address. A confirmed address means that the ship-to address indicated by the buyer is the same as the billing address on the credit card the buyer chose to register with PayPal. On the Accept or Deny page, information about the buyer is shown, including verification status, account creation date, and participation number (same as your reputation number).

✔ PayPal assesses your account $10 for any chargeback. The fee is waived if you've fulfilled the requirements in the PayPal Seller Protection policy (see the next bullet). To specify whether you want to accept a credit card payment from a buyer without a confirmed address, log on, go to your account, and then click the Profile tab. Next, scroll down Selling Preferences and click Payment Receiving Preferences. If you accept payment from a nonconfirmed address, that transaction will not be covered by the PayPal Seller Protection policy.

✔ The PayPal Seller Protection policy provides up to $5000 in annual chargeback protection, unauthorized card use, and nonshipments. To qualify for this protection, you must do the following:

- **Be a verified member of PayPal with a premier or business account:** Allow PayPal to confirm with your bank that your checking account and address are your own.

- **Ship only to a confirmed address:** PayPal confirms that the buyer's ship-to address coincides with the address to which the credit company sends monthly bills. Fraudulent shoppers often ask you to ship to another address — don't do it.

- **Keep proof of shipping that can be tracked online:** Here's where those delivery confirmation things come in handy. See Chapter 14 to find out how you can get them for free. For transactions greater than $250, you must get a signed proof of delivery from the shipper.

- **Ship tangible goods:** PayPal doesn't cover goods that are transmitted electronically.

- **Accept only single payments from a single account:** Don't let a buyer try to pay portions of a purchase from different e-mail addresses. Someone who's trying to pay using several accounts may be attempting to defraud you.

- **The transaction must be between U.S., U.K., or Canadian buyers and sellers:** Seller protection isn't extended to other international shipments.

Other requirements change from time to time. Check PayPal's help area for updates. But know that if a transaction is eligible, Seller Protection Policy Eligible will appear on the individual Transaction Details page.

If you have a personal PayPal account, you may still be able to accept credit card payments, but you will have to pay a hefty fee. You'll pay 4.9 percent of the total amount collected, plus the standard $0.30 transaction fee. Seller's fee tiers for business and premier accounts are adjusted based on the prior month's transaction volume. Look at Table 13-4 for the updated PayPal fee tiers.

Table 13-4	PayPal Domestic (U.S.) Transaction Fees by Sales Tier
Monthly Sales	*Fee*
$0 to $3,000.00	2.9% plus $0.30 USD
$3,000.01 to $10,000.00	2.5% plus $0.30 USD
$10,000.01 to $100,000.00	2.2% plus $0.30 USD
$100,000.01 and over	1.9% plus $0.30 USD

To receive the lower rates from PayPal, you must apply for merchant rate pricing. Once your sales go over $3000 a month, you must log into your PayPal account and apply. If you can't find the link, call PayPal sales at 866-836-1648. If your sales dip below the minimum tier of $3000, you do not need to reapply.

A brilliant feature of PayPal is the ability to download your sales and deposit history to your computer. Although PayPal also offers files that integrate with QuickBooks (for more on QuickBooks, see Chapter 16), the standard downloads are rich in features. Rather than importing just sales figures, you see each and every detail of your transaction — dates, names, addresses, phone numbers, amounts, and more. Even fees and taxes (if you charge sales tax) are broken down separately, making bookkeeping a breeze. The download imports into Microsoft Works and Excel.

Downloading your history will help you calculate income taxes and sales taxes, reconcile your accounts, predict sales trends, calculate total revenues, and perform other financial reporting tasks. It will also give you an excellent customer database. The deposits download gives you detailed information for all the deposits that you receive: payments, PayPal transaction and deposit fees, refunds, rebates, and any adjustments made to your account.

Follow these steps to download your sales and deposit histories:

1. **On your PayPal Main Overview page, click the History tab.**

2. **Click the Download My History link, on the left side of the page.**

3. **Enter the time span and the file format for the information that you want to view.**

4. **Click the Download History button.**

   The information appears on the screen. Or if the servers are busy, you'll receive an e-mail (usually in a minute or two) when the reports are ready.

5. **Save the file in a directory that you can conveniently access for bookkeeping.**

You can just double-click the file to open it in Excel or Microsoft Works. You now have all the information you could possibly need to apply to your book-keeping program.

Registering with PayPal

If you aren't registered with PayPal yet (what's holding you up?), use the convenient Selling link on the All Selling page, which you reach from your My eBay page. To get more information, just click the PayPal link to arrive at the PayPal overview page (see Figure 13-5), and then click the Sign Up for a PayPal Account button to begin registration, as shown in Figure 13-6.

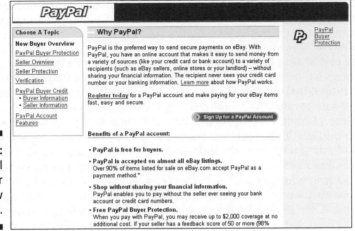

Figure 13-5:
The PayPal
seller
overview
page.

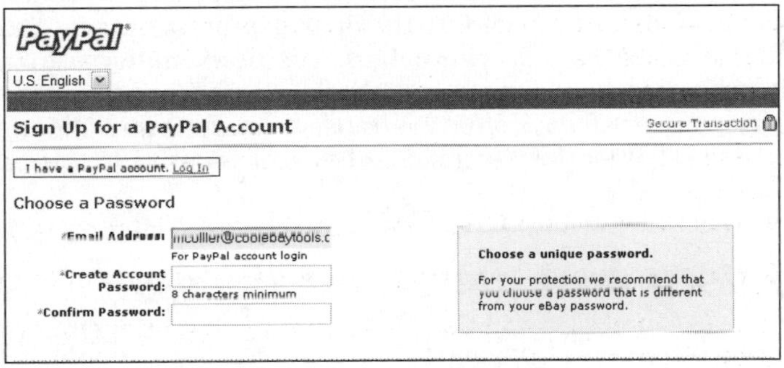

Figure 13-6:
This is
where you
begin your
registration.

The convenience of PayPal integration into the eBay site shines when your item is purchased. Winners just click a Pay Now button that pops up on your auction page immediately after the listing closes. When you list auctions, you pre-set the shipping and handling charges that appear in the shipping box at the bottom of the page. When winners click the Pay Now button (see Figure 13-7), they're taken directly to a payment page set up with your information. The process is as easy as purchasing something through Buy It Now.

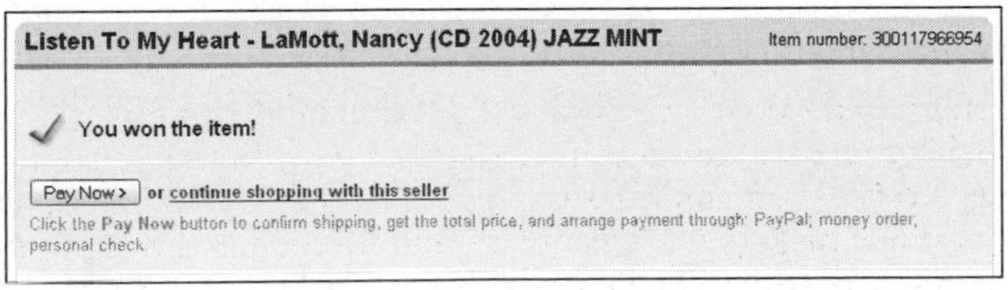

Figure 13-7:
The Pay
Now button
appears
when the
buyer wins.

Listen To My Heart - LaMott, Nancy (CD 2004) JAZZ MINT   Item number: 300117966954

✓ You won the item!

[Pay Now >] or continue shopping with this seller

Click the **Pay Now** button to confirm shipping, get the total price, and arrange payment through PayPal, money order, personal check

When a purchase is made and the payment is deposited in your PayPal account, the system holds the money until you choose how you want to withdraw it.

Because credit card and identity theft is so prevalent on the Internet — and an expensive burden to e-commerce — PayPal uses the extra security measure provided by Visa and MasterCard called CVV2. Most credit cards have three (or four) additional numbers listed on the back, immediately following the regular 16-digit number. Merchants use these numbers for security or verification but aren't allowed to store them, so they're presumably protected from hackers. However, in the unlikely event your credit card doesn't have these numbers yet, PayPal still allows you to use your card by verifying it through a procedure known as *random charge*. PayPal charges a few cents or so to your card and asks you to disclose the pin number printed on your statement. Then PayPal knows that you control the card and didn't steal it.

Withdraw your funds from the PayPal account on a regular basis; you need that money to operate your business. Don't let it become a temporary savings account — unless you choose the PayPal interest-bearing account (check out www.PayPal.com for details). Also, any money you have in your account can be extricated for a chargeback — and chargebacks can be applied as many as 60 days after the transaction. For more about chargebacks, see the "Forget the buyer: Seller beware!" sidebar, in this chapter.

Your very own merchant account

If your eBay business is bringing in more than $20,000 a month, a credit card merchant account may be for you. At that level of sales, discounts kick in and your credit card processing becomes a savings to your business rather than an expense. Before setting up a merchant account, however, I recommend that you look at the costs carefully. I get at least one e-mail each week begging me to set up a merchant account, and each one offers lower fees than the last. But charges buried in the small print make fees hard to calculate and even harder to compare. Even those who advertise low fees often don't deliver. Be sure to look at the entire picture before you sign a contract.

The best place to begin looking for a merchant account may be your own bank, where they know you, your credit history, and your business reputation and have a stake in the success of your business. If your credit isn't up to snuff, I recommend building good credit before pursuing a merchant account because your credit rating is your feedback to the offline world.

If your bank doesn't offer merchant accounts for Internet-based businesses, find a broker to evaluate your credit history and hook you up with a bank that fits your needs and business style (or join Costco as a last resort; see the following section). These brokers make their money from your application fee, from a finder's fee from the bank that you finally choose, or both.

Payment services that eBay won't allow

To maintain a safe marketplace, eBay likes to check out and approve the many new payment methods that crop up on the Internet from time to time. They like to be sure that the service offers substantial financial, privacy, and antifraud protection for buyers and sellers, amongst other requirements.

Before you add a new payment method (other than checks, money orders, or PayPal), go to the Help area and search accepted payments. You can also go directly to `http://pages.ebay.com/help/policies/accepted-payments-policy.html`. Although this policy may seem limiting to sellers, keep in mind that we are selling on eBay's site. If we choose not to follow the rules, we can go elsewhere.

Assuming you want to continue selling on eBay, I'd stay away from the following payment services that can get your listings ended (or get you suspended) for offering them: AlertPay.com, anypay.com, AuctionChex.com, BillPay.ie, ecount.com, cardserviceinternational.com, CCAvenue, ecount, e-gold, eHotPay.com, ePassporte.com, EuroGiro, FastCash.com, Google Checkout, gcash, GearPay, Goldmoney.com, graphcard.com, greenzap.com, ikobo.com, Liberty Dollars, Moneygram.com, neteller.com, Netpay.com, paychest.com, payingfast.com, Payko.com, paypay, Postepay, Qchex.com, rupay.com, sendmoneyorder.com, stamps, Stormpay, wmtransfer.com, and xcoin.com.

After you get a bank, you'll be connected to a *processor,* or transaction clearinghouse. Your bank merely handles the banking; the clearinghouse is on the other end of your Internet connection when you're processing transactions, checking whether the credit card you're taking is valid and not stolen or maxed out.

The next step is setting up your *gateway,* the software (ICVerify or PCAuthorize, for example) with which you transmit charges to the clearinghouse. Some gateways use HTML Web sites and take the transactions directly on Web-based forms (Cybercash or VeriFone, among others). Web-based gateways connect your Web forms to real-time credit card processing.

In Table 13-5, I highlight various possible costs associated with setting up and maintaining a merchant account.

Table 13-5	Possible Internet Merchant Account Fees
Fee	*Average Amount*
Setup fee	$25.00 to $250.00
Monthly processing fee to bank	2.5% (1.5% to 5%)
Fee per transaction	$0.20 to $0.50

(continued)

Table 13-5 *(continued)*

Fee	Average Amount
Processor's fee per transaction	$0.35 to $0.50
Internet discount rate	2% to 4%
Monthly statement fee	$9.00 to $15.00
Monthly minimum processing fee	$15.00 to $30.00
Gateway monthly processing fee	$20.00 to $40.00
Application fee	$50.00 to $500.00
Software purchase	$350.00 to $1000.00
Software lease	$25.00 per month
Chargeback fee	$15.00

Remember that some merchant accounts will charge you some of these fees and others may have a bunch of little snipes at your wallet. In the following list, I define some of the fees in Table 13-5:

- ✔ **Setup fee:** A one-time cost that you pay to either your bank or to your broker.

- ✔ **Discount rate:** A percentage of the transaction amount (a discount from your earnings), taken off the top along with the transaction fee before the money is deposited into your account.

- ✔ **Transaction fee:** A fee per transaction that's paid to the bank or to your gateway for the network.

- ✔ **Gateway or processing fee:** Your fee for processing credit cards in real time that's paid to the Internet gateway.

- ✔ **Application fee:** A one-time fee that goes to the broker or perhaps to the bank.

- ✔ **Monthly minimum processing fee:** If your bank's cut of your purchases doesn't add up to this amount, the bank takes it anyway. For example, if your bank charges a minimum monthly fee of $20 and you don't hit $20 in fees because your sales aren't high enough, the bank charges you the difference.

If you're comfortable with all the information in the preceding list and in Table 13-5, and you're looking for a broker, heed my advice and carefully read everything a broker offers. Be sure you aren't missing any hidden costs.

PayPal's Virtual Terminal

If you want your own merchant account and want all the benefits of PayPal, you can apply for their solution: Virtual Terminal. With Virtual Terminal you can accept credit card payments by phone, fax, or mail. All this for only an additional $20 a month over your regular PayPal fees. No extras and no equipment to buy or rent. What a deal! Just log into your PayPal business account online at `www.paypal.com/vt` and fill in the Virtual Terminal form. You can also apply for the terminal through that link. You must have a Business account to use the Virtual Terminal feature.

Virtual Terminal fees are the same as PayPal merchant tiers and are based on the total amount of money you put through PayPal per month — including regular PayPal payments. The buyer's credit card charge will appear on their bill with the name of your business.

Costco member's credit card processing

Here's some true discount credit card processing: a one-stop merchant account and gateway! You can not only buy tuna fish in bulk with a Costco membership, but also obtain a reasonably priced way to handle a merchant account (check out Table 13-6) through the NOVA Network. Costco got together with Nova Information Systems, one of the nation's largest processors of credit card transactions, to offer Costco Executive members a discounted Internet credit card processing service. Costco Executive membership brings the cost of a Costco membership up from $45 to $100, but you get the benefit of receiving 2 percent back for most purchases (not including tobacco, gas, food, and some other purchases).

Table 13-6	Costco Executive Member Internet Credit Card Processing Fees
Fee	*Amount*
Telephone order fee	1.99% plus $0.27
Internet sales fee	1.99% plus $0.27
Transaction fee to NOVA per transaction	$0.27
NOVA monthly fees minimum	$20.00

To get an Internet commerce account, you should already have the following in place:

- ✔ Products and pricing
- ✔ A return and refund policy
- ✔ An active customer service phone number
- ✔ Posted delivery methods and shipment time
- ✔ A privacy policy stating that you will not share your customer's information with any other entity
- ✔ A registered domain in your name or in the name of your business
- ✔ A secure order page with https and lock

To begin the application process, follow these steps:

1. **Go to www.costco.com.**

2. **At the top of the home page, click the Services link.**

3. **Scroll to the Services for Your Business area and click the Merchant Credit Card Processing link.**

4. **Read the information and click the Apply Now link.**

5. **Type your Executive Membership number, and fill out the secure form.**

   Filling out the form speeds up the application process.

After sending your form, you'll receive a full application package by two-day air. A representative will also contact you by telephone. For further information or to apply by phone, call NOVA at 1-800-551-0951 and mention promotion code 83500.

Chapter 14

Shipping Your Items: Sending Them Fast and Saving Money

. . . .

. . . .

1 think the most satisfying part of an eBay transaction is making the sale and receiving payment. After that comes the tedious process of fulfilling your orders. You shouldn't feel bad if this is the point that makes you take pause and sigh. Order fulfillment is one of the biggest challenges (and yuckiest chores) that face any mail order or online entrepreneur. The onerous task of packing and mailing is the bane of almost all businesses.

But as an eBay businessperson, you *must* attend to these tasks, however much you'd rather not. So in Chapter 17, I detail what you need for packing (boxes, bubble pack, and so on) and some options for purchasing online postage. And in this chapter, I explain just how your items will get to their destinations, exploring your shipping options, costs, and insurance coverage along the way.

Finding the Perfect Shipping Carrier: The Big Four

When you're looking at your shipping options, you need to first determine what types of packages you'll generally be sending (small packages that weigh less than 2 pounds or large and bulky packages), and then decide how you'll package your items. Planning this before listing the item is a good idea.

Deciding on your carrier can be the most important decision in your eBay business. You need to decide which one is more convenient for you (close to your home base, provides pickup service, gives better customer service) and which is the most economical (leverages your bottom line). The efficiency of your shipping is only as good as the people who service your account. If the UPS man dumps packages at your door without ringing the bell, perhaps he's not the right person to entrust with the heart and soul of your business. Maybe your letter carrier knows you by name and gives you good service; if that's the case, maybe the United States Postal Service (USPS) is the best choice for the bulk of your shipments. Many eBay sellers send packages using ground services rather than airmail or overnight, but a shipper who can give you both options may be offering you a good deal because you don't have to deal with more than one vendor.

Settling on one main shipper to handle your shipments is important because you'll be able to have the bulk of your records on one statement or in one area. You might also need a secondary shipper (most sellers do) for special types of packages. One shipper can't be everything to every business, so having an account with more than one can be to your advantage. Also, shippers may not sign up new accounts as readily in the middle of a strike or work slowdown.

In this section, I give you the lowdown on the four major carriers — DHL, FedEx, UPS, and the USPS — so you can see who fits your requirements. For a summary of shipping costs from these four, see Table 14-1. Note that FedEx and UPS include tracking numbers for delivery confirmation. The USPS charges extra; delivery confirmation is $0.65 for Priority mail and $0.75 for Parcel Post. For info on eliminating this fee for Priority mail, check out Chapter 17.

Table 14-1	Shipping Costs from Coast to Coast (Residence Delivery)				
Delivery Service	*2 lbs.*	*5 lbs.*	*10 lbs.*	*15 lbs.*	*Flat-Rate Box*
UPS 3-Day Select (1–3 days)	$10.10	$24.86	$36.74	$48.17	n/a
USPS Priority mail (2– 3 days)	$7.50	$15.85	$25.05	$30.50	$8.95
DHL@ Home (2–4 days)	$6.55	$8.72	$10.88	$14.33	n/a
FedEx Home Delivery (4 days)	$7.73	$9.21	$11.50	$15.15	n/a
UPS on Demand (1–6 days)	$10.41	$12.56	$12.85	$17.25	n/a
USPS Media mail (2–9 days)	$2.14	$3.16	$4.86	$6.56	n/a
USPS Parcel Post (2–7 days)	$6.15	$10.50	$16.17	$20.40	n/a

Shipping the really big stuff!

When it comes to shipping heavy or big stuff, you have a few options. Because I like using FedEx, I generally check FedEx Freight first. A friend of mine once purchased four large heavy-equipment tires on eBay, and there was no way he could go with a regular carrier. We called FedEx Freight and told the seller to place the tires on a pallet and secure them. FedEx Freight picked them up at their location in one shipment. Shipping costs were reasonable, but the only caveat was that the shipment had to be delivered to a place of business, not a residential location.

This is easy to overcome, especially if you have a friend with a retail store or a gym you go to.

A Web site called www.freightquote.com negotiates rates with several major freight forwarders and will give you a free quote on your large shipment right on their Web site. Before attempting to sell a heavy item, you can sign onto their home page and enter the weight and dimensions of your shipment, and they'll give you a free quote on the spot.

You can now prepare UPS or USPS shipping documents online through PayPal and on Web sites for the other carriers. See Chapter 17 for the ins and outs (and pros and cons) of shipping through PayPal.

When you start shipping a few dozen packages a week, you might want to check out *eBay Timesaving Techniques For Dummies,* by yours truly, for an in-depth analysis of the big four and their variable shipping rates.

DHL@Home

Once considered the outsider in the shipping arena for eBay sellers, DHL has come up with a class of service that makes sense dollarwise. Most sellers consider DHL as the guy for big companies and their very big time logistical needs, but this is no longer the case.

The company was founded in 1969 in San Francisco by Adrian Dalsey, Larry Hillblom, and Robert Lynn (see the DHL?) and is now owned by the German Deutsche Post.

DHL partnered with the U.S. Postal Service to create a service for shipments to residences as part of the DHL/USPS. Drop off your parcels at a DHL location, and the trackable package is delivered by the local post office, including delivery to P.O. boxes.

You can sign up for an account and print your labels online at www.dhl-usa.com.

DHL has many benefits to the shipper, here are a few:

- ✔ Each shipment is covered for $100.00 in declared value. Additional insurance is $0.35 per $100.00 or a fraction thereof.
- ✔ Residential deliveries are limited to 70-pound packages.
- ✔ Daily pickup service adds an additional charge to your account.
- ✔ Dropping off packages at DHL counters incurs no additional charge.
- ✔ DHL@Home delivers Monday through Saturday through the USPS.

Federal Express

Federal Express (FedEx) is world famous for its reliable service. It's the number-one choice for all major companies who "Absolutely, positively have to get it there on time." FedEx also has a reputation for some of the highest costs in the business — but only to the untrained eye. FedEx acquired Roadway Package Service (RPS) and formed FedEx Ground, which has a separate division called FedEx Home Delivery that delivers to residences. For the services they provide, you'll be happy to pay what you do. Read on.

FedEx Ground and Home Delivery

When FedEx's residential ground delivery service began, their slogan was "The neighborhood-friendly service that fits the way we live, work, and shop today." Although I rarely get warm fuzzies from my package deliveries, this slogan brought meaning to the philosophy behind their service: to bring professional shipping to your home residence. FedEx Home Delivery offers low rates and a high-quality service. They're the only shipper that offers a money-back guarantee on home service. They deliver until 8 p.m. *and* on Saturdays but not on Monday.

To open an account, visit the FedEx Home Delivery Web site and sign up for an account at www.fedex.com/us/services/us/homedelivery. Even if you have a current Federal Express account, you need to sign on to add the Ground service (which includes Home Delivery). Registering for Ground service is even easier than registering on eBay, so give it a shot.

I opened my FedEx Home Delivery account through a link on the main FedEx home page, and got the skinny on how to use the service. The online calculator allows you to choose the option of Home Delivery, so you don't even have to look up alternative rates and charts. And just as other shippers do, FedEx Home Delivery gives you a service schedule to let you know how long it will take your package to arrive at its destination.

Here are a few fast facts about FedEx Ground services:

- You print your own labels and barcodes for your packages and track them online.

- FedEx Home Delivery works on a zone system based on your ZIP code and how far the package is going. Refer to the FedEx Home Delivery zone chart or get the cost online through the online calculator.

- Each shipment is covered for $100.00 in declared value.

- Residential deliveries are limited to 70-pound packages.

- Daily *pickup* service adds an additional weekly charge to your account.

- Dropping off packages at Federal Express counters incurs no additional charge.

- FedEx Home Delivery delivers Tuesday through Saturday till 8 p.m. within one to five business days.

If FedEx Ground shipping charges seem to be a great deal, they are! But you can get an even better deal if you charge your FedEx shipping to an American Express Business card (one that gives you access to the American Express Open Network). You save an additional 5% on all FedEx shipments when you use online shipping and place your orders online. If you have the Amex card, be sure it is officially linked so you get the discount.

FedEx Online

FedEx has one of the most intuitive online applications for shipping. The FedEx Ship Manager interface will turn your computer into a one-person shipping shop. You can generate labels for all forms of FedEx in one place. The site allows you to search for rate quotes and track packages, and it includes a shipping notification option to send tracking information e-mails to your recipients.

Larger businesses can get the Ship Manager workstation, complete with a PC and printer. The workstation has the unique ability to choose from other carriers. Aside from FedEx Express and FedEx Ground, you can also access UPS shipping services, which allow you to rate, track, report, and ship for multiple carriers on one system.

United Parcel Service

Everyone's familiar with the big brown trucks that tool around town delivering packages hither and yon. Those trucks belong to the United Parcel Service, or UPS, whose home page is shown in Figure 14-1.

Figure 14-1:
The UPS
United
States hub.

UPS offers three levels of service based on your shipping needs:

- ✔ **Internet account (on Demand):** Print your own bar-coded labels so that you can drop off packages at the UPS retail counter or store (you can also do that without an account) or give packages to a UPS driver. You can also use Internet account rates when shipping through PayPal.

- ✔ **Occasional shipper account:** Use UPS for the rare large box or heavy shipment. An occasional shipper can call UPS for a next-day pickup. You have to pay an additional fee per package for the driver to pick up from you if you don't feel like bringing the package to the UPS local counter.

- ✔ **Pickup account:** When you hit the big time, you're able to get the lowest UPS rates and have a driver make daily stops to pick up your packages. Fees for a pickup account may run as much as $20.00 per week (based on the amount of packages you ship each week) over the cost of your package shipping.

For big shippers, UPS offers its Application Program Interface (API), which can be integrated into a company's home servers.

To register for UPS online, visit `www.ups.com/content/us/en/index.jsx` or go to your PayPal account. After typing your personal or business information and answering a few basic questions, *UPS* will decide what account is right for you. By registering, you can also track packages and ship online.

Here are some quick facts about UPS:

- ✔ Shipping with UPS requires that you pay a different rate for different zones in the country (the same as the other shippers). The cost of your package is based on its weight, your ZIP code (where the package ships from), and the addressee's ZIP code (where the package is going). To figure out your cost, use the handy eBay shipping calculator shown in Figure 14-2.

✔ The UPS Web site offers a chart that defines the shipping time for your ground shipments (remember, no weekend deliveries).

✔ Each package has a tracking number that you can input online to verify the location of a package in transit and the time of delivery.

✔ Delivery to a residence is more expensive than delivery to a commercial location.

✔ UPS delivers packages Monday through Friday.

✔ $100.00 in insurance is included with every shipment. Valuations from $100.01 to $300.00 cost $1.50, and valuations over that are an additional $0.50 per $100.00.

Figure 14-2:
The eBay shipping calculator.

United States Postal Service

Whether you call it snail mail, POPS (plain old postal service), or whatever nickname you like, the United States Postal Service has been delivering the mail since 1775, when our first postmaster (Benjamin Franklin) took the reins. The USPS has attempted to get every piece of mail delivered to every part of our country. Check out its Web site in Figure 14-3.

The USPS is open to everyone. You don't have to set up an account to use its services. To get a basic idea of what you'll pay to send a package, you can access a rate calculator on the USPS Web site (www.usps.gov). The post office provides many services; in this section, I go over the most popular forms of mail used by eBay sellers.

Distance and weight aren't the only measure for postal shipping fees; shape matters too. Because the cost of handling each mail shape varies, letters, large envelopes (flats), and packages (parcels) of different sizes can incur different rates.

Figure 14-3:
The United
States
Postal
Service
Web site.

First Class mail

eBay sellers often forget that items that weigh 13 ounces or less can be shipped by super-speedy First Class mail at considerable savings. I send my First Class shipments in bubble-lined mailer envelopes and they arrive swiftly. Delivery confirmation is available for First Class mail for $0.75 at the post office counter or $0.18 when you print your postage electronically.

For use of delivery confirmation, First Class mail (large envelopes, flats, and packages) must be greater than ¾-inch thick at the thickest point, unless the item is packaged in strong, rigid fiberboard or in a container that becomes rigid after the contents are enclosed and the container is sealed. The package must be able to maintain its shape throughout the mail process without collapsing.

Priority mail

The two-to-three-day Priority mail service is the most popular form of shipping for eBay packages. You can get free cartons in many sizes, stickers, and labels from the post office. (See Chapter 17 for a complete list of what the USPS supplies for your mailing needs.) You can also print postage online through PayPal, Endicia.com, or Stamps.com (again, see Chapter 17).

Priority mail rates are perfect for 1-pound packages ($4.60 flat rate cross-country) and 2-pound packages (from $4.80 to $7.50, based on distance). There's a flat-rate Priority envelope in which you can jam as much as possible (regardless of the final weight) for the same $4.60. And you can use two sizes of flat-rate boxes and load them chock-full of heavy books or whatever and pay only $8.95 to get your items delivered — anywhere in the country.

The Priority mail rates (including free shipping materials) are attractive until you get into the larger, heavier packages that won't fit into the flat-rate boxes (refer to Table 14-1). Also, if you don't print your postage online, delivery confirmation costs an additional $0.65 for Priority mail ($0.75 for Parcel Post and Media mail). Delivery confirmation tells you only *if* the package was delivered; it doesn't trace the package along its route.

Media mail

To stay hip, the post office has renamed its old Book Rate to Media mail, causing many eBay sellers to mistakenly miss out on this valuable mailing tool. The savings are immense (refer to Table 14-1). The drawback is that you must mail only books, cassettes, videos, or computer-readable media. Transit time on Media mail can be up to three weeks, but the cost savings on heavy packages are worth it.

Parcel Post

If you want to use USPS and have a heavy package (up to 70 pounds) that doesn't fit the requirements for Media mail, use Parcel Post. However, USPS Parcel Post rates don't save you much when you compare them to UPS or FedEx Ground rates.

USPS Application Program Interface

If you want to print your own postage, you can use USPS Click-n-Ship, PayPal, Endicia.com, or Stamps.com — that is, unless you're a large corporation and you'd like to incorporate the post office tools into your own Web site. USPS has an application program interface (API) that allows your Web site to interact with USPS servers, as shown in Figure 14-4. With this software, big businesses can get delivery confirmation (among other services) at no charge and print their own barcodes. The USPS Web Tools page is at www.usps.com/webtools.

Figure 14-4: USPS Web Tools Documentation Center.

TIP

The integration of USPS APIs isn't for the meek and small (like me — and maybe you?), but you can use a reliable independent service such as Endicia.com or Stamps.com. They're perfect for the e-commerce entrepreneur.

Protecting Packages with Universal Parcel Insurance Coverage

If you think that printing your own postage is slick, you're gonna love Universal Parcel Insurance Coverage (U-PIC), a service that automates the post office insurance hassle. U-PIC has been in the package insurance business since 1989, mainly insuring packages for large shippers. U-PIC has expanded its business to the online auction arena, and you can insure packages that you send through USPS, UPS, FedEx, and other major carriers. If you use its insurance on USPS-shipped packages, you can save as much as 80 percent on insurance rates. If you use U-PIC, you can stop purchasing package insurance from your carriers.

The U-PIC service also enables you to print your postage through an online postage service and, if you have just a few packages, give the packages directly to your USPS mail carrier. (You don't have to stand in line to get your insurance form stamped.) If you have a ton of boxes, you'll need to drive them to the post office and shove them over the counter. No waiting in line, no hassle!

To apply for the U-PIC service, you must fill out a Request to Provide (RTP) form. Go to their Web site at www.u-pic.com and click the Apply link (see Figure 14-5). You must answer questions about who you are, how many packages you send, how many insurance claims you've filed in the past two years, and your average value per package.

Figure 14-5:
The U-PIC home page.

After you fill out the online form and agree to the policy (Evidence of Insurance), a U-PIC representative will contact you within forty-eight hours. The representative will answer your questions and help you decide which of their programs will work best for your eBay business. (I give you some details about these in just a bit.)

Your U-PIC sales representative will explain to you exactly how to declare value with U-PIC based on your present system. At the end of each shipping month, you fax, e-mail, or snail mail your shipping reports to U-PIC.

To place a claim with U-PIC on a USPS shipment, you must do so no sooner than thirty days after the date of mailing, and you must supply the following:

- ✔ A signed letter, stating the loss or damage from the consignee
- ✔ A copy of the monthly insurance report you turned in to U-PIC reflecting the insured value
- ✔ A completed U-PIC claim form (one claim form per claim)
- ✔ A copy of the original invoice or the end of auction form

Because you're paying for private insurance, U-PIC suggests that you include in the package a copy of your insurance policy (or at the very least a note explaining that you have an insurance policy covering your shipments) so that your buyer doesn't think you're overcharging (which makes some folks a bit cranky).

Table 14-2 compares USPS and U-PIC insurance rates. UPS charges $0.35 cents per $100.00 package value (after the initial $100.00). U-PIC charges only $0.14 per $100.00 UPS shipment value. FedEx charges $0.50 per $100.00 value with a $2.50 minimum. By using U-PIC, you can insure your FedEx packages for $0.20 per $100.00 value.

Table 14-2	USPS and U-PIC Domestic Insurance Coverage Rate Comparison		
Coverage	*USPS*	*U-PIC Standard*	*U-PIC with USPS Delivery Confirmation*
$0.01 to $50.00	$1.10	$0.75	$0.50
$50.01 to $100.00	$2.00	$0.75	$0.50
$100.01 to $200.00	$3.00	$1.50	$1.00
$200.01 to $300.00	$4.00	$2.25	$1.50
$300.01 to $400.00	$5.00	$3.00	$2.00

U-PIC will also insure international shipments. The cost to insure international USPS parcels is only $1.00 per $100.00, with no deductible.

If you're a high-volume shipper, you can negotiate an even lower rate with U-PIC. To reach U-PIC, call toll-free at 800-955-4623 or visit their Web site at `www.u-pic.com`.

Occasional shipper program

The occasional shipper program is for the person who ships one to five packages per month. You can pay for your insurance online using a credit card, but the rates are not as attractive as those for the standard program.

Offline standard program

The offline standard program is the service for eBay businesspeople who ship a large amount of packages per month. At the end of each shipping month, you generate an insurance report and use it to calculate your premium. You can pay the premium by check or through PayPal. You can get a discount when shipping with the post office when you use a delivery confirmation.

Part IV
Your eBay Back Office

The 5th Wave   By Rich Tennant

"I think we ought to check first to see if eBay has a category for 'Fertility gods: Ancient.'"

In this part . . .

Do you have all your licenses? You know, those silly government required things that allow you to legally run a business — or, better yet, allow you to buy at wholesale.

Setting up your eBay business as a real business entity involves some unpleasant paperwork. Applying for licenses, organizing, and record keeping are never fun. Even though you should talk to a professional, I fill in the blanks and get you started on the right track. I also provide a handy checklist of the items you need to run your business online, such as your legal status, bookkeeping requirements, and software to automate shipping.

Chapter 15

Getting Legal: Understanding Taxes and Licenses

"*L*egal business format?" you ask. "What's a legal business format?" I hate to be the one to tell you: You can't just say, "I'm in business," and be in business. When you started selling on eBay, maybe you were happy just adding a few dollars to your income. Now that the money is coming in faster, you have a few more details to attend to. Depending how far you're going to take your business, you have to worry about taxes, bookkeeping, and possible ramifications down the line.

I want to remind you that I am *not* a lawyer or an accountant. The facts I give you in this chapter are from what I've learned over the years. When you begin a formal business, it's best to involve an attorney and an Enrolled Agent or a CPA. At the very least, visit www.nolo.com, a great Web site that offers some excellent business startup advice and forms.

One of the rules in the eBay User Agreement reads ". . . you may not transfer your eBay account (including feedback) and User ID to another party *without our consent*" (emphasis mine). This means if you begin your business on eBay with another person, you'd better have some kind of agreement up front about who gets the user ID in case of a sale. And if you sell your business, the person with the original ID had best be involved actively with the new company — as the rules say, your feedback can never be transferred or sold without eBay's permission. eBay's official permission may be a long time coming or may not happen at all, and you don't want to leave these details until the last moment of signing a deal with a new owner. Otherwise, the new owner would have to start a new account on eBay with a new name — unless the principal from the old company was contractually involved and was the actual eBay member.

To my knowledge, no one has tested this rule lately, and I'll bet you don't want to be the first to face eBay's top-notch lawyers. Know that this is the rule and plan for it.

Types of Businesses

Businesses come in several legal forms, from a sole proprietorship all the way to a corporation. A corporation designation isn't as scary as it sounds. Yes, Microsoft, IBM, and eBay are corporations, but so are many individuals running businesses. Each form of business has its plusses and minuses — and costs. I go over some of the fees involved in incorporating later in this chapter. For now, I detail the most common types of businesses, which I encourage you to weigh carefully.

Before embarking on any new business format, be sure to consult with a certified professional in the legal and financial fields.

Sole proprietorship

If you're running your business by yourself part-time or full-time, your business is a *sole proprietorship*. Yep, doesn't that sound official? A sole proprietorship is the simplest form of business. Nothing is easier or cheaper. Most people use this form of business when they're starting out. Many then graduate to a more formal type of business as things get bigger.

If a husband and wife file a joint tax return, they *can* run a business as a sole proprietorship (but only one of you can be the proprietor). However, if both you and your spouse work equally in the business, running it as a partnership — with a written partnership agreement — is a much better idea. (See the next section, "Partnership," for more information.) A partnership protects you in case of your partner's death. In a sole proprietorship, the business ends with the death of the proprietor. If the business has been a sole proprietorship in your late spouse's name, you may be left out in the cold.

Being in business adds a few expenses, but you can deduct many of those expenses (relating to your business) from your state and federal taxes. A sole proprietorship *can* be run out of your personal checking account (although I don't advise it). The profits of your business are taxed directly as part of your own income tax, and the profits and expenses are reported on Schedule C of your tax package. As a sole proprietor, you're at risk for the business liabilities. All outstanding debts are yours, and you could lose personal assets if you default.

There's also the issue of Uncle Sam. When you're a sole proprietor, you are required to pay a self-employment tax, over and above your regular state and federal taxes. This tax covers the Social Security and Medicare taxes that are normally paid by your employer. Currently, the self-employment tax is 15.3% (for the first $94,200). That means the profits you make from your online enterprise get taxed additionally! Yowsers!

You *can* deduct half of your self-employment tax in figuring your adjusted gross income. This deduction affects only your income tax. It does not affect either your net earnings from self-employment or your self-employment tax. Other legal business forms can work around this scourge. For up-to-date data on this tax, visit the IRS Web site at `www.irs.gov/businesses/small/article/0,,id=98846,00.html`.

Also, you must consider the liability of the products you sell on eBay. If you sell foodstuff, vitamins, or neutraceuticals (new-age food supplements) that make someone ill, you may be personally liable for any court-awarded damages. If someone is hurt by something you sell, you may also be personally liable as the seller of the product.

Partnership

When two or more people are involved in a business, it can be a *partnership*. A general partnership can be formed by an oral agreement. Each person in the partnership contributes capital or services, and both share in the partnership's profits and losses. The income of a partnership is taxed to both partners, based on the percentage of the business that they own or upon the terms of a written agreement.

You'd better be sure that you can have a good working relationship with your partner: This type of business relationship has broken up many a friendship. Writing up a formal agreement when forming your eBay business partnership is an excellent idea. This agreement is useful in solving any disputes that may occur over time.

In your agreement, be sure to outline things such as

- ✔ Division of profits and losses
- ✔ Compensation to each of you
- ✔ Duties and responsibilities of each partner
- ✔ Restrictions of authority and spending
- ✔ How disputes should be settled
- ✔ What happens if the partnership dissolves
- ✔ What happens to the partnership in case of death or disability

One more important thing to remember: As a partner, you're jointly and severally responsible for the business liabilities and actions of the other person or people in your partnership — as well as of your own. Again, this is a personal liability arrangement. You are both personally open to any lawsuits that come your way through the business.

The partnership has to file an informational return with the IRS and the state, but the profits of the partnership are taxed to the partners on their personal individual returns.

LLC (Limited Liability Company)

A *limited liability company,* or LLC, is similar to a partnership, but also has many of the characteristics of a corporation. An LLC differs from a partnership mainly in that the liabilities of the company are not passed on to the members (owners). Unless you sign a personal guarantee for debt incurred, the members are responsible only to the total amount they have invested into the company. But all members *do* have liability for the company's taxes.

You'll need to put together an operating agreement, similar to the partnership agreement. This also will help establish which members own what percentage of the company for tax purposes. Most states will require you to file Articles of Organization forms to start this type of business.

An LLC is taxed like a sole proprietorship, with the profits and losses passed on to the members' personal tax returns. An LLC may opt to pay taxes like a corporation and keep some of the profits in the company, thereby reducing the tax burden to the individual members. Although members pay the LLCs taxes, it must still file Form 1065 with the IRS at the end of the year. This gives the IRS extra data to be sure that the individual members properly report their income.

More information on LLCs can be found on the Web site of my friend, Seattle accountant Stephen L. Nelson, CPA. He's the author of the bestselling books *QuickBooks For Dummies* and *Quicken For Dummies*. He also publishes *Do-It-Yourself Limited Liability Company: LLC Formation Kits*. Check out his informative (state-by-state) site at www.llcsexplained.com.

Corporation

A *corporation* has a life of its own: its own name, its own bank account, and its own tax return. A corporation is a legal entity created for the sole purpose of doing business. One of the main problems a sole proprietor faces when incorporating is realizing that he or she can't help themselves to the assets of the business. Yes, a corporation can have only one owner: the shareholder(s). If you can understand that you can't write yourself a check from your corporation, unless it's for salary or for reimbursement of legitimate expenses, you may be able to face the responsibility of running your own corporation.

The full brunt of that nasty self-employment tax on income doesn't rear its ugly head when you have a corporation. Because you become an employee of your corporation, you pay yourself a salary. The Medicare and Social Security taxes (approximately 15%) are paid only on the part of your profit that you call wages. Niiiice.

You have your choice of either a C or an S corporation. They each have different tax situations. An S corporation enables you to treat profits as distributions and pass them directly to your personal tax return. The C corporation files its own returns and treats you like an employee. This is a pretty tricky area and I suggest you consult with a professional before making a decision on which type of corporation to form.

The state in which you run your business sets up the rules for the corporations operating within its borders. You must apply to the Secretary of State for the state in which you want to incorporate. Federal taxes for corporations presently range from 15 to 35 percent, and they're generally based on your net profits. Often employee owners of corporations use the company to shelter income from tax by dividing the income between their personal and corporate tax returns. This is frequently called *income splitting* and involves setting salaries and bonuses so that any profits left in the company at the end of its tax year will be taxed at only the 15 percent rate. It's kind of fun to see how much the big guys pay and how much you'll pay in taxes if you leave profits in a small corporation, so check out Table 15-1 for the rates.

Table 15-1	Federal Tax Rates through 2007 for C Corporations
Taxable Income	**Tax Rate**
$0 to $50,000	15%
$50,001 to $75,000	25%
$75,001 to $100,000	34%
$100,001 to $335,000	39%
$335,001 to $10,000,000	34%
$10,000,001 to $15,000,000	35%
$15,000,001 to $18,333,333	38%
$18,333,334 and over	35%

Getting your legal documents prepared online

You just *knew* legal services would go online eventually, didn't you? If you're thinking of setting up one of the business formats described in this chapter, you might be interested in putting things together online. Real lawyers are there to help you. A new venture, `www.legalzoom.com`, will handle legal document preparation for business incorporation, partnerships, and more for incredibly low prices. This online venture was developed by a group of experienced attorneys, cofounded by Robert Shapiro (yes, *that* Robert Shapiro — of O.J. fame).

They feature an amazing online law library that can answer many of your questions and help you make informed decisions. Documents are prepared according to how you answer online questionnaires, which are designed to cover most legal transactions. LegalZoom checks your work and then e-mails your documents or mails them printed on quality acid-free paper for your signature.

You may want to also do at least a phone consultation with an attorney in your area, perhaps one who is a member of the local Chamber of Commerce.

Often in small corporations, most of the profits are paid out in tax-deductible wages and benefits. The most important benefit for a business is that any liabilities belong to the corporation. Your personal assets remain your own, because they have no part in the corporation.

Taking Care of Regulatory Details

Let me give you some important words to make your life easier in the long run: Don't ignore city, county, state, and federal regulatory details. Doing so may make life easier at the get-go, but if your business is successful, one day your casual attitude will catch up with you. Ignorance is no excuse. To do business in this great country, you must comply with all the rules and regulations that are set up for your protection and benefit.

Fictitious business name statement

If you plan on running your business under a name different from your own, you may have to file a *fictitious name statement* regardless of the legal format of your business. Your fictitious name (or *DBA, doing business as*) is the name under which the government and the general public know your business. In most states, every person who regularly transacts business for profit under a fictitious business name must file. Depending on where you live, you generally file this form with the county clerk. You can run a Google search for your county's clerk office to find out the exact procedures and fees for your area.

After a certain length of time after you file, your fictitious name will be published in a newspaper that has a section of fictitious names in its classified section. Usually the newspaper files with county agencies and publishes for you in one procedure.

If you have a small community or neighborhood newspaper, check with it to see whether it files fictitious name statements or DBAs. These newspapers also have the lowdown on all the licenses and certificates that you'll need for your locality. Choosing small newspapers to handle these issues for you is a smart idea because they tend to charge a lot less than big-city dailies. Plus, you get to help another small business in your area.

Business license or city tax certificate

Business licenses are the official-looking pieces of paper you see behind the register at local stores. Every business must have one, and depending on your local laws, you may have to have a *city license* or a *city tax registration certificate*. Yes, even if you're running a business out of your home and have no one coming to do business at your home, you may still need this. If you don't have one, the authorities may charge you a bunch of penalties if they ever find out. Avoiding this step isn't worth the risk.

To save you hanging on the phone, listening to elevator music, and being transferred and disconnected ad nauseam, I'm supplying you with the direct links to apply for your licenses (see Table 15-2). These URLs are accurate at the time of this writing, but as everybody knows, URLs change frequently. Check the following for updates:

```
www.sba.gov/hotlist/license.html
```

Table 15-2	Web Sites for Business License Information
State	*URL*
Alabama	www.ador.state.al.us/licenses/index.html
Alaska	http://www.state.ak.us/local/bus1.html www.dced.state.ak.us/occ/home.htm

(continued)

Table 15-2 *(continued)*

State	URL
Arizona	www.aztaxes.gov/default.aspx
Arkansas	www.arkansas.gov/dfa/income_tax/tax_guide_overview.html
California	www.calgold.ca.gov/
Colorado	www.advancecolorado.com/small-business/index.cfm
Connecticut	www.ct-clic.com
Delaware	www.delaware.gov/egov/portal.nsf/CategoryPages/Business--Start-Up
District of Columbia	brc.dc.gov/licenses/licenses.asp
Florida	www.stateofflorida.com/portal/desktopdefault.aspx?tabid=8
Georgia	www.sos.state.ga.us/firststop
Guam	www.admin.gov.gu
Hawaii	www.hawaii.gov/portal/business/all.html
Idaho	http://business.idaho.gov/
Illinois	business.illinois.gov/step_by_step_guides.cfm
Indiana	www.state.in.us/sic/owners/ia.html
Iowa	www.sos.state.ia.us/business/buslicenseinfo.html
Kansas	www.ksrevenue.org/busregistration.htm
Kentucky	www.thinkkentucky.com/
Louisiana	www.sec.state.la.us/comm/fss/fss-index.htm
Maine	www.maine.gov/portal/business/licensing.html
Maryland	www.blis.state.md.us/BusinessStartup.aspx

State	URL
Massachusetts	www.mass.gov/?pageID=dorhomepage&L=1&L0=Home&sid=Ador
Michigan	www.michigan.gov/businessstartup
Minnesota	www.deed.state.mn.us/bizdev/license.htm http://www.dted.state.mn.us/01x00f.asp
Mississippi	www.olemiss.edu/depts/mssbdc/going_intobus.html
Missouri	www.missouribusiness.net/startup/
Montana	http://mt.gov/business.asp
Nebraska	www.nebraska.gov/howdoi.php
Nevada	www.nv.gov/FAQ.htm
New Hampshire	www.revenue.nh.gov/business/dra_licenses.htm
New Jersey	www.state.nj.us/njbusiness/index.shtml
New Mexico	www.nj.gov/njbusiness/license/
New York	www.tax.state.ny.us/sbc/starting_business.htm
North Carolina	http://www.secretary.state.nc.us/blio/default.asp www.nccommerce.com/servicenter/blio/startup/
North Dakota	www.nd.gov/businessreg/license/index.html
Ohio	www.odod.state.oh.us/onestop/index.cfm
Oklahoma	www.okcommerce.gov/
Oregon	www.filinginoregon.com/obg/index.htm
Pennsylvania	www.paopenforbusiness.state.pa.us
Rhode Island	www2.sec.state.ri.us/faststart/
South Carolina	sc.gov/Portal/Category/BUSINESS_TOP
South Dakota	www.state.sd.us/drr2/newbusiness.htm

(continued)

Table 15-2 *(continued)*

Tennessee	`www.tennesseeanytime.org/online/` `#biz_license`
Texas	`www.governor.state.tx.us/ecodev/` `sba/guide`
Utah	`www.utah.gov/business/starting.html`
Vermont	`www.thinkvermont.com/start/`
Virgin Islands	`www.dlca.gov.vi/blsteps.htm`
Virginia	`http://www.dba.state.va.us/launchpad/` `www.dba.state.va.us/licenses/`
Washington	`www.dol.wa.gov/business/licensing.html`
West Virginia	`www.state.wv.us/taxrev/busreg.html`
Wisconsin	`www.wisconsin.gov/state/byb/`
Wyoming	`uwadmnweb.uwyo.edu/SBDC/starting.htm`

Sales tax number

If your state has a sales tax, a *sales tax number* (the number you use when you file your sales tax statement with your state) is required before you officially sell anything. If sales tax applies, you may have to collect the appropriate sales tax for every sale that ships within the state that your business is in.

Some people also call this a *resale certificate* because when you want to purchase goods from a wholesaler within your state, you must produce this number (thereby certifying your legitimacy) so that the dealer can sell you the merchandise without charging you sales tax.

To find the regulations for your state, try the following terrific site, which should have the answers to your questions: `www.taxadmin.org/fta/` `link/forms.html`.

Don't withhold the withholding forms

Aye, caramba. I swear it feels like the rules and regulations are never going to end, but if you have regular employees, you need to file *withholding forms* to collect the necessary taxes that you must send to the state and the IRS on behalf of your employees. You're also expected to deposit those tax dollars with the IRS and your state on the date required, which may vary from business to business. Many enterprises go down because the owners just can't seem to keep their fingers out of withheld taxes, which means the money isn't available to turn in when the taxes are due (another reason why you should have a separate bank account for your business).

If you have employees, you probably need to get the following:

- **Federal Employee Tax ID number:** File IRS form SS-4. You can apply for this number online, by going to the following:

  ```
  www.irs.gov/businesses/small/article/0,,id=102767,
       00.html
  ```

  For more information, call 1-800-829-1040. For forms to fill out the old-fashioned way, call 1-800-829-3676.

- **State Employer number:** You need this for withholding taxes if your state has an income tax. Check the following site for more information:

  ```
  www.taxadmin.org/fta/forms.ssi
  ```

Chapter 16

Savvy Record Keeping — Keeping the Tax Man at Bay

. . . .

In This Chapter

▶ Understanding first things first: Bookkeeping basics

▶ Saving your records to save your bacon

▶ Finding bookkeeping software

▶ Using QuickBooks for your bookkeeping needs

. . . .

*B*ookkeeping, *bah!* You'll get no argument from me that bookkeeping can be the most dreaded and time-consuming part of your job. You may feel that you just need to add your product costs, add your gross sales, and bada-bing, you know where your business is. Sorry, not true. Did you add that roll of tape you picked up at the supermarket today? Although it cost only $1.29, it's a business expense. How about the mileage driving back and forth from garage sales and flea markets? Those are expenses, too. I suspect that you're also not counting quite a few other "small" items just like these in your expense column.

Once I actually get into the task, I must confess that I enjoy posting my expenses and sales. It gives me the opportunity to know exactly where my business is at any given moment. Of course, I'm not using a pencil-and-paper ledger system; I use a software program that's easy enough. In this chapter, I give you the lowdown on the basics of bookkeeping, emphasize the importance of keeping records in case Uncle Sam comes calling, and explain why using QuickBooks is the smart software choice. Keep reading: This chapter is *required*.

Keeping the Books: Basics That Get You Started

Although posting bookkeeping can be boring, clicking a button to generate your tax information is a lot easier than manually going over pages of sales information on a pad of paper. That's why I like to use a software program, particularly QuickBooks (more about that in the section titled "QuickBooks: Making Bookkeeping Uncomplicated").

I suppose that you *could* use plain ol' paper and a pencil to keep your books; if that works for you, great. But even though that might work for you now, it definitely won't in the future. Entering all your information into a software program now — while your books may still be fairly simple to handle — can save you a lot of time and frustration in the future, when your eBay business has grown beyond your wildest dreams and no amount of paper can keep it all straight and organized. I discuss alternative methods of bookkeeping in the "Bookkeeping Software" section. For now, I focus on the basics of bookkeeping.

To effectively manage your business, you must keep track of *all* your expenses — down to the last roll of tape. You need to keep track of your inventory, how much you paid for the items, how much you paid in shipping, and how much you profited from your sales. If you use a van or the family car to pick up or deliver merchandise to the post office (I can load eight of the light kits that I sell on eBay in my car), you should keep track of this mileage as well. When you're running a business, you should account for every penny that goes in and out.

Bookkeeping has irrefutable standards called GAAP (Generally Accepted Accounting Procedures) that are set by the Financial Accounting Standards Board. (It sounds scary to me too.) Assets, liabilities, owner's equity, income, and expenses are standard terms used in all forms of accounting to define profit, loss, and the fiscal health of your business.

Every time you process a transaction, two things happen: One account is credited while another receives a debit (kind of like yin and yang). To get more familiar with these terms (and those in the following list), see the definitions in the chart of accounts later in this chapter (in Table 16-2) and in Appendix A (a mini-glossary I've included for your convenience). Depending on the type of account, the account's balance either increases or decreases.

Hiring a professional to do your year-end taxes

When I say that you must hire a professional to prepare your taxes, I mean a certified public accountant (CPA), if your business format is a corporation, or an enrolled agent (EA), for a sole proprietorship or partnership. An *enrolled agent* is a tax professional who's licensed by the Federal government and specializes solely in taxation and current tax laws. Enrolled agents must pass an annual two-day exam (less than a third of the people who take the test pass it) and are required to fulfill continuing education requirements to maintain their standing. Just like a CPA or a tax attorney, EAs are authorized to appear before the IRS on your behalf in the event of an audit. Unlike a CPA or an attorney, however, EAs don't charge an arm and a leg. They're a valuable addition to your business arsenal.

Although the folks at your local "We Do Your Taxes in a Hurry Store" may be well meaning and pleasant, they may have gone through only a six-week course in the current tax laws. This does not make them tax professionals. When business taxes are at stake, a professional with whom you have a standing relationship is the best choice. If you don't know one, ask around or call your local Chamber of Commerce.

Posting bookkeeping can be boring. At the end of the year when you have a professional do your taxes, however, you'll be a lot happier — and your tax preparation will cost you less — if you've posted your information cleanly and in the proper order. That's why using QuickBooks is essential to running your business. (See the "QuickBooks: Making Bookkeeping Uncomplicated" section.)

One account that increases while another decreases is called *double entry accounting:*

- ✔ When you post an expense, the debit *increases* your expenses and *decreases* your bank account.

- ✔ When you purchase furniture or other assets, it *increases* your asset account and *decreases* your bank account.

- ✔ When you make a sale and make the deposit, it *increases* your bank account and *decreases* your accounts receivable.

- ✔ When you purchase inventory, it *increases* your inventory and *decreases* your bank account.

- ✔ When a portion of a sale includes sales tax, it *decreases* your sales account, and *increases* your sales tax account.

Manually performing double-entry accounting can be a bit taxing (no pun intended). A software program automatically adjusts the accounts when you input a transaction.

As a business owner, even if you're a sole proprietor (see Chapter 15 for information on business types), you should keep your business books separate from your personal expenses. (I recommend using a program such as Quicken to keep track of your *personal* expenses for tax time.) By isolating the business records from the personal records, you can get a snapshot of what areas of your sales are doing well and which ones aren't carrying their weight. But that isn't the only reason keeping accurate records is smart; there's the IRS to think about, too. In the next section, I explain Uncle Sam's interest in your books.

Records Uncle Sam May Want to See

One of the reasons we can have a great business environment in the United States is because we all have a partner, Uncle Sam. Our government regulates business and sets the rules for us to transact our operations. To help you get started with your business, the IRS maintains a small-business Web site at www.irs.gov/businesses/small.

In this section, I highlight what information you need to keep and how long you should keep it (just in case you're chosen for an audit).

Supporting information

Aside from needing to know how your business is going (which is really important), the main reason to keep clear and concise records is because Uncle Sam may come knocking one day. You never know when the IRS will choose *your* number and want to examine *your* records. In the following list, I highlight some of the important pieces of *supporting information* (things that support your expenses on your end-of-year tax return):

✔ **Receipts:** Dear reader, heed this advice: Save every receipt that you get. If you're out of town on a buying trip and have coffee at the airport, save that receipt — it's a deduction from your profits. Everything related to your business may be deductible, so you must save airport parking receipts, taxi receipts, receipts for a pen that you picked up on your way to a meeting, *everything*. If you don't have a receipt, you can't prove the write-off.

- **Merchandise invoices:** Saving all merchandise invoices is as important as saving all your receipts. If you want to prove that you paid $400 and not the $299 retail price for that Nintendo Wii that you sold on eBay for $500, you'd *better* have an invoice of some kind. The same idea applies to most collectibles, in which case a retail price can't be fixed. Save all invoices!

- **Outside contractor invoices:** If you use outside contractors — even if you pay the college kid next door to go to the post office and bank for you — you should also get an invoice from them to document exactly what service you paid for and how much you paid. This is supporting information that will save your bacon, should it ever need saving.

- **Business cards:** It may sound like I'm stretching things a bit, but if you use your car to look at some merchandise, pick up a business card from the vendor. If you're out of town and have a meeting with someone, take a card. Having these business cards can help substantiate your deductible comings and goings.

- **A daily calendar:** This is where your handheld comes in. Every time you leave your house or office on a business-related task, make note of it in your handheld. Keep as much minutia as you can stand. A Palm Desktop can print a monthly calendar. At the end of the year, staple the pages together and include them in your files with your substantiating information.

- **Credit card statements:** You're already collecting credit card receipts (although mine always seem to slip through the holes in my purse). If you have your statements, you have monthly proof of expenses. When you get your statement each month, post it into your bookkeeping program and itemize each and every charge, detailing where you spent the money and for what. (QuickBooks has a split feature that accommodates all your categories.) File these statements with your tax return at the end of the year in your year-end envelope (shoe box?).

I know that all this stuff will pile up, but that's when you go to the store and buy some plastic file storage containers to organize it all. To check for new information and the lowdown on what you can and can't do, ask an accountant or a CPA. Also visit the IRS Tax Information for Business site at www.irs.ustreas.gov/businesses.

How long should you keep your records?

How long do you have to keep all this supporting information? I hate to tell you, but I think I've saved it all. I must have at least ten years of paperwork in big plastic boxes and old files in the garage. But you know, I'm not too extreme;

the period in which you can amend a return or in which the IRS can assess more tax is never less than three years from the date of filing — and can even be longer. As of my last visit to the IRS Web site, the information in Table 16-1 applied.

Table 16-1	How Long to Keep Your Tax Records
Circumstance	*Keep Records This Long*
You owe additional tax (if the following three points don't apply)	3 years
You didn't report all your income and what you didn't report is more than 25% of the gross income shown on your return	6 years
You file a fraudulent tax return	No limit
You don't bother to file a return	No limit
You file a claim of refund or credit after you've filed	3 years or 2 years after tax was paid (whichever is longer)
Your claim is due to a bad debt deduction	7 years
Your claim is from worthless stock	7 years
You have information on assets	Life of the asset

Even though I got this information directly from the IRS Web site and literature (Publication 583, "Starting a Business and Keeping Records"), it may change in the future. You can download a PDF copy of the booklet by going to www.irs.gov/pub/irs-pdf/p583.pdf. (The download requires Adobe Acrobat Reader. If it isn't installed on your computer, you can download the software for free from the IRS Web site.) It doesn't hurt to store your information for as long as you can stand it and stay on top of any changes the IRS may implement.

Bookkeeping Software

Keeping track of your auctions is hard without software, but keeping track of the money you make without software is even harder (and more time consuming). If using software to automate your auctions makes sense, so does using software to automate your bookkeeping. You can afford to make a mistake here and there in your own office, and no one will ever know. But if you make a mistake in the books, your partner (Uncle Sam) will notice — and be quite miffed. He may even charge you a penalty or two so that you'll remember not to make those mistakes again.

Those penalties aren't small either. A three-day-late tax deposit will cost you an additional 10 percent tax penalty. That can be an expensive lesson.

When I started my business, I used accounting ledger pads (which had just replaced the chisel and stone format). I soon found that I had way too many ledgers to keep track of and cross reference. A calculator was useful, based on the assumption that I typed the correct figures to start with.

Spreadsheet software can be a boon when you're just starting out. A program such as Microsoft Office Excel is an excellent way to begin posting your business expenses and profits. The program can be set up to calculate your expenses, profits, and (I hope not too many) losses. Microsoft Works comes with several free financial worksheet templates that you can easily adapt for an eBay small business. Also, you can find current Excel templates to get you started at office.microsoft.com. There's no need to spend any extra money on templates when you're first starting!

With official bookkeeping software, reconciling a checkbook is a breeze. You merely click off the deposits and checks when the statement comes in. If I made a mistake originally when inputting the data, the software (comparing my balance and my bank's) lets me know. This kind of efficiency would have put Bob Cratchit out of a job!

I researched various Web sites to find which software was the best selling and easiest to use. I had many discussions with CPAs, enrolled agents, and bookkeepers. The software that these professionals most recommend for business is Intuit's QuickBooks. (Thank goodness that's the one I use.) QuickBooks is considered the best, which is why I devote so much of this chapter to it. Some people begin with Quicken and later move to QuickBooks when their business gets big or incorporates. My theory? Start with the best. It's not that much more expensive — on eBay, I've seen new, sealed QuickBooks Pro 2007 software for as low as $135 and QuickBooks for as low as $65 — and it will see you directly to the big time.

QuickBooks: Making Bookkeeping Uncomplicated

QuickBooks offers several versions, from basic to enterprise solutions tailored to different types of businesses. QuickBooks Simple Start and QuickBooks Pro have a few significant differences. QuickBooks Pro adds job costing and expensing features, payroll, and the ability to keep track of your inventory through your sales receipts and purchases (making it a sound upgrade for eBay sellers). QuickBooks Simple Start does a darn good job too, so check out the comparison at `quickbooks.intuit.com` and see which version is best for you. I use (and highly recommend) QuickBooks Pro, so that's the version I describe in the rest of this section.

Stephen L. Nelson wrote *QuickBooks 2007 For Dummies* (published by Wiley). His book is amazingly easy to understand. I swear that neither Steve nor my publisher gave me a nickel for recommending his book. (Heck, I even had to pay for my copy.) I recommend it simply because it answers — in plain English — just about any question you'll have about using the program for your bookkeeping needs. Spend the money and get the book. Any money spent on increasing your knowledge is money well spent (and may be a tax write-off).

I update my QuickBooks software yearly, and every year it takes me less time to perform my bookkeeping tasks (because of product improvements). If you find that you don't have time to input your bookkeeping data, you may have to hire a bookkeeper. The bonus is that professional bookkeepers already know QuickBooks, and the best part is that they can print weekly reports for you that keep you apprised of your business condition. Also, at the end of each year, QuickBooks will supply you with *all* the official reports and data your enrolled agent or certified public accountant will need to do your taxes. (Yes, you really do need an EA or a CPA; see the "Hiring a professional to do your year-end taxes" sidebar elsewhere in this chapter.) You can even send them a backup on a zip disk or a CD-ROM. See how simple bookkeeping can be?

QuickBooks integrates with PayPal

PayPal can provide your payment history in QuickBooks format. They even offer a settlement and reconciliation system download that breaks up your PayPal transactions into debits and credits. A handy feature! One warning though: These are only financial transactions. When you use QuickBooks to its fullest, you will have your inventory in the program. When you purchase merchandise to sell, QuickBooks sets up the inventory — and deducts from it each time you input an invoice or a sales receipt. This way your inventory receipts follow GAAP. In my books, *eBay Timesaving Techniques For Dummies* and *eBay PowerSeller Practices For Dummies,* I show you my procedures for posting your weekly (or daily) sales in QuickBooks by using sales receipts versus clogging up your program with thousands of customer listings. Which, by the way, received an approving nod from Stephen Nelson when I showed him my system.

QuickBooks Pro

When you first fire up QuickBooks Pro, you must first answer a few questions to set up your account. Among the few things you need to have ready before you even begin to mess with the software are the following starting figures:

- ✓ **Cash balance:** This may be the amount in your checking account (no personal money, please!) or the amount of money deposited from your eBay profits. Put these profits into a separate checking account to use for your business.

- ✓ **Accounts receivable balance:** Does anyone owe you money for some auctions? Outstanding payments make up this total.

- ✓ **Account liability balance:** Do you owe some money? Are you being invoiced for some merchandise that you haven't paid for? Total it and enter it when QuickBooks asks you.

If you're starting your business in the middle of the year, gather any previous profits and expenses that you want to include, because you'll have to input this information for a complete annual set of diligently recorded books. I can guarantee that this is going to take a while. But after you've gathered together your finances, even if it takes a little sweat to set it up initially, you'll be thanking me for insisting you get organized. It just makes everything work smoother in the long run.

Firing up QuickBooks for the first time

The first thing you need to do is organize finances. Put all your expenses in one folder and sales information in another, and then you can proceed with the QuickBooks setup interview. The interview is designed to give those with accounting-phobia and those using a bookkeeping program for the first time a comfort level.

QuickBooks asks you questions about your business and you fill in the very intuitive form. If you mess things up, you can always use the back arrow and change what you've input. If you need help, simply click the Help button and the program will answer many of your questions. Hey, if worse comes to worst, you can always delete the file from the QuickBooks directory and start over.

If you're new to bookkeeping, you may want to go through the QuickBooks startup interview step by step with a tutor at your side. For more details, remember to check out *QuickBooks 2007 For Dummies* — this book can teach you almost everything you need to know about QuickBooks.

Learning about COGS

No, no, I'm not talking about Cogswell's Cogs (the company that George Jetson worked for); I'm talking about Cost of Goods Sold. It's a special type of expense and often varies depending on the type of business. The general definition of COGS reflects the cost of purchasing raw materials and manufacturing finished products. Some accountants look at it slightly differently in an eBay business: encompassing credit card (PayPal) fees, eBay fees, and shipping costs, making it include all direct costs of products sold and shipped to customers.

I like it this way, because in the financial profit & loss statement, QuickBooks lists COGS ahead of other expense accounts. This gives me a snapshot view of the sales profitability of my eBay business without clouding things by including telephone, payroll, travel, and all the other expenses that affect the gross profits.

QuickBooks chart of accounts

After you've finished the setup and have successfully set yourself up in QuickBooks, the program presents a chart of accounts. Think of the *chart of accounts* as an organization system, such as file folders. It keeps all related data in the proper area. When you write a check to pay a bill, it deducts the amount from your checking account, reduces your accounts payable, and perhaps increases your asset or expense accounts.

You have a choice of giving each account a number. These numbers, a kind of bookkeeping shorthand, are standardized throughout bookkeeping; believe it or not, everybody in the industry seems to know what number goes with what item. To keep things less confusing, I like to use titles as well as numbers.

To customize your chart of accounts, follow these steps:

1. **Choose Edit⇨Preferences.**
2. **Click the Accounting icon (on the left).**
3. **Click the Company preferences tab and indicate that you'd like to use account numbers.**

   An editable chart of accounts appears. Because QuickBooks doesn't assign account numbers as a default, you'll need to edit the chart to create them.
4. **Go through your QuickBooks chart of accounts and add any missing categories.**

   You may not need all these categories, and you can always add more later. In Table 16-2, I show you a chart of accounts that a CPA wrote for an eBay business.

Table 16-2	eBay Business Chart of Accounts	
Account Number	**Account Name**	**What It Represents**
1001	Checking	All revenue deposited here and all checks drawn upon this account
1002	Money market account	Company savings account
1100	Accounts receivable	For customers to whom you extend credit
1201	Merchandise	COGS: Charge to cost of sales as used, or take periodic inventories and adjust at that time
1202	Shipping supplies	Boxes, tape, labels, and so forth; charge these to cost as used or take an inventory at the end of the period and adjust to cost of sales
1401	Office furniture & equipment	Desk, computer, telephone
1402	Shipping equipment	Scales, tape dispensers
1403	Vehicles	Your vehicle if it's owned by the company
1501	Accumulated depreciation	For your accountant's use
1601	Deposits	Security deposits on leases
2001	Accounts payable	Amounts owed for the stuff you sell, or charged expenses
2100	Payroll liabilities	Taxes deducted from employees' checks and taxes paid by the company on employee earnings
2200	Sales tax payable	Sales tax collected at time of sale and owed to the state
2501	Equipment loans	Money borrowed to buy a computer or other equipment
2502	Auto loans	When you get that hot new van for visiting your consignment clients
3000	Owner's capital	Your opening balance
3902	Owner's draw	Your withdrawals for the current year

(continued)

Table 16-2 *(continued)*

Account Number	Account Name	What It Represents
4001	Merchandise sales	Revenue from sales of your products
4002	Shipping and handling	Paid by the customer
4009	Returns	Total dollar amount of returned merchandise
4101	Interest income	From your investments
4201	Other income	Income not otherwise classified
5001	Merchandise purchases	All the merchandise you buy for eBay; you'll probably use subaccounts for individual items
5002	Freight in	Freight and shipping charges you pay for your inventory, not for shipments to customers
5003	Shipping	COGS: Shipping to your customers: USPS, FedEx, UPS, and so on
5004	Shipping supplies	COGS: Boxes, labels, tape, bubble pack
6110	Automobile expense	When you use your car for work
6111	Gas and oil	Filling up the tank!
6112	Repairs	When your business owns the car
6120	Bank service charges	Monthly service charges, NSF charges, and so forth
6140	Contributions	Charity
6142	Data services	Do you have an outside firm processing your payroll?
6143	Internet service provider	What you pay to your Internet provider
6144	Web site hosting fees	Fees paid to your hosting company
6150	Depreciation expense	For your accountant's use
6151	eBay fees	COGS: What you pay eBay every time you list an item and make a sale

Account Number	Account Name	What It Represents
6152	Discounts	Fees you're charged for using eBay and accepting credit card payments; deducted from your revenue and reported to you on your eBay statement
6153	Other auction site fees	COGS: You may want to set up subcategories for each site where you do business, such as Yahoo! or Amazon.com
6156	PayPal fees	COGS: Processing fees paid to PayPal
6158	Credit card merchant account fees	COGS: If you have a separate merchant account, post those fees here
6160	Dues	If you join an organization that charges membership fees (relating to your business)
6161	Magazines and periodicals	Books and magazines that help you run and expand your business
6170	Equipment rental	Postage meter, occasional van
6180	Insurance	Policies that cover your merchandise or your office
6185	Liability insurance	Insurance that covers you if someone slips and falls at your place of business (can also be put under Insurance)
6190	Disability insurance	Insurance that will pay you if you become temporarily or permanently disabled and can't perform your work
6191	Health insurance	If provided for yourself, you may be required to provide it to employees
6200	Interest expense	Credit interest and interest on loans
6220	Loan interest	When you borrow from the bank
6230	Licenses and permits	State and city licenses
6240	Miscellaneous	Whatever doesn't go anyplace else
6250	Postage and delivery	Stamps used in your regular business
6251	Endicia.com fees	COGS: Fees for your eBay business postage service

(continued)

Table 16-2 *(continued)*

Account Number	Account Name	What It Represents
6260	Printing	Your business cards, correspondence stationery, and so on
6265	Filing fees	Fees paid to file legal documents
6270	Professional fees	Fees paid to consultants
6280	Legal fees	If you have to pay a lawyer
6650	Accounting and bookkeeping	Bookkeeper, CAP, or EA
6290	Rent	Office, warehouse, and so on
6300	Repairs	Can be the major category for the following subcategories
6310	Building repairs	Repairs to the building where you operate your business
6320	Computer repairs	What you pay the person who sets up your wireless network
6330	Equipment repairs	When the copier or phone needs fixing
6340	Telephone	Regular telephone, FAX lines
6350	Travel and entertainment	Business-related travel, business meals
6360	Entertainment	When you take eBay's CEO out to dinner to benefit your eBay business
6370	Meals	Meals while traveling for your business
6390	Utilities	Major heading for the following subcategories
6391	Electricity and gas	Electricity and gas
6392	Water	Water
6560	Payroll expenses	Wages paid to others
6770	Supplies	Office supplies
6772	Computer	Computer and supplies

Account Number	Account Name	What It Represents
6780	Marketing	Advertising or promotional items you purchase to give away
6790	Office	Miscellaneous office expenses, such as bottled water delivery
6820	Taxes	Major category for the following subcategories
6830	Federal	Federal taxes
6840	Local	Local taxes
6850	Property	Property taxes
6860	State	State taxes

QuickBooks on the Web

If you want to handle everything on the Web, use QuickBooks online service. The online QuickBooks program offers fewer features than the Pro version, but if your accounting needs are simple, it may be right for you. Before you decide, however, consider that while your accounting needs may be simple now, they may not be so simple later.

Intuit charges from $19.95 a month for the service, which is comparable to buying the QuickBooks Pro version — but at least you can continue to use purchased software for more than one year. The online version also requires you to have a broadband connection to the Internet so that you're always online (dial-up connections need not apply). The online edition doesn't include integrated payroll, purchase orders, online banking, and bill payments.

Chapter 17

Building an eBay Back Office

· ·

In This Chapter

▶ Organizing your stock

▶ Keeping inventory

▶ Exploring shipping materials

▶ Becoming your own post office

· ·

*T*he more items you sell, the more confusing things can get. As you build your eBay business, the little side table you use for storing eBay merchandise isn't going to work. You must think industrial. Even part-time sellers can benefit by adding a few professional touches to their business areas.

In this chapter, I emphasize the importance of setting up and organizing your back office. Organization will save you huge amounts of time when it comes to fulfilling your orders. I cover everything from stacking your stock to keeping inventory to indispensable packing materials and online postage services. Organization will be your byword. Dive right in. The sooner you read this chapter, the sooner you can build your eBay back office and get down to business.

The Warehouse: Organizing Your Space

Whether you plan to sell large items or small items, you need space for storing them. As you make savvy purchases, maintaining an item's mint condition will be one of your greatest challenges. Organized storage is an art in itself, so in this section I cover the details of what you'll need to safeguard your precious stock.

Shelving your profits

Before you stock the shelves, it helps to have some! You also need a place to put the shelves: your garage, a spare room, or somewhere else. You have a choice between two basic kinds of shelves:

- ✔ **Plastic:** If you're just starting out, you can always go to the local closet and linen supply store to buy inexpensive plastic shelves. They're light and cheap — but they'll buckle in time, rendering them useless.

- ✔ **Steel:** If you want to do it right the first time, buy steel shelving. The most versatile steel shelving is the wire kind (versus solid-steel shelves), which is lighter and allows air to circulate around your items. Steel wire shelving assembles easily; I put mine together without help. They come with leveling feet or four-inch casters, so you can move the unit, if necessary. Installing the casters is up to you. You can combine steel wire shelving units to create a full wall of shelves. Each shelf safely holds as much as 500 pounds of merchandise.

Search eBay for **shelving** to find sellers offering this kind of industrial shelving. The main problem with ordering this product online is that the shipping usually costs more than the shelving.

To save you time, dear reader, I researched the subject and found some readily available, reasonably priced shelves. Just go to Target or Costco and look for steel wire four-shelf commercial shelving, sold in 36- and 48-inch-wide units. Each shelf will hold up to 500 pounds. These shelves are available also on the Costco Web site, but you have to pay for shipping.

Box 'em or bag 'em?

Packing your items for storage can be a challenge. As long as you're picking up your shelving (see preceding section), pick up some plastic bags in snack, sandwich, quart, and gallon sizes. The snack baggies are perfect for storing the smallest of items. When items are stored in plastic, they can't pick up any smells or become musty before you sell them. The plastic also protects the items from rubbing against each other and causing possible scratches. If you package them one item to a bag, you can then just lift one off the shelf and put it directly into a shipping box when the sale is made. Also, when you ship the item, the plastic protection may save the package from a rainy day.

Your bags of items will have to go into boxes for storage on the shelves. Clear plastic storage boxes, the kind you often find at superstores, are great for bulky items. They're usually 26 inches, so before you buy these big plastic containers, be sure that they'll fit on your shelving easily and that you'll have easy access to your items. Using cardboard office-type file storage boxes from an office supply store is another option. These cardboard boxes are 10 x 12 x 16 inches, which is a nice size for storing medium-size products. At around $1 each, they're the most economical choice. The downside is that you can't see through cardboard boxes, so if your label falls off, you have to take the box off the shelf and open it to check its contents. Smaller see-through plastic boxes with various compartments, such as the kind home improvement stores carry for storing tools, work great for storing very small items.

When using these large plastic bins, it's always a good idea to tape a pad of Post-it notes on the end of the box so you can quickly identify the contents. You *can* use regular sticky labels, but changing them will leave large amounts of paper residue over time, and your storage will look sloppy and icky.

Inventory: Keeping Track of What You Have and Where You Keep It

Savvy eBay sellers have different methods of handling inventory. They use everything from spiral-bound notebooks to sophisticated software programs. Although computerized inventory tracking can simplify this task, starting with a plain ol' handwritten ledger is fine, too. Choose whichever works best for you, but keep in mind that as your eBay business grows, a software program that tracks inventory for you may become necessary. If you use QuickBooks for your bookkeeping, this all-in-one software will also keep track of your inventory (every time you post your purchases and sales).

Ledger systems wouldn't work for a company with a warehouse full of stock, but will work nicely in a beginning eBay sales environment. Many sellers tape sheets of paper to their boxes to identify them by number, and use that as a reference to a simple Excel spreadsheet for selling purposes. Excel spreadsheets are perfect for keeping track of your sales as well, but if you're using a management service or software, you don't need both for physical inventory. After you're running a real business, however, you have to keep Uncle Sam happy with a dollars and cents accounting of your inventory, so keep your inventory records in a standardized program such as QuickBooks (discussed in Chapter 16). In Chapter 9, I detail a variety of auction management software and Web sites, many of which include physical inventory tracking features.

Planning: The key to good organization

When it became time for me to put my eBay merchandise in order, I was busy with my regular job, so I hired people to organize my eBay area. This decision turned out to be one massive mistake. They organized everything and put all my items in boxes — but didn't label the boxes to indicate what was stored in each. The boxes also weren't placed in an intuitive manner for me to quickly assemble my packages. It took me months to recover.

A bit of advice: Think things out and plan where you'll put everything. Organize your items by theme, type, or size. In my eBay business area, I have books in one area, DVDs in another, photographic equipment on shelves, and so on. If you organize before planning, you might end up with organized disorganization.

You may also want to use Excel spreadsheets for your downloaded PayPal statements, to hold information waiting to transfer to your bookkeeping program, or merely for archival purposes at the end of the year.

The Shipping Department: Packin' It Up

If you've read *eBay For Dummies,* you know all about the various ways to pack your items. I hope you've become an expert! In this section, I review some of the things you must have for a complete, smooth-running shipping department, such as cleaning supplies and packing materials. The *handling fee* portion of your shipping charges pays for these kinds of items. Don't run low on them and pay attention to how you store them. They must be kept in a clean environment.

Packaging clean up

Be sure the items you send out are in tip-top shape. Here are a few everyday chemicals that can gild the lily:

- ✔ **WD-40:** This decades-old lubricant works incredibly well at getting price stickers off plastic and glass without damaging the product. The plastic on a toy box may begin to look scratchy and nasty, even when stored in a clean environment. A quick wipe with a paper towel containing a dash of WD-40 will make it shine like new. WD-40 also works well for untangling jewelry chains and shining up metallic objects. (It also removes ink and crayon marks from many items.)

- ✔ **Goo Gone:** Goo Gone works miracles in cleaning up gooey sticker residue from nonporous items.

- ✔ **un-du:** This amazing liquid easily removes stickers from cardboard, plastic, fabrics, and more without causing damage. It comes packaged with a patented miniscraper top that you can use in any of your sticker-cleaning projects. You can also use lighter fluid (which is, of course, considerably more dangerous and may damage your item).

Packing materials

So that you can always be sure that your items will arrive at their destinations in one piece, you'll want to keep the following on hand at all times:

Removing musty odors from apparel items

Clothing can often pick up odors that you just don't notice. I once bought a designer dress on eBay from a seller who had the typical disclaimer in her description: "No stains, holes, repairs, or odors. Comes from a smoke-free, pet-free home." Unfortunately, the minute I opened the box I could smell the musty odor of an item that had been stored for a long time.

To prevent that icky, storage odor, keep a package of Dryel Fabric Care System around. This is a safe, do-it-yourself, dry-cleaning product. Just toss your eBay clothing items in the patented Dryel bag with the special sheet and toss the bag in the dryer as per the instructions on the box. Your garment will come out smelling clean — and wrinkle free. For more information, visit their Web site at www.Dryel.com.

✔ **Bubble wrap:** A clean, puffy product that comes in rolls (see Figure 17-1), bubble wrap is available in several sizes. Depending on your product, you may have to carry two sizes of bubble wrap to properly protect your goods. Bubble wrap can be expensive, but check out vendors at eBay; you'll find quite a lot of them (and possibly a deal). The best part about bubble wrap is that it's highly recyclable, and the packing material that comes in with your merchandise orders can be reused on your outgoing items.

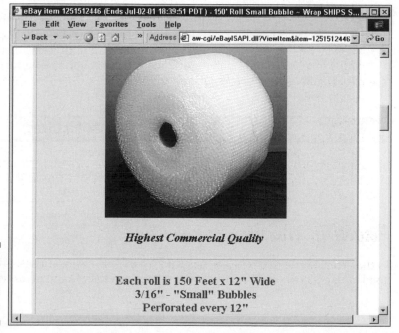

Figure 17-1: Bubble wrap in its pure form.

✔ **Styrofoam packing peanuts:** Why they call them peanuts, I'll never know — I guess somebody thought they look like peanuts. Nonetheless, Styrofoam peanuts protect just about everything you ship. Storing them is the tricky part. I store mine by putting the peanuts into 33-gallon drawstring plastic trash bags, and then I hang the bags on cup hooks (available at the hardware store) around the walls and rafters of my garage. When packing your items with peanuts, be sure that you place the item carefully and use enough peanuts to fill the box *completely;* leaving any airspace defeats the point of using the peanuts in the first place. (Don't go short in the land of plenty.)

✔ **Plastic bags:** Buy plastic bags in bulk to save money. Make sure you buy various sizes and use them for both shipping and storing. Even large kitchen or trash bags are good for wrapping up posters and large items before shipping; the plastic protects the item from inclement weather by waterproofing it.

✔ **Two- or three-inch shipping tape:** You'll need clear tape for finishing up packages. You'll also need the clear tape to place over address labels to protect them from scrapes and rain. I once received a package with an address label completely soaked with rain and barely legible. Don't risk a lost package for want of a few inches of tape.

✔ **Bubble mailer envelopes:** If you send items that fit nicely into bubble-lined envelopes, use them (see Figure 17-2). This type of envelope — with paper on the outside and bubble wrap on the inside — is perfect for mailing small items or clothing using First Class or Priority mail. The envelopes are available in quantity by the case (an economical choice) and don't take up much storage space. Table 17-1 shows you the industry-standard sizes of bubble mailer envelopes and their suggested uses. To get a real-world idea of how these mailers fit your items, bring the items to a local office super store and buy one each of several different sizes of envelopes before ordering.

Table 17-1	Standard Bubble Mailer Sizes	
Size	*Measurements*	*Suggested Items*
#000	4" x 8"	Collector trading cards, jewelry, computer diskettes, coins
#00	5" x 10"	Postcards, paper ephemera
#0	6" x 10"	Doll clothes, CDs, DVDs, Xbox or PS2 games
#1	7¼" x 12"	Cardboard sleeve VHS tapes, jewel-cased CDs, DVD sets
#2	8½" x 12"	Clamshell VHS tapes, books

Size	Measurements	Suggested Items
#3	8½" x 14½"	Toys, clothing, stuffed animals
#4	9½" x 14½"	Small books, trade paperbacks
#5	10½" x 16"	Hardcover books, dolls
#6	12½" x 19"	Clothing, soft boxed items
#7	14¼" x 20"	Much larger packaged items, framed items and plaques

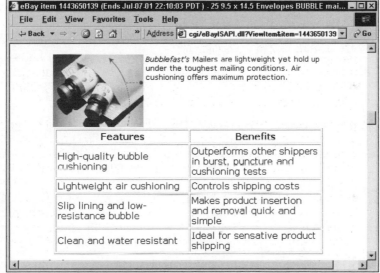

Figure 17-2:
Bubble-wrap-lined mailer envelopes for sale on eBay.

Packaging — the heart of the matter

Depending on the size of the item you sell, you can purchase boxes in bulk at reliable sources. Because you have a resale number (see Chapter 15), look in your local yellow pages for wholesale boxes. (You still have to pay tax, but the resale number identifies you as a business and often can get you a lower price.) Try to purchase from a manufacturer that specializes in B2B (business to business) sales. Some box companies specialize in selling to the occasional box user. Knowing the size that you need enables you to buy by the case lot.

You can save big money if your items fit into boxes that the post office supplies without charge (that's *free*, my friends) and you plan on using Priority mail. The USPS will give you all the boxes and mailing envelopes you need free, and it offers plenty of sizes. See handy Table 17-2 for available sizes.

Table 17-2	Free Priority Mail Packaging	
Size	*Description*	*Minimum Quantity*
8⅝" x 5⅜" x 1⅝"	Small video box 10965	25
9¼" x 6¼" x 2"	Large video box 1096LX	10
11¼" x 14" x 2¼"	Medium 1097	10
12½ x 15½" x 3"	Large 1095	10
12.125" x 13.375" x 2.75"	Medium 1092	10
6" x 38"	Triangle tube 14F	10
6" x 25"	Triangle tube 1098S	10
7" x 7" x 6"	Small square cube BOX4	25
12" x 12" x 8"	Square cube BOX7	25
11⅞" x 3⅜" x 13⅝"	Flat rate rectangle box FRB2	20
11" x 8.5" x 5.5"	Flat rate cube box FRB1	20
7.5 x 5.125 x 14.375	Shoe box	10
11.625" x 15.125"	Tyvek envelope EP14	10
6" x 10"	Cardboard envelope 14B	10
12½" x 9½"	Flat rate cardboard envelope 14-F	10
5" x 10"	Cardboard window envelope	1

Go to `http://shop.usps.com/` and then click the For Mailing/Shipping link (see Figure 17-3). Scroll down near the bottom of the page and click the Priority_Mail link to order your boxes, labels, forms, and just about anything else you'll need to ship Priority mail. Be sure to order a month or so in advance to make sure that you'll have what you need when you need it.

Figure 17-3:
Order
shipping
supplies
from the
USPS.

The Mail Room: Sendin' It Out

In August of 1999, the United States Postal Service announced a new service: information-based indicia (IBI). Targeted at the SOHO (small office/home office) market, IBI is USPS-certified postage that you can print on envelopes and sticker labels right from your PC. In this section, I give you the lowdown on the main Internet postage vendors: Endicia.com, Stamps.com, and PayPal.

I'm a savvy consumer and businesswoman. I don't believe in paying for extras, nor do I believe in being a victim of hidden charges. The online postage arena — while providing helpful tools that make running your eBay business easier — is fraught with bargains, deals, and introductory offers. I urge you to read these offers carefully so that you know what you're getting yourself into: Evaluate how much it will cost you to start and to maintain an ongoing relationship with the company. Although you may initially get some free hardware and pay a low introductory rate, the fine print might tell you that you have agreed to pay unreasonably high prices six months down the line. I always double-check pricing before getting into anything, and I urge you to do the same.

Your old pal the United States Postal Service has Web tools that enable you to print postage and delivery confirmations online. One caveat: This is a no-frills online service, and you often get what you pay for. Keep in mind that you can't print the labels on a label printer. You must print to regular 8½ x 11 paper. For more details, go to www.usps.com/clicknship.

Free USPS package pickup

Yes! Some things *are* free! If you print electronic postage through one of the vendors mentioned in this chapter, you can go the post office Web site at http://carrierpickup.usps.com and request a free pickup for your items (as long as you have at least one Priority mail package). If you misplace the URL, go to the Post Office main page and type **carrier pickup** in the search box. You can request a next-day pickup as late as 2 a.m.

Printing labels on your printer is convenient until you start sending out a dozen packages at a time — then cutting the paper and taping the label gets a bit too time consuming. I highly recommend that you do yourself a favor and get a label printer. Yes, they can be expensive, but you can find some great deals on eBay. I bought my heavy-duty, professional Eltron Zebra 2844 thermal label printer on eBay for one-fourth the retail price. (Search eBay for *zebra 2844*.) It's saved me countless hours. Dymo also makes a very good label printer for beginners.

If you're asking yourself why I haven't included a world famous, popular postage meter service in this book, you have a good question. Purchasing and printing online postage is just about the defacto standard in the online selling industry. Postage meters not only eat up your profits in fees, but the ink is *sooo* expensive. Inkjet ink is expensive enough (I know I don't have to tell *you* that), so if you're going to print your labels on paper, try to use a laser printer and put clear tape over the address. That's another reason why I love that Zebra label printer. No ink! It's thermal and prints over and over without ever needing ink.

Printing online postage with handy software

In the early days of online commerce, I had to scour the Internet to find places to conveniently print my shipping postage. Previous editions of this book listed each service individually, but now I examine how the current services can save you time and money. Online postage labels have a unique look. Figure 17-4 shows you a typical online 4 x 6 postage label printed from Endicia's DAZzle software.

Printing your postage the twenty-first-century way makes life a lot simpler:

✔ **Online postage purchases:** With a click of your mouse, you can purchase postage instantly using your credit card or by direct debit from your checking account. You can register your preferences when you sign up with Endicia.com.

✔ **Hidden postage:** A *stealth indicia* (also known as the postage-paid indicia) is an awesome tool for the eBay seller. By using this feature, your customer will not see the exact amount of postage that you paid. This allows you to add reasonable shipping and handling costs to your invoice and not inflame the buyer when they see final costs on the label.

✔ **Free delivery confirmations on Priority mail:** Delivery confirmations may be printed for First Class, Parcel Post, and Media Mail. Priority mail delivery confirmation is free (that's right — no more $0.65 each) when you print postage online. (First Class delivery confirmation is only $0.18 cents online versus $0.75 cents at the post office counter.)

✔ **Address validation:** Before printing any postage, the software contacts the USPS database of every valid mailing address in the United States. This Address Matching System (AMS) is updated monthly.

✔ **ZIP code check:** The software runs a check on your addresses and corrects any ZIP code errors you've made.

✔ **Addition of the extra four digits to your addressee's ZIP code:** This nifty feature helps ensure swift delivery while freeing you of the hassle of having to look up the extra digits.

✔ **Packages are ready for the letter carrier pickup:** Once you've used the online services, you have all your mail ready to go. No more socializing in the Post Office lines!

Figure 17-4:
A custom label, instantly printed on my thermal printer.

As you can see, the benefits hugely outweigh any possible service costs. The two major players that cater to online sellers are Endicia.com and Stamps.com. I give you a bit of background on both.

Endicia.com

At the beginning of PC graphics in the early '90s, I attended a cutting-edge industry trade show. I had a successful graphics and advertising business, so I was interested in the latest and greatest innovations to bring my business off the light table and onto my computer. In a smallish booth were a couple of guys peddling new software to enable artists to design direct-mail pieces from the desktop. Wow! What an innovation! Their inexpensive software even let you produce your own bar coding for the post office. I fell in love with that software and used it throughout my graphics career.

Today's Endicia Internet Postage is based on DAZzle, their award-winning mailpiece design tool that lets you design envelopes, postcards, and labels with color graphics, logos, pictures, text messages, and rubber stamps. You can print your mailing label with postage and delivery confirmation on anything from plain paper (tape it on with clear tape) to fancy 4 x 6 labels in a label printer from their extensive list of label templates.

DAZzle, combined with their patented Dial-A-Zip, became the basis for today's version of the software, which is distributed to all Endicia.com customers. There isn't a more robust mailing program on the market.

Their service also makes International mailings a breeze. From Anniston, Alabama, to Bulawayo, Zimbabwe, the DAZzle software not only prints postage but also lists all your shipping options and applicable rates. For international mailing, it will also advise you as to any prohibitions (for example, no prison-made goods can be mailed to Botswana), restrictions, necessary customs forms, and areas served within the country.

A nifty thing that I love about Endicia is that you can highlight the buyer's name and address from an e-mail or from your PayPal history, click Copy, and the data is automatically transferred to their DAZzle software in the address field area. No pasting needed.

Endicia offers their own private (third-party) package insurance. They also support U-PIC (one of the first private package insurers catering to online sellers). The insurance cost is charged to you automatically. Or, in the case of U-PIC, you can send your monthly insurance logs electronically to U-PIC at the end of the month — a service that's integrated into the DAZzle software. That way, there's no need to print insurance logs to mail.

If you're using an auction management service or software, Endicia integrates directly with the most popular: Channel Advisor, MarketWorks, Andale, Blackthorne, Dek, and more. Visit www.endicia.com/endicia-usa/Site/integratedpartners.cfm for the current list.

All the features just listed come with Endicia's standard plan. Their premium plan adds customizable e-mail, enhanced online transaction reports and statistics, business reply mail, return shipping labels (prepaid so your customer won't have to pay for the return), and stealth indicias.

With all this, you'd think their service would be expensive, but it's not. The standard plan is $9.95 a month ($99.95 if paid annually), and the premium plan is $15.95 a month ($174.94 annually). For a free sixty-day trial just for my readers, go to www.endicia.com/coolebaytools.

Stamps.com

Stamps.com purchased thirty-one Internet postage patents from e-stamp, making its services a combination of the best of both sites. (I was a big fan of e-stamp, but they discontinued their online postage service late in 2000.) Many eBay sellers moved their postage business over to Stamps.com, which is shown in Figure 17-5.

Stamps.com works with software that you probably use every day, integrating itself into many programs, such as Microsoft Word, Outlook, and Office, Corel WordPerfect, Palm Desktop, and Quicken.

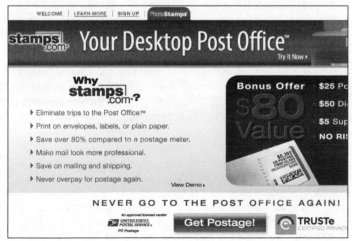

Figure 17-5:
The
Stamps.com
home page.

Stamps.com offers all the standard features of an online postage service, and purchasing postage is as easy as going to www.stamps.com and clicking your mouse. With Stamps.com, you don't *need* any extra fancy equipment, although most introductory deals come with a free 5-pound-maximum scale. Serious users should get a better quality postage scale from a seller on eBay or through an office supply store.

To find the Stamps.com introductory deal of the month, visit its Web site. They charge a flat rate of $15.99 per month. The site regularly offers sign-up bonuses that include as much as $25.00 free.

Because Office Depot, Staples, and OfficeMax deliver any order more than $50.00 free the next day, it's a great place to get paper and labels. Better buys on scales, though, can be found on eBay, especially if you search *postage scale*. I use a super small, 13-pound-maximum scale that I bought on eBay for only $29.95, complete with a five-year warranty.

Figuring out the best solution for your business

Before deciding which service is the one for you, check out the current fees and features offered by each. Following are some of the specialized features you might want to look for:

✔ **Mac compatibility:** If you use a Mac in your daily business, you need to be sure that your postage vendor has easy-to-use Mac-compatible software that performs all the features the service offers on the PC platform.

✔ **Print customs forms for international mail:** Printing postage for international mail isn't enough. You must be able to print the associated customs forms that go with each package and their particular level of service.

✔ **Mailpiece design:** It's nice to be able to add your own logo or even slightly customize a label (within postal guidelines).

✔ **Use your printer to print envelopes:** If your printer allows it, you can even print logo-designed envelopes along with bar-coded addresses, your return address, and postage. This saves quite a bit in label costs.

✔ **Third-party insurance:** Save time and money using a private postal insurance company (get the lowdown on this money saver in Chapter 14). Software that automatically integrates this feature is worth its weight in gold.

✔ **Integrated package tracking:** It's nice to have all your shipping data in one place, and a sophisticated mailing system will allow you to simply click a button or link to discover whether your package has been delivered.

✔ **Hard drive records of shipping:** Software that permits you to keep your shipping records on your computer is important. That way, you can check records even if the server on the Internet is down.

Postage online through PayPal

PayPal continues to add great features for sellers. Now you can not only buy postage or ship with UPS through PayPal, but also print labels on your own printer. If you ship lots of items and use a different service for printing your shipping data (such as the other services mentioned in this chapter), PayPal allows you to input the tracking information on the site even if you've printed your delivery confirmations with postage elsewhere. Just click the <u>Details</u> link for the transaction, and then click the <u>Add Tracking Info</u> link that appears. Input the tracking or delivery confirmation information from USPS, UPS, or another shipping company on the resulting page, as shown in Figure 17-6, and PayPal sends an e-mail to your buyer with that information.

Figure 17-6:
Input your tracking information, and PayPal sends an e-mail to your buyer.

The information you added appears in both the record of your PayPal transaction list and the buyer's transaction list in their account, as shown in Figure 17-7. (You can check whether the package has progressed by clicking the `Check Shipment` link on the Transaction list.)

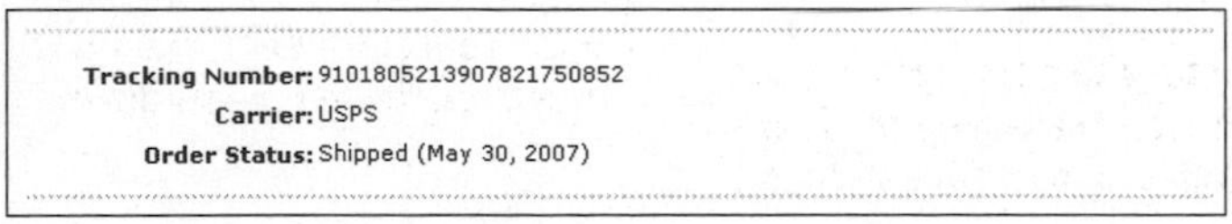

Figure 17-7:
The tracking information becomes part of the sales record on PayPal.

PayPal shipping services work great when you're just starting out in your eBay business, but once you get rolling, you need a mailing service that includes e-mail and record keeping, such as Endicia or Stamps.com. When you process your shipping (UPS or USPS) through PayPal, the shipping amount is deducted from your PayPal (sales revenue) balance. This is an important issue.

If you're starting a business in earnest, you need to keep track of your online expenses separately (see Chapter 16). Allowing PayPal to deduct your shipping costs from your incoming revenue creates a bookkeeping nightmare. You need to have exact figures for expense and income — and it really helps keep confusion to a minimum when your deposits (withdrawals from your PayPal account to your bank) match your sales receipts. If you want to ship through PayPal, be sure you withdraw your sales amount from your checking account *before* you process your shipping. That way, your shipping can be charged to your business credit card for easier tracking.

To purchase postage and print your label for a specific purchase, click the Print Shipping Label button next to the payment record in your PayPal account overview, as shown in Figure 17-8. You'll be taken through a step-by-step process for paying for your shipping and printing the appropriate label on your printer.

Figure 17-8: You can buy postage and print a label for a specific purchase.

All Activity - Advanced View from May 6, 2007 to Jun. 5, 2007

Date	Type	To/From	Name/Email	Status	Details	Action	Gross
Jun. 4, 2007	Payment	From		Completed	Details	Check Shipment	$28.98 USD
Jun. 4, 2007	Payment	To		Completed	Details		-$8.74 USD
Jun. 4, 2007	Payment	From		Completed	Details	Check Shipment	$172.99 USD
Jun. 3, 2007	Payment	From		Completed	Details	Check Shipment	$8.98 USD
Jun. 1, 2007	Payment	From		Completed	Details		$25.74 USD
Jun. 1, 2007	Payment	From		Completed	Details	Check Shipment	$28.45 USD
Jun. 1, 2007	Payment	From		Completed	Details		$301.99 USD
Jun. 1, 2007	Payment	From		Completed	Details	Print shipping label	$185.19 USD
May 28, 2007	Payment	From		Completed	Details	Check Shipment	$15.97 USD

Part V
The Part of Tens

The 5th Wave   By Rich Tennant

"You've opened an insect-clothing shop on eBay?
Neat! Where do you get buttons that small?"

In this part . . .

Not everyone is a shooting star or even a PowerSeller on eBay, but they are good goals. For your inspiration, I've included profiles on some interesting people — from all walks of life — who've turned eBay into a profitable enterprise, some working only part-time. These are not people in big companies. Instead, they're people like us, working hard to expand their income through a business on eBay. In the second chapter, I provide information on moving merchandise that you think you might never sell.

Chapter 18

Ten (or So) Sellers Who've Made the Jump from Hobby to Profits

In This Chapter

▶ People who make their living selling at eBay . . .

▶ . . . and love it!

1 love hearing stories about how much people like eBay. I enjoy it even more when I hear that they're doing something that they get pleasure from while earning a good living. One of the best parts of writing and teaching at eBay University is talking to the hundreds of sellers who attend my seminars and send me e-mails. I get the opportunity to bounce ideas around with them and find out about the creative ways they spend their time at eBay.

I thought you might like to know more about some of the people at eBay, too, so I interviewed them; it was so much fun getting to know about each of them. They have different backgrounds and lifestyles — but they all have one thing in common: eBay!

In favor of highlighting some regular folks at eBay, I dispensed with the customary writer thing (you know, finding the largest PowerSellers at eBay to interview). No one's a success overnight, and the people I discuss in this chapter certainly have been plugging away at eBay, increasing their businesses and becoming successful. I dug through some old feedbacks (all the way back to 1997) and contacted sellers to see how they're doing these days. Here are their stories (and their advice).

Beachcombers!

Member since December 2002; Feedback 4977; Positive feedback 99.7%

eBay store: `stores.ebay.com/Beachcombers-Bazaar`

Beachcombers! eBay store came into my search when I was looking for some reasonably priced holiday gifts. I've shopped with them continuously since. The store is run by Jody Rogers and her other half, Asad Bangash.

Asad started on eBay selling car parts for his previous employer. He was successful, and after he got addicted to making a profit, he suggested to Jody that they clean out their house in Ohio and sell things on eBay. After their house emptied out, they went to neighbors' houses.

Jody and Asad decided to move to Florida. Changing their home made them think twice, and rather than getting new jobs, they decided to go into eBay full-time.

Jody loved Indian glass bangles and khussa shoes and thought that mehndi (Indian temporary tattoos) were a fun idea. She looked around for sources and started selling these products on eBay. Now Jody even designs them for the American market — making popular handmade khussa shoes beautiful and in sizes that fit the larger U.S. foot. Funny thing, she's also sold them to people in India who can't get the shoes to fit their larger feet! The glass bangles they sell are custom made and are available only in limited quantities.

They're strong on customer service; they offer a full return policy and have a toll-free incoming number. They include complete instructions with their mehndi kits. They've also come up with unique ways to get repeat business, such as the bangle of the month club, where the recipient gets a handmade bangle stand and Indian glass bangles for the first shipment, and then gets a new bangle set every month for the duration of their membership. There is also a Build-A-Bangle line, where you create and design your own bracelet set.

They started with Turbo Lister and now use MarketWorks.

 Jody agrees with what I've been saying since 1998. Success in an eBay business means selling what you know and enjoy. Mailing out merchandise every day that doesn't make you happy won't make for a happy, profitable business in the long run.

Bubblefast

Member since May 1999; Feedback: 20,597; Positive feedback 100%

eBay store: `stores.ebay.com/Bubblefast`

I first met the Bubblefast "family" when I needed to move my mother's things from Florida to California. When I got the price quote from the moving company for rolls of cushioning, it was so high I nearly fell over! I knew that I could find a better price at eBay — and I did. Bubblefast prices were 50 percent less than the moving company had quoted, and they shipped the wrap directly to my mom's house so that I could meet it there to wrap her valuables.

The Bubblefast business began with Robin and her husband Alan. Their first transaction on eBay took place in early 1999, when Alan bought a Macintosh computer. When it came to finally selling, Alan figured that all eBay sellers would need shipping supplies. At first, they sold just one product, a 150-foot roll of ³⁄₁₆" (small size) bubble cushioning. Now they sell more than sixty-five variations of eight products: bubble cushioning, antistatic bubble wrap, bubble bags, bubble-lined mailers, rolled shipping foam, boxes, sealing tape, and stretch film.

Alan passed away in 2001, and Robin and her family carried on the business. On the bright side, Robin remarried, and now (with a combined family) they have even more indentured employees. The Le Vine Family — Robin, Mark, Jenny 20, Steven 14, Sara 12, Michelle 23, and Grandma Gloria — and family friend Syble work closely together, putting in 70 to 80 hours a week.

A seller with many repeat customers (more than 39,000 positives; repeat customers help build businesses!), they decided to branch out and go into consignment selling. They registered on eBay as Trading Assistants and now they're "up to their eyeballs in new business." It works out well for them, because they're already in the shipping supply business. No package is a challenge!

They use Turbo Lister for listing their items. Fashion mavens Jenny and Michelle help write descriptions for consignment listings. Robin still handles order entry and answers the phone and e-mail. Grandma Gloria and her friend Syble handle the packing and shipping. They ship anywhere from one hundred to two hundred orders a day. The family has customers from around the world who buy from their auctions, eBay store, and Web site (www. bubblefast.com). Last year, their business grossed $650,000. The profit margin on the Bubblefast products is low, so they have to make it up in volume.

eBay has totally changed this family's lives. Alan used to say "Our family is together all the time now; we've learned to pull together for a common goal." It's still true today with the family business he started.

The Le Vine family's tip for eBay sellers: "If you want to create a thriving eBay business and are willing to put the time and energy into it, the possibilities are endless. With a minimal investment of money, you have the potential to reach the world! Treat every customer like you want to be treated. After all this time, the customer is still always right."

Dans Train Depot

Member since January 1999; Feedback: 20,738; Positive feedback 100%

eBay store: `stores.ebay.com/Dans-Train-Depot`

Dan Glasure started selling comic books on eBay. Then he sold Legos and they did well. But his real passion was model trains (and his wife was tired of a living room full of Legos), so he branched out. He found a train collection for sale in a local newspaper. He and his father checked out the collection and were wowed by the price; $27,000.00! Their innate sales sense said that this was still a good deal, so dad put a second mortgage on the house and they took the plunge.

He sold trains out of his office at home, and the spare bedroom was the packing facility. They quickly learned the importance of going above and beyond in packaging the precious trains carefully.

He did well on the trains and continued purchasing collections locally. Then he branched out again, buying six brass model trains — having no idea what they were — and then selling them for about $600 each on eBay. Getting even braver, they purchased a large brass train collection for $45,000.00. Now brass trains make up the largest percentage of their sales (`www.brasstrains.com`).

Dan's father passed away in 2000. His employees and his mom still keep up the great service. They still buy out estates and hobby shops and large collections, so you'll never know what treasures they will find and put up for sale on eBay.

Dan's tip for eBay sellers: "Watch your cash flow. Treat your business professionally. Keep your profits separate so that you can make it through the slow times."

EvanP

Member since December 1998; Feedback: 28,155; Positive feedback 100%

eBay store: `stores.ebay.com/evanp-Discount-Musical-Instruments`

Evan and Sandra Prytherch run their family business and homeschool their children from their mountaintop home in rural Pennsylvania. Their careers previously required long hours away from home, so when they became parents in 1996, they decided to look for a way to make a living that would allow them to be home with their daughter. They also wanted to escape suburban traffic so they could safely ride their tandem bicycle.

They had experience in the music industry and had an interest in computers, technology, and the Internet. This led them to the eBay venue. They started selling in 1998, made their big move in 2001, and have continued to "live their dream."

EvanP is a musical instrument and accessories business. They carry musical gear from Fender, Bach, Yamaha, Lone Star, Danelectro, Dennis Wick, MXR, Johnson, Gibson, Warwick, Martin, Harmon, Selmer, Marshall, Hohner, Jo-Ral, Korg, Line 6, Zildjian, Sabian, Hosa, and Rico & Vox, and they ship worldwide.

Sandra suggests that you "be exceedingly well organized; to make sure to make time to integrate your life and business."

GalleryNow

Member since June 1999; Feedback: 3,955; Positive feedback 100%

eBay store: `stores.ebay.com/GalleryNow`

Stephen Kline has been an artist for more than thirty-five years. He's a self-representing artist who runs his own eBay store. He designed the State of Florida's "State of the Arts" license plate and his work has been exhibited worldwide and featured in "Art in America" and the American Kennel Club.

Kline's eBay store specializes in offering his signature dog and animal art along with his renowned paintings. It all started one Christmas, when he sent out a Santa lithograph drawn with the words "Season's Greetings." When the next Christmas rolled around, many friends had framed and displayed the art as part of their holiday celebration. So he decided to try a dog drawing out of the breed's name. When he placed the art on eBay, the response was overwhelming. He sells pictures of more than one hundred breeds now, along with other charming animals that his buyers love. He's sold to every state in the union and more than twenty countries around the world.

Stephen personally operates all functions of his eBay store, with marketing support from his wife Kris. He's hands-on all the way, from packing all the art (guaranteeing a safe delivery) to answering all e-mail requests, questions, and comments.

He lists manually with his own template.

Stephen's tip for sellers: "Make sure that you treat the customer like gold. Good feedback will be the key to success in your business." Stephen also follows my advice by sending a note along with every order assuring the customer that he appreciates their business.

Magic-By-Mail

Member since October 2001; Feedback 6,059; Positive feedback 99.8%

eBay store: stores.ebay.com/MAGIC-by-MAIL

After twenty years on the job, Jonathan retired from his position as a police officer in England, came to America, and met his lovely wife Ellen. They discovered eBay together. Jonathan's lifelong hobby was magic, so he developed his own magic products and put them up for sale — they sold immediately. What started as a means to supplement Jonathan's pension became a burgeoning full-time business. They even opened their own Web site at www.magicbymail.biz.

The best day they ever had on eBay was when they sold more than $3500 of magic in ten hours! They once made a $1000 plus sale to a magician in Australia and have had several other single sales between $500 and $900.

Although they devote many hours a day to their eBay business, it has allowed them to be flexible with their schedules. Ellen is just finishing her Bachelors degree in Professional Business Communication. She's applied much of what she's learned to their eBay business.

They enjoy buying on eBay too. Their most treasured purchase is an 1857 first edition magic book, "Magician's Own Book," which had been previously owned by a relative of Martha Washington (the wife of America's first president).

The biggest challenge in their business is keeping up with its growth! They've had such a steady increase in monthly sales that they're looking to move their business to larger quarters. That's a tough problem to have.

Magic-By-Mail's tip for new sellers: "Plan ahead, start small, and let your business grow. Look after your customers; they are your single biggest asset. Without customers you would not have a business." I think those are good words to live by.

MaryJoRoz_Aroma_Galaxy

Member since June 2005; Feedback: 4,855; Positive feedback 99.8%

eBay store: stores.ebay.com/maryjorozs-aroma-galaxy

September 11 changed a lot of lives. It also put three family members — Mary, Joanne, and Roz — out of work. So they founded an eBay business. Running a business with three people makes everything easier, and the combined strength of the three women "has kept us going." They've also opened a Web site, www.aromagalaxy.com.

They strive to share their love for quality candles, oils, soaps, and lovely accessories. They also sell the famous line of Yankee Candles, carrying a large selection of current, retired, and hard-to-find scents.

They travel wherever they hear there is a good bargain. They visit trade shows to meet with distributors and artists who create unique candle products. This way, they can form a relationship with their sources so that they're always abreast of what is new for the next season.

They ship as soon as they receive payment. They believe that as soon as you have paid for an item you want to have the item in your hands, so shipping the item is equally as important as the merchandise.

What tip do Mary, Joanne, and Roz have for sellers? "We look towards what we would want for ourselves and how we would want to be treated. This is the philosophy we strive to put in practice with our customers."

McMahanPhoto

Member since June 2002; Feedback: 7694; Positive feedback 99.9%

eBay store: stores.ebay.com/Robert-McMahan-Photography

Robert McMahan was (and is) a talented freelance New York photographer. Originally from Los Angeles, he began shooting pictures in 1991. Since 2001, he has concentrated most of his work in the area of journalism. He continues to build a body of travel, scenic, and holiday images, which lead to many photographs for sale. Like many other people living in New York on September 11, 2001, his life was changed. Heading down to the twin towers with his camera, Robert caught a now-famous photo of firefighters entering the smoke and dust of the collapsed World Trade Center, named "Walk of Courage."

Photography is his passion, "be it on the street capturing the often-overlooked moments of everyday life, or in the lab producing the most stunning print possible." That's what Robert sells on eBay. He sells quality photographs from both the Robert McMahan Collection and his RMP Archive Collections, producing high-quality prints of some of the greatest documentary photos ever taken.

He stocks more than five thousand historic and documentary photographs by hundreds of photographers, as well as photographic greeting cards and note cards. (I even bought a set of his stunning holiday cards.) His customers include museums, archives, galleries, publishers, collectors, and interior decorators. All of his prints, unless otherwise noted, are glossy chemically-processed lab photographs. He's proud of the prints and says they are the sharpest, brightest, most stunning photos available anywhere.

Robert also runs his own Web site at www.mcmahanphoto.com.

Melrose_Stamp

Member since March 1998; Feedback 13,678; Positive feedback 100%

eBay store: stores.ebay.com/ Melrose-Stamp-Co

A while back, I needed a rubber stamp or two for my business and didn't have time to go out to a printing store and place an order. I thought surely someone on eBay sells custom rubber stamps! I was right. That's when I met Jeff Stannard of Melrose Stamp Company. He specializes in self-inking custom rubber stamps and also sells stock design stamps.

Jeff was an assistant in a New York State economic development agency when he started his part-time business on eBay. Being around entrepreneurs gave him the inspiration he needed to quit his job and take his part-time sales to the next level.

He's had his eBay store since 2001 and works the business with his wife, Donna, and his Mom, Diane. His biggest sale came from a Chamber of Commerce in South Carolina. They ordered sixty-five custom stamps to use for a promotional day, where various merchants stamp a customer's card indicating that the customer visited the store.

eBay has changed his life. No longer a nine-to-fiver, Jeff works more than sixty hours a week. All his life he wanted to run his own business. "My business model would fail if it were locally based only. With eBay, I'm living my dream and selling my products globally. It's a life of independence, free from the corporate rat race!"

Jeff's advice to new eBay sellers? "Invest time to create a business plan. A business plan will help you identify your strengths and weaknesses, threats and opportunities. Build into the plan a set of financial projections as well; this will help you to clearly identify investment and working capital needs. Treat your eBay operation as a real, sustainable business and you will go far!"

Perpetual-Vogue

Member since April 2002; Feedback 5039; Positive feedback 99.9%

eBay store: `stores.ebay.com/Perpetual-Vogue`

Looking around eBay for some unique items, I ran across Clarissa Parashar's eBay store, Perpetual Vogue. Clarissa, a native Southern Californian, has developed a store with a style of its own. The store specializes in rock 'n roll, musician, tattoo design, biker, and streetwear apparel and accessories.

She discovered eBay as a buyer and found it to be a fabulous marketplace to find great items. After six months, she thought she'd like to become a seller. That timing coincided with the first eBay Live Convention in Anaheim California, which she attended. She was inspired to take a chance on an eBay business. (She attended my class too!)

Her eBay business took off and she opened an eBay store to further expand her sales. Although Clarissa runs the business, she gets quite a bit of help from her family. Her husband often serves as the model for menswear. Her mom is retired with lots of energy and helps when new shipments come in — unpacking items, inventorying sizes, and folding the items away into their bins.

This shrewd businesslady increases sales through marketing. She promotes through a page on MySpace and sends out a regular newsletter to her customers. Two years after she started sales on eBay, she opened her own Web site, `www.tattooapparel.com`. The retail bug really hit her and she just opened a retail store in LaHabra, California.

TIP

Clarissa bonds her transactions through BuySAFE so that her customers receive a surety bond on their purchase that guarantees performance. "This takes the risk out of shopping online for my customers. The customer pays nothing for this added benefit. It is paid for by me as I feel the most important thing I as a merchant can do is to give the customer confidence so that they have the freedom to shop online without worry."

SallyJo

Member since January 1998; Feedback: 6,855 Positive feedback: 99.9%

eBay store: `stores.ebay.com/SALLYJOS-DIAMOND-COLLECTIBLES`

Sally Severance is an eBay seller, a mother of four valedictorians, and a rancher specializing in purebred Charolais cattle (her ranch Web site is `www.sdcbulls.com`). She also runs a North Dakota farm with her husband. She gave up a successful ten-year banking career to stay home with her family, and by the way, she buys and sells at eBay.

From her ranch in North Dakota, Sally sells collectibles and general merchandise on eBay to supplement her income. The twenty-five to thirty hours a week that she spends on eBay earn her the money to buy things that she wants.

Sally also shops for her family on eBay and considers that part of her business. She can save money by finding special things for her children and grandchildren. She has one daughter, Robyn, who is married with two children, and three sons: Ryan, an engineer; Randy, a recent college graduate working on the farm; and Rod, in the Army and recently returned after serving his second tour in Iraq. She has made many friends on eBay and enjoys personal contact with customers. Sally spent an entire year using her eBay earnings sending weekly care packages to our troops in Iraq.

Her new eBay store is slowly filling with items. She does not use software to list her auctions but may do so in the future as her inventory grows.

Sally's tip for eBay sellers: "My #1 tip on setting up a business on eBay is to be honest, especially when writing a description of what you are selling!"

Chapter 19

Ten Other Places to Move Your Merchandise

*W*hen a corner of your eBay merchandise area becomes the graveyard of unsold stuff (at some point it will — believe me), whatcha gonna do? Inevitably, you'll find yourself holding on to some merchandise that you feel may never scrape together a profit, and you'll become sick of looking at it. (Besides, you undoubtedly have *some* cash tied up in it.) Whether you have hundreds of salad spinners that are suddenly appearing in multiple auctions or you jumped on the opportunity to buy a truckload (literally) of bargain-priced cat-scratching posts, you have to make room for this stuff immediately or sell it fast.

Every business has a problem with excess inventory, so don't feel bad about it. You can't expect to bat a thousand every time you select a product to sell. The key is getting rid of excess merchandise while losing minimal amounts on your investment. None of your merchandise is trash — I hope — so someone out there will want it and will pay *something* for it. If not, you can always donate it and take a tax write-off. In this chapter, I highlight the top ten ways to move that superfluous merchandise and still save your investment.

Donate to Charitable Organizations

Charitable donations are my favorite way of unloading unwanted items. Not only are you doing something good for someone else, but your donation may be a 100-percent business write-off. My community — no doubt yours too — has many private schools, churches, and synagogues. What these places all have in common are putting on fundraisers (auctions, raffles, tournaments, bingo) and welcoming donations. You have to give the best stuff to your schools or churches — especially if your item will be some sort of prize. Some organizations even make up gift baskets of varied items to put together a higher-value prize. Charities will often gratefully take boxes of miscellaneous stuff (think Salvation Army and Goodwill).

Classy gifting

Something I like to do is put together little gift baskets for charity auctions. I'll take a bunch of female-related, male-related, or kids' items and put them in a basket on a base of shredded Sunday comics. I keep a roll of clear cellophane on hand to wrap the entire thing. I then top it off with a nice big bow. It's always an appreciated donation and, wrapped up this way, it always gets a higher price at bazaars or silent auctions.

Online charities

One of my favorite Web sites, `MissionFish.com` (see Figure 19-1), joined with eBay to organize eBay Giving Works. MissionFish helps nonprofit organizations support their missions by teaching them to fish and to build their own fisheries (to paraphrase the parable). Select your charity from the more than ten thousand on their approved list, and MissionFish does the rest. See Chapter 2 for more on charity auctions on eBay.

When an item sells, you (the donor) are responsible for shipping the item. You must use a shipping company that supplies a tracking number, which you submit to eBay Giving Works. (In addition to the item, the entire cost of shipping is tax deductible.) After the winner receives the item, all proceeds are sent from MissionFish to the designated nonprofit. You then receive a thank-you letter as proof of your gift for IRS tax purposes. You'll have a write-off, and you'll feel good about what you did to help others.

Figure 19-1:
The eBay
Giving
Works
charity
auctions
home page.

eBay Giving Works (through MissionFish) has raised more than $34 million for nonprofits to date. Many sellers have found that by participating in this program and contributing a portion of their sales to a charity, they've increased their bids and final sale prices. This merchandising model makes a lot of sense because it helps your other listings as well. By donating your proceeds (or a portion of them) to a charity, you build an image of being a caring business on eBay rather than just another seller. Remember these facts:

- Listings stand out with a Giving Works ribbon icon.

- Your chosen nonprofit's mission statement is on every listing that benefits them.

- Each donation is tax deductible (MissionFish provides the receipt for you).

- The eBay fee credit policy rewards your generosity.

Many other charities accept *gifts-in-kind,* items that are new or gently used that they resell to raise funds. I've brought excess eBay inventory to the American Cancer Society's Discovery Shop, and they've been very gracious about the donations. Now they also sell on eBay (aside from their many retail locations) under their own user ID.

Have a Garage Sale

Garage sales draw big crowds when promoted properly, and you'll be surprised at the amount of stuff you'll unload. An especially good time to have a garage sale is late fall or early winter — just in time for the holidays. (Before it freezes)!

Because you've probably been to a bunch of garage sales but maybe haven't given one in a long time, here are a few reminders:

- **Plan the sale at least three weeks in advance:** Decide on the weekend of your sale well beforehand and be sure to set a specific opening time. If you welcome *early birds* (people who like to show up at 6 or 7 a.m.), be sure to put that in your ad and flyers.

- **Invite neighbors to participate:** The more the merrier, right? Also, the bigger the sale, the more customers you're likely to entice. Everyone can drum up at least a few items for a garage sale.

- **Gather and price items to go in the sale:** After you set a date, immediately start putting things aside and pricing them with sticky tags. This way, you won't have to scramble the day before to find things.

- **Place a classified ad:** Call your local newspaper a week before the sale and ask the friendly classified department people when the best time is to run an ad. Take their advice — they know what they're talking about! Also consider placing the ad on their online site.

- **Make flyers to post around the neighborhood:** Fire up your computer and make a flyer; include your address, a map, the date, and the starting time. Be sure to mention special items that you've thrown into the sale to bring 'em in and mention also that many items are new. If two or three families are participating in the sale, mention that too. If you have small throwaway types of items, include the line "Prices start at 25 cents." Hang the flyers in conspicuous places around your neighborhood.

- **Post large signs on nearby corners:** The day before the sale, put up *large* posters advertising the sale. (You can pick up 22 x 28 poster board from an art store or office supply store.) When you make the posters, use thick black shipping markers on brightly colored boards. Use few words, including only the basic details, for example: "Garage Sale June 22–24, 8 a.m., Tons of Stuff, 1234 Extra Cash Blvd." Also make a sign to hang at the sale location "Sale Continues Tomorrow. New Items Will Be Added!"

- **Clean up any dusty or dirty items:** If you want someone to buy an item for a good price, you have to make it look good.

✔ **Gather supplies:** Get lots of change; make sure you have plenty of tens, fives, a ton of singles, and several rolls of coins. Get a calculator for each person who will be taking money. Set aside a box to use as the cash box. (Cigar boxes work nicely.) Collect all the supermarket shopping bags that you can for those with multiple purchases.

✔ **Hang helium balloons to draw attention to your signs:** The day of the sale, go to the busiest corner near your sale and tie some helium balloons to your sign — that's sure to attract attention. Do the same thing at the corner near your sale and also at the curb of the sale.

✔ **Display everything in an orderly fashion:** Pull out your old card tables and arrange items so that people can easily see what's there; a literal pile of junk'll turn them off. Hang clothes on a temporary rack (or use a clothesline on the day of the sale).

✔ **Get ready to negotiate:** Talk to people when they approach, use your selling talents, and *make that sale!*

At the end of your sale, be sure to take down the signs you've plastered all over the neighborhood. It's the nice thing to do.

Rent a Table at the Local Flea Market

Local *swap meets* or *flea markets* (regularly scheduled events where you can rent space for a token fee and sell your wares) can be a great place to meet other eBay sellers. But whatever you do, don't mention that you sell on eBay. Let the customers think that you're a rube and that they can get the best of you. Offer great deals; give 'em a discount if they buy a ton of stuff. Just like with a garage sale (see the preceding section), you can move lots of merchandise here.

Don't forget to try to unload your goods to other sellers; perhaps they can do with a little extra inventory. Check the classifieds of local newspapers for swap meets, which occur once a month in some towns.

If you have a weekly Farmer's Market in your area, check it out. This might be a great place to buy a table for a few hours — especially if you're selling related (culinary or home) items.

Consign Merchandise to the Local Antique Mall

An *antique mall* is a retail store that's often run by several people who take your merchandise on consignment. You can probably find a few in your area. Your items are sold in the store (good for you), and the storeowners take a commission on each sale (good for them). They take your items, tag them with your own identifying tag, and display them for sale. Antique malls usually see an enormous amount of foot traffic, and this may be as close to having a retail store that you'll ever get.

Take a Booth at a Community Event

Where I live, the local business community often holds special events: street fairs, Fourth of July extravaganzas, pumpkin festivals, and more. As a vendor, you can buy a booth at such events to peddle your wares. For seasonal events, purchasing a bunch of holiday-related items to make your table match the festivities is a savvy marketing idea. Your excess eBay inventory will just be part of the display — and a big part of your sales. You might even consider donating a percentage of your sales to a local nonprofit to help boost traffic.

 If the event is in the evening, purchase a few hundred glow-in-the-dark bracelets on eBay (you can often get one hundred for $20). The kids love them and will drag their parents to your booth. Be creative and think of other ways to make your booth stand out. Support your community, have a barrel of fun, and make some money!

Resell to Sellers on eBay

Sell your items to other eBay sellers. Hee hee, only kidding (maybe not). Maybe another seller (your competition) is selling the same items but is doing a better job with those items than you. If so, offer to sell your stock to that seller. It's a win-win situation. Perhaps some of the stuff you have may appeal to the locals in your community (some of whom probably sell on eBay).

Package up your items into related lots that will appeal to sellers who are looking for merchandise online. Take a tip from the successful eBay seller that often combines many lost packages into single lots to sell on eBay: the Post Office Mail Recovery Center. If you're overstocked with stuffed animals, put together a lot of a dozen. If you don't have a dozen of any one item, make packages of related items that will appeal to a certain type of seller.

Be sure to use the words *liquidation, wholesale,* or *resale* (or all three) in your title. A world of savvy sellers is out there looking for items to sell. Maybe another seller can move the items later or in a different venue.

Note that eBay has Wholesale subcategories for almost every sort of merchandise.

Visit a Local Auctioneer

Yes, when I say you should visit a local auctioneer, I mean a real live auctioneer, one who holds live auctions at real auction houses that real people attend. Many people enjoy going to live auctions. (I recommend that you go occasionally to acquire unique items to resell on eBay.) Shopping at auctions can be addictive (duh), and live auctions attract an elite group of knowledgeable buyers.

The basic idea is to bring your stuff to an auctioneer, who auctions off lots for you. Good auctioneers, such as those at the Los Angeles Bonhams & Butterfields (www.bonhams.com), can get a crowd going, bidding far more than an item was expected to sell for. Bonhams & Butterfields Appraisal Days page is shown in Figure 19-2.

Figure 19-2:
Bonhams consignment information.

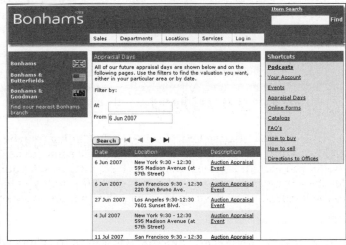

Here are a few facts about real live auctioneers and some pointers to keep in mind when looking for one:

- ✔ **Make sure that the auction house you choose is licensed to hold auctions in your state, insured, and bonded.** You don't want to leave your fine merchandise with someone who will pack up and disappear with your stuff before the auction.

- ✔ **Get the details before agreeing to the consignment.** Many auction houses give you at least 75 percent of the final hammer price. Before you consign your items, ask the auctioneer's representative about the details, such as

  - When will the auction be held?

  - How often are the auctions held?

  - Have you sold items like this before? If so, how much have they sold for in the past?

  - Will there be a printed catalog for the sale, and will my piece be shown in it?

  Get the terms and conditions in writing and have the rep walk you through every point so that you thoroughly understand each one.

- ✔ **Search the Internet.** Type *licensed auctions* and see what you come up with; it can't hurt.

- ✔ **Contact local auctioneers.** If your items are of good quality, a local auction house may be interested in taking them on consignment.

Find Specialty Auction Sites

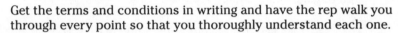

If you have some specialized items that just don't sell very well on eBay, you might look for a different venue. Although eBay is the best all-purpose selling site in the world, you may have an item that only a specialist in the field can appreciate.

For example, I've seen some fine works of art not sell on eBay. But don't fret, you'll find many other places online where you can sell these items. For example, I searched Yahoo! for *art auctions*. Under the Web Results heading, I found more than six million Web sites that auction artwork. You might want to refine your search with your telephone area code so that you find auction locations in your immediate area.

You may find an online auctioneer who specializes in the particular item you have for sale, something too esoteric for the eBay crowd. I've found some incredible bargains for myself on elegant new sunglasses made by a company in Italy called Persol, a company world famous for crystal lenses and ultra-fine quality. The super-famous wear these sunglasses: Robert De Niro, Tom Cruise, Donald Trump, Sharon Stone, Mel Gibson, and Cindy Crawford. These sunglasses normally retail from $150–$300 a pair, but you can sometimes find them on eBay for as low as $40. Unless you're buying them dirt cheap, you're not making your profits on eBay. Maybe the crowd just doesn't know about them, but they sell well elsewhere.

Run a Classified Liquidation Ad

Sell your special items in the appropriate categories of the classifieds. Sell the rest of them in preassigned bulk lots for other sellers. When you write the ad, make your lots sound fantastic; give the reader a reason to call you. When they call, be excited about your merchandise. But be honest and tell them you're just selling the stuff to raise cash.

Sell Everything on eBay for a $.99 Opening Bid . . .

. . . and take what you get.

Part VI
Appendixes

"How many times have I told you that you can't sell your brother on eBay?"

In this part . . .

It's not really a reference book without an Appendix, so I wanted to be sure you got your money's worth. Appendix A will clue you in on terms you may not know — but will definitely hear as you make your rise to entrepreneurdom. Appendix B updates you on the latest in networks. You absolutely must have one — that way you can print your labels from a lounge chair in the garden — one of the clear benefits of having a home-based eBay business.

Appendix A

Glossary

1099: An end-of-year form that you file with the IRS to record your payments to outside contractors. A 1099 must be filed for anyone to whom you pay more than $600 in a calendar year.

About Me: The free Web page given to every eBay user. An excellent promotional tool.

absentee bid: A bid that an auction house employee places on a lot (or lots) — up to a maximum amount that you designate — in your absence. When you want to participate in a live auction but can't attend it physically, you can arrange to have the auction house place absentee bids for you.

accounts payable: The amount your business owes to vendors, office supply stores, your credit card charges, and the like. This includes any money your business owes.

accounts receivable: The money people owe you, such as the checks and money orders you're expecting in the mail and the money sitting in your PayPal account that you haven't transferred to your checking account.

announcements pages: eBay pages where you get all the latest eBay information. You need to check these pages periodically. If you follow the Announcements link, which is at the bottom of every eBay page, you end up at the Community announcements page at www2.ebay.com/aw/marketing.shtml. If you're wondering whether it's your computer's problem or an eBay problem when the search engine isn't working, check out the System Status Announcements Board at www2.ebay.com/aw/announce.shtml.

as is/where is: An item that comes with no warranty, implied or otherwise, speaking to the merchantability of the product.

bid increment: The minimum amount that a bid must advance, based on the auction's high bid.

bid retraction: A cancelled auction bid. Retractions can occur only under extreme circumstances (such as when you type the wrong numerals).

bid shielding: An illegal process wherein two bidders work together to defraud a seller out of high bids by retracting a bid at the last minute and granting a confederate's low bid the win. Not as much of an issue anymore due to eBay's new bid retraction policy; *see also* bid retraction.

bonding: A surety bond can be issued by a third party (usually an insurance company) to guarantee a seller's performance in a transaction.

card not present: Credit card services use this term to describe transactions that typically happen over the Internet or by mail order. It means that the seller hasn't seen the actual card. This is the opposite of *swiped,* where the seller had possession of the card.

caveat emptor: Latin for *let the buyer beware.* If you see this posted anywhere, proceed cautiously — you're responsible for the outcome of any transaction in which you take part.

chargeback: When someone calls his or her credit card company and refuses to pay for a transaction. The credit card company will credit the card in question and make you pay back the amount.

consignment: When someone hands over merchandise to you, which you then auction on eBay. You make a little commission and the other person sells something without the hassle. Become an eBay Trading Assistant to get more leads in this area (`http://pages.ebay.com/tahub/index.html`).

cookie: A small text file that may be left on your computer to personalize your experience on a particular Web site. When you sign on to eBay and check the box to remain signed on, a cookie is placed on your computer that keeps your user ID and password active for the next 24 hours.

corporation: A separate entity set up to do business.

CPA: Certified Public Accountant. Someone who has been educated in accounting and has passed a certification test. CPAs are at the top of the accounting professional heap.

CTR: Click-through rate. It's a ratio of the times a visitor clicks on a Web ad, versus those who view and don't click through.

DBA: Doing business as. These letters appear next to the common name of a business entity, sole proprietorship, partnership, or corporation that conducts business under a fictitious name.

DOA: Dead on arrival. The product you purchased doesn't work from the moment you opened the package.

DUNS number: Data Universal Numbering System number. An identification number issued to businesses from a database maintained by the great and powerful Dun and Bradstreet. These numbers are issued to allow your business to register with more than fifty global, industry, and trade associations, including the United Nations, the U.S. Federal Government, the Australian Government, and the European Commission. My business has had a DUNS number for years. You can get yours at no cost by calling Dun and Bradstreet at 800-333-0505 (`https://eupdate.dnb.com/requestoptions.html`).

EA: Enrolled agent. Enrolled agents are the only tax professionals tested by the IRS on their knowledge of tax law and regulations. They specialize in taxes, not corporate accounting. They (like CPAs) are required by the IRS to take Continuing Professional Education and are governed by Treasury Circular 230 in their practice before the IRS.

EIN: Employer identification number. If you run your business as a partnership or a corporation, you need an EIN number from the IRS. If you're a sole proprietor, your Social Security number is your EIN because you file all your business on your personal tax return.

entrepreneur: That's you! An entrepreneur is someone who takes the financial risk to start a business. Even if you're buying and reselling garage sale items, you're still an entrepreneur.

FOB: Free on board. When you begin purchasing large lots of merchandise to sell, you'll encounter this term. The FOB location technically means the place where the seller delivers the goods. If the price you're quoted is FOB Chicago, you're responsible for all shipping costs to get the goods from Chicago to your home city.

FTP: File transfer protocol. The protocol used to transfer files (such as images) from one server to another.

hammer fee: A fee that the auction house charges at a live auction. Be sure to read the information package *before* you bid on an item in a live auction. Hammer fees usually add 10–15 percent to the amount of your bid.

HTF: Hard to find. An abbreviation that commonly appears in eBay auction titles to describe items that are, uh, hard to find.

invoice: A bill that outlines the items in a specific transaction, who the item is sold to, and all costs involved.

ISBN number: International Standard Book Number. Just like a car's VIN or the UPC on a can of beans, the ISBN identifies a book by a universal number.

keystone: In the brick-and-mortar retailing world, 100 percent markup. A product sells for keystone if it sells for twice the wholesale price. Products that you can sell at keystone are very nice to find.

live auctions: Auctions held online in real time. Check out www. ebayliveauctions.com.

LLC: Limited liability corporation. A form of corporation that's a little less formal than a regular C corporation. This type of corporation has become popular in the e-commerce world.

mannequin: A representation of the human form made of wood, fiberglass, or plastic. Essential for modeling clothing for your eBay apparel sales.

MIB: Mint in box. Okay, the item inside the box is mint, but the box looks like an eighteen-wheeler ran over it.

MIMB: Mint in mint box. Not only is the item in mint condition, but it's in a perfect box as well.

mint: An item in perfect condition is described as mint. This is truly a subjective opinion, usually based on individual standards.

MSRP: Manufacturer's suggested retail price. The price hardly anybody pays.

NARU: Not a registered user. A user of eBay or other online community who has been suspended for any number of reasons.

OOP: Out of print. When a book or CD is being published, it usually has its own lifetime in the manufacturing process. When it is no longer being made, it's out of print.

provenance: The story behind an item, including who owned it and where it came from. If you have an interesting provenance for one of your items, be sure to put it in the auction description because it adds value to the item.

QuickBooks: A top-of-the-heap accounting program that helps you keep your records straight.

register: Similar to a checkbook account listing, a register goes up and down depending on the amount of flow in an account balance.

ROI: Return on investment. A figure expressed as a percentage that stands for your net profit after taxes and your own equity.

STR: Sell through rate. The percentage of your successful listings over a prescribed period of time, usually a month.

sniping: The act (or fine art) of bidding at the very last possible second of an auction. You can do this manually or you can subscribe to any number of services that can do it for you in the last six seconds of an auction.

sole proprietorship: A business that's owned by only one person. The profits and losses are recorded on that person's personal tax return.

split transaction: A transaction that you must assign to more than one category. If you pay a credit card bill and a portion of the bill went to purchase merchandise, a portion to gas for business-related outings, and yet another portion to eBay fees, you must post each amount to its own category.

tax deduction: An expenditure on your part that represents a normal and necessary expense for your business. Before you get carried away and assume that *every* penny you spend is a write-off (deduction), check with your tax professional to outline exactly what is and what isn't.

TOS: Terms of service. eBay has a TOS agreement; check it out at `pages. ebay.com/help/policies/user-agreement.html`.

W-9: A form that must be filled out by any outside contractor you pay for services. This form includes the contractor's Social Security number and address. Your outside contractors must give you an invoice for each payment that you make to them. You use the information from this form to issue your 1099s at the end of the year. *See also* 1099.

wholesale: Products sold to retailers (that's you) at a price above the manufacturer's cost, allowing for a mark-up to retail. I hope you buy most of your merchandise at wholesale. Stores such as Costco or Sam's Club sell items in bulk at prices marginally over wholesale. You must get a resale number from your state to buy at true wholesale.

Appendix B

The Hows and Whys of a Home Network

• •

*W*hat is a network? A *network* is a way to connect computers so that they can communicate with each other — as if they were one giant computer with different terminals. The best part is that a network enables high-speed Internet connection sharing, as well as the sharing of printers and other peripherals. By setting up a computer network, one computer might run bookkeeping, another might run a graphics server, and others might be used as personal PCs for different users. From each networked computer, it's possible to access programs and files on all other networked computers.

Today's technologies allow you to perform this same miracle on the *home network.* You can connect as many computers as you like, and run your business from anywhere in your home — you can even hook up your laptop from the bedroom if you don't feel like getting out of bed.

Now for the *whys* of a home network. A network is a convenient way to run a business. All big companies use them, and so should you. You can print your postage, for example, on one printer from any computer in your home or office. You can extend your DSL line or Internet cable connection so that you can use it anywhere in your home — as well as in your office.

In a network, you can set certain directories in each computer to be *shared.* That way, other computers on the network can access those directories. You can also password-protect certain files and directories to prevent others — your children or your employees — from accessing them.

I devote the rest of this appendix to a quick-and-dirty discussion of home networks installed on Windows-based PCs. I give you a lesson on what I know works for most people. (Hey, if it doesn't work, don't e-mail me — head back to the store and get your money back!)

At this point, I want to remind you that I'm not a techno-whiz (just like I'm not a lawyer or an accountant). For more information about anything you'd think to ask about home networking, I defer to Kathy Ivens, author of *Home Networking For Dummies,* 4th Edition (published by Wiley).

What I know about home networks, I've found out the hard way — from the school of hard knocks. A lot of research went into this appendix as well, so humor me and read on.

Variations of a Home Network

Basically, you have a choice of three types of home networks: Ethernet, powerline, and wireless. See Table B-1 for a quick rundown of some pros and cons of each.

Table B-1	Network Pros and Cons	
Type	*Pros*	*Cons*
Traditional Ethernet	Fast, cheap, and easy setup	Computers and printers must be hardwired; cables run everywhere
Powerline	Fast; your home is already prewired with outlets	Electrical interference may degrade the signal
Wireless network	Pretty fast; wireless (no ugly cords to deal with)	Expensive; may not be reliable because of interference from home electrical devices

Many people still use an Ethernet connection to hardwire their main (desktop) computer to connect to a wireless router. If you have an office, it's nice to know that Ethernet cabling will work over 300 feet in distance. You can then connect laptops (and desktops) throughout the house via wireless and powerline.

The wireless network is the hot ticket and highly touted by the world in general these days. However, in a home office setting, the wireless signal may experience interference because many networks run with the same 2.4 GHz technology as some home wireless telephones. I have a wireless network and it works great. My primary network hookup is via Ethernet. But it's actually a hybrid, combining Ethernet, powerline, and wireless.

With broadband over powerline, you get high-speed Internet directly into your home electrical system. Just plug in your powerline boxes (more on that later) and you're up and running!

All networks need the following two devices:

- **Router:** A router allows you to share a single Internet IP address among multiple computers. A router does exactly what its name implies; it routes signals and data to the different computers on your network. If you have one computer, the router can act as a firewall or even a network device leading to a print server (a gizmo that attaches to your router and allows you to print directly to a printer without having another computer on).

- **Modem:** You need a modem for an Internet connection. You get one from your cable or phone company and plug it into an outlet with cable (just like your TV) or into a special phone jack if you have DSL. The modem connects to your router with an Ethernet cable.

If you have broadband, you don't even need to have a main computer turned on to access the connection anywhere in the house. If you keep a printer turned on (and have a print server), you can also connect that to your router and print from your laptop in another room — right through the network.

Hooking up with wireless

Wireless networking — also known as WiFi or, to the more technically inclined, IEEE 802.11 — is the hot technology for all kinds of networks. It's an impressive system when it works, with no cables or connectors to bog you down.

If you're worried about your next-door neighbor hacking into your computer through your wireless connection, stop worrying. Wireless networks are protected by their own brand of security, called WEP (or Wired Equivalent Privacy). WEP encrypts your wireless transmissions and prevent others from getting into your network. Another flavor of security is WPA, which is even more secure. Although super-hackers have cracked this system, it's the best currently available for the home office user.

To link your laptop or desktop to a wireless network with WEP (or WPA) encryption, you have to enter a key code from the wireless access point. Just enter it into your wireless card software on every computer (or system-based software) that uses the network, and you should be good to go.

You may get confused when you see the different types of wireless available. Here's the lowdown on the variations:

✓ **802.11a:** This wireless format works really well — fast with good connectivity. It's also very expensive. This format is used when you have to connect a large group, such as at a convention center or in a dormitory. It delivers data at speeds as high as 54 Mbps (megabits per second). It runs at the 5 GHz band (hence its nickname, WiFi5), so it doesn't have any competition for bandwidth with wireless phones or microwave ovens.

✓ **802.11b:** My laptop has a built-in 802.11b connection, so I can log on to the popular hotspots in Starbucks and airports. It's the most common wireless type, and it's used on the most platforms. It travels over the 2.4 GHz band. The 802.11b version is slower than the 802.11a version, transferring data at only 11 Mbps.

The lower frequency of 2.4 GHz drains less power from laptops and other portable devices, so laptop batteries will last longer. Also, 2.4 GHz signals travel farther and can work through walls and floors more effectively than 5 GHz signals.

✓ **802.11g:** This flavor is based on the 2.4 GHz band. It speeds data up to a possible 54 Mbps, and it's backward compatible with 802.11b service.

✓ **802.11n:** The latest fastest form of wireless, 802.11n is a dual frequency that works through MIMO (multiple input/multiple output) technology. It travels further and faster than any of the other formats — I'm using it now as I write this, and it's amazing!

Installing your wireless network isn't a gut-wrenching experience either (although it can be if the signal doesn't reach where you want it). You hook up your computer (a laptop works best) to the wireless access point (the gizmo with the antenna that broadcasts your signal throughout your home or office) to perform some setup tasks such as choosing your channel and setting up your WEP (or WPA) code. (The wireless access point comes with its own instructions.)

After you complete the setup and turn on your wireless access point, you have a WiFi hotspot in your home or office. Typically, a hotspot provides coverage for about 100 feet in all directions, although walls and floors cut down on the range.

Here are some simplified steps on configuring your network:

1. **Run a cable from your cable connection, or a phone cord from your DSL line, to your modem.**

2. **Connect one Ethernet cable from your modem to your router.**

3. **Connect one Ethernet cable to your wireless access point.**

Take a look at the network diagram from Netgear in Figure B-1.

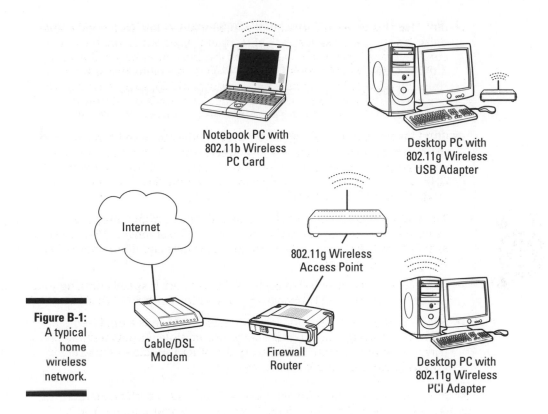

Notebook PC with
802.11b Wireless
PC Card

Desktop PC with
802.11g Wireless
USB Adapter

Internet

802.11g Wireless
Access Point

Figure B-1:
A typical
home
wireless
network.

Cable/DSL
Modem

Firewall
Router

Desktop PC with
802.11g Wireless
PCI Adapter

Extending wireless with powerline

An ingenious invention, a powerline wireless extender uses your existing
home powerlines to carry your network and your high-speed Internet connection. You access the network by plugging a powerline adapter wired to
your router into an electrical outlet on the wall. Then, another little box can
be placed farther away in your home to broadcast an additional wireless
signal. Standard powerline networks have been around for a while; this is the
second round of technological advances.

I have a powerline wireless extender so I can bring my network out to the
garage and to far points in my home.

Hooking up a wireless powerline extender is so easy that it's a bit disappoint-
ing — you'll wonder why it isn't more complicated. Most installations work
immediately right out of the box. Hooking up the wireless/powerline network
goes like this:

1. The high-speed connection comes in through your DSL or cable line.

2. Plug the cable line (or phoneline for DSL) into your modem.

3. Connect one "in" Ethernet cable from your modem to a router.

4. Connect the "out" Ethernet cable to the wireless powerline extender.

5. Plug the wireless powerline extender into a convenient wall outlet.

6. Plug the wireless powerline receiver box into a convenient wall outlet wherever you want to extend the signal.

That's it!

Index

• *M* •

BUSINESS, CAREERS & PERSONAL FINANCE

0-7645-9847-3

0-7645-2431-3

Also available:
- Business Plans Kit For Dummies
  0-7645-9794-9
- Economics For Dummies
  0-7645-5726-2
- Grant Writing For Dummies
  0-7645-8416-2
- Home Buying For Dummies
  0-7645-5331-3
- Managing For Dummies
  0-7645-1771-6
- Marketing For Dummies
  0-7645-5600-2

- Personal Finance For Dummies
  0-7645-2590-5*
- Resumes For Dummies
  0-7645-5471-9
- Selling For Dummies
  0-7645-5363-1
- Six Sigma For Dummies
  0-7645-6798-5
- Small Business Kit For Dummies
  0-7645-5984-2
- Starting an eBay Business For Dummies
  0-7645-6924-4
- Your Dream Career For Dummies
  0-7645-9795-7

HOME & BUSINESS COMPUTER BASICS

0-470-05432-8

0-471-75421-8

Also available:
- Cleaning Windows Vista For Dummies
  0-471-78293-9
- Excel 2007 For Dummies
  0-470-03737-7
- Mac OS X Tiger For Dummies
  0-7645-7675-5
- MacBook For Dummies
  0-470-04859-X
- Macs For Dummies
  0-470-04849-2
- Office 2007 For Dummies
  0-470-00923-3

- Outlook 2007 For Dummies
  0-470-03830-6
- PCs For Dummies
  0-7645-8958-X
- Salesforce.com For Dummies
  0-470-04893-X
- Upgrading & Fixing Laptops For Dummies
  0-7645-8959-8
- Word 2007 For Dummies
  0-470-03658-3
- Quicken 2007 For Dummies
  0-470-04600-7

FOOD, HOME, GARDEN, HOBBIES, MUSIC & PETS

0-7645-8404-9

0-7645-9904-6

Also available:
- Candy Making For Dummies
  0-7645-9734-5
- Card Games For Dummies
  0-7645-9910-0
- Crocheting For Dummies
  0-7645-4151-X
- Dog Training For Dummies
  0-7645-8418-9
- Healthy Carb Cookbook For Dummies
  0-7645-8476-6
- Home Maintenance For Dummies
  0-7645-5215-5

- Horses For Dummies
  0-7645-9797-3
- Jewelry Making & Beading For Dummies
  0-7645-2571-9
- Orchids For Dummies
  0-7645-6759-4
- Puppies For Dummies
  0-7645-5255-4
- Rock Guitar For Dummies
  0-7645-5356-9
- Sewing For Dummies
  0-7645-6847-7
- Singing For Dummies
  0-7645-2475-5

INTERNET & DIGITAL MEDIA

0-470-04529-9

0-470-04894-8

Also available:
- Blogging For Dummies
  0-471-77084-1
- Digital Photography For Dummies
  0-7645-9802-3
- Digital Photography All-in-One Desk Reference For Dummies
  0-470-03743-1
- Digital SLR Cameras and Photography For Dummies
  0-7645-9803-1
- eBay Business All-in-One Desk Reference For Dummies
  0-7645-8438-3
- HDTV For Dummies
  0-470-09673-X

- Home Entertainment PCs For Dummies
  0-470-05523-5
- MySpace For Dummies
  0-470-09529-6
- Search Engine Optimization For Dummies
  0-471-97998-8
- Skype For Dummies
  0-470-04891-3
- The Internet For Dummies
  0-7645-8996-2
- Wiring Your Digital Home For Dummies
  0-471-91830-X

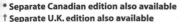

* Separate Canadian edition also available
† Separate U.K. edition also available

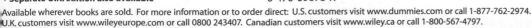

Available wherever books are sold. For more information or to order direct: U.S. customers visit www.dummies.com or call 1-877-762-2974.
U.K. customers visit www.wileyeurope.com or call 0800 243407. Canadian customers visit www.wiley.ca or call 1-800-567-4797.

SPORTS, FITNESS, PARENTING, RELIGION & SPIRITUALITY

0-471-76871-5

0-7645-7841-3

Also available:

- Catholicism For Dummies
  0-7645-5391-7
- Exercise Balls For Dummies
  0-7645-5623-1
- Fitness For Dummies
  0-7645-7851-0
- Football For Dummies
  0-7645-3936-1
- Judaism For Dummies
  0-7645-5299-6
- Potty Training For Dummies
  0-7645-5417-4
- Buddhism For Dummies
  0-7645-5359-3

- Pregnancy For Dummies
  0-7645-4483-7 †
- Ten Minute Tone-Ups For Dummies
  0-7645-7207-5
- NASCAR For Dummies
  0-7645-7681-X
- Religion For Dummies
  0-7645-5264-3
- Soccer For Dummies
  0-7645-5229-5
- Women in the Bible For Dummies
  0-7645-8475-8

TRAVEL

0-7645-7749-2

0-7645-6945-7

Also available:

- Alaska For Dummies
  0-7645-7746-8
- Cruise Vacations For Dummies
  0-7645-6941-4
- England For Dummies
  0-7645-4276-1
- Europe For Dummies
  0-7645-7529-5
- Germany For Dummies
  0-7645-7823-5
- Hawaii For Dummies
  0-7645-7402-7

- Italy For Dummies
  0-7645-7386-1
- Las Vegas For Dummies
  0-7645-7382-9
- London For Dummies
  0-7645-4277-X
- Paris For Dummies
  0-7645-7630-5
- RV Vacations For Dummies
  0-7645-4442-X
- Walt Disney World & Orlando
  For Dummies
  0-7645-9660-8

GRAPHICS, DESIGN & WEB DEVELOPMENT

0-7645-8815-X

0-7645-9571-7

Also available:

- 3D Game Animation For Dummies
  0-7645-8789-7
- AutoCAD 2006 For Dummies
  0-7645-8925-3
- Building a Web Site For Dummies
  0-7645-7144-3
- Creating Web Pages For Dummies
  0-470-08030-2
- Creating Web Pages All-in-One Desk
  Reference For Dummies
  0-7645-4345-8
- Dreamweaver 8 For Dummies
  0-7645-9649-7

- InDesign CS2 For Dummies
  0-7645-9572-5
- Macromedia Flash 8 For Dummies
  0-7645-9691-8
- Photoshop CS2 and Digital
  Photography For Dummies
  0-7645-9580-6
- Photoshop Elements 4 For Dummies
  0-471-77483-9
- Syndicating Web Sites with RSS Feeds
  For Dummies
  0-7645-8848-6
- Yahoo! SiteBuilder For Dummies
  0-7645-9800-7

NETWORKING, SECURITY, PROGRAMMING & DATABASES

0-7645-7728-X

0-471-74940-0

Also available:

- Access 2007 For Dummies
  0-470-04612-0
- ASP.NET 2 For Dummies
  0-7645-7907-X
- C# 2005 For Dummies
  0-7645-9704-3
- Hacking For Dummies
  0-470-05235-X
- Hacking Wireless Networks
  For Dummies
  0-7645-9730-2
- Java For Dummies
  0-470-08716-1

- Microsoft SQL Server 2005 For Dummie
  0-7645-7755-7
- Networking All-in-One Desk Referenc
  For Dummies
  0-7645-9939-9
- Preventing Identity Theft For Dummies
  0-7645-7336-5
- Telecom For Dummies
  0-471-77085-X
- Visual Studio 2005 All-in-One Desk
  Reference For Dummies
  0-7645-9775-2
- XML For Dummies
  0-7645-8845-1